Bentley Farm Cookbook

By Virginia Williams Bentley

Let Herbs Do It
Bentley Farm Cookbook

BENTLEY FARM COOKBOOK

by Virginia Williams Bentley

Drawings by Virginia Hoyt Cantarella
Photographs by Dick Carpenter of Jenks Studio

Houghton Mifflin Company Boston

1975

Library of Congress Cataloging in Publication Data
Bentley, Virginia Williams
        Bentley farm cookbook.

        1. Cookery.   I. Title.
TX715. B4817   641.5   74-13108
ISBN 0-395-19446-6
ISBN 0-395-19394-X (pbk.)

Printed in the United States of America
            First Printing M

To my granddaughter
Victoria Williams Bentley,
as a torch-passing gesture across the generations

not forgetting
Emma Lou Rothman,
who corrected and cosseted me
through a year of monkish seclusion
reminiscent of the Venerable Bede

Contents

Introduction

The yellowed pages of a grandmother's cookbook are what gave the impetus for the writing of this one. The more brown and spotted a page appears, the more is the message conveyed that here was a favorite recipe — a strange sort of hieroglyph to reach across the years. How I wish she had written down little messages concerning the homely day-to-day techniques that are a part of meal preparation, had transmitted some of what she must have known about practical matters of the kitchen, and of the things she thought about as she went her busy way. Even if some of her methods would be outmoded today, they would be of great historical interest. There are only the frayed pages and the spots, eloquent in their way, but tantalizing, because her culinary lore is lost forever.

So now, having a granddaughter of my own, I've tried to do for her what I wish my grandmother might have done for me. And in the doing, get that horrifying kitchen midden of unorganized recipes (that haunt most of us) into A-1 shape. And while I organize, try to convey the joy I have experienced in providing that basic ingredient of life, food, for family and friends.

Two experiences in childhood set the course for this kitchen hangup, as I look back; one delightful, the other traumatic. It was in about the sixth grade in Newton Centre, Massachusetts, where I grew up, that a cooking course for girls was augmented by a Bread Club for the real eager beavers who wanted to stay after school and learn how to make bread. Did I want to? I remember falling all over myself as I raced down the school corridor to sign up for this offer. When I was not only accepted, but elected President of the Mason Grammar School Bread Club, my cup ran over. We were thrill-

ingly costumed in white caps and coverall aprons, which were belted at the waist, and from the belt hung two pot holders that swung around our knees as we walked. These were ready for instant service as we removed honest-to-goodness fragrant loaves of bread from the school ovens in the basement. Incidentally, we had made these outfits in sewing class the previous year, getting ready for matriculation into the wonders of cooking.

But to switch from delight to trauma; in the seventh grade I ran away from home. I had to. My stepmother made me eat stew for lunch that was full of fat, bones, gristle, and what appeared to be a few main arteries. I issued an ultimatum that if I were forced to eat it I'd have to leave home. Kids never won such battles in those days. It was clean-your-plate-or-else. So, with revulsion, as the tears streamed, I obeyed, but laid plans for a get-away. I sent a note home from the afternoon session of school, by a friend. It stated, jauntily, that I had headed North, in case they wanted to send the police after me, and that I found a home where stew was so poorly made quite unbearable. I went as far North as two houses from home, where I hid in the note-bearing accomplice's cellar. Hunger, and fright

at my own audacity, forced me home shortly after the supper hour. I was in disgrace for weeks, and can't recall the punishment meted out, but poorly made stew turned me into a purist about such matters. Evidences of early twig-bending are apparent throughout this book.

Cooking, to me, is one of the fine arts, and the limitless creativity it involves has sustained me in sickness and health, joy and sorrow. It's also a magic carpet to making others happy, so the cry of certain over-zealous Women's Liberationists to "get out of the kitchen" puzzles me. In a far more subtle and lasting way, the power and action are with the hand that stirs the kettle, rather than the one that pounds a typewriter (though many women successfully do both). And if it isn't one of woman's chief roles to feed people, then Mother Nature certainly gave us the wrong signal.

A warm, welcoming, clean home, with a meal ready, and enchanting odors emanating from the kitchen, is not easily come by. It takes a lot of hard work and a high degree of organizational ability. Many women aren't up to it, or want to escape this form of creativity. This is fine with me. I'm all for women "doing their own thing," so long as they let me do mine. But I hate to think what some are missing, so one of the aims of this book is to sell the idea that cooking, being creative, therapeutic, and charitable, one had better take a second look, and learn how to do it well enough to like it. No one ever hated to do anything at which he is really proficient. Be like the old Romans, who, it is said, enjoyed reading cookbooks as much as odes. Start a collection. Anyone who can read can cook. Reading about food tends to stir enthusiasm, and overcome that what-shall-we-have-to-eat syndrome. I've been a compulsive collector of cookbooks, and would blush to count them, but if I were allowed only one to take to some desert island, it would be Fannie Farmer, with Joy of Cooking a close runner-up. These are definitive cookbooks that no household should be without. This is not, nor does it attempt to be, but I hope it has other merits.

The often-heard complaint that one spends all day getting a good meal, only to have it gone in moments so what's-the-use, is not valid. The food may be gone, but the memories linger on and become a part of the tyranny and treasure of brain recordings that last a life-time. (It is no happenstance that the supreme sacrament of the Church is the breaking of bread and drinking of wine together. Or that Confucius and Lao-tse turned their deepest thoughts to the kitchen.) Modern psychiatry corroborates the overwhelming importance of the ceremonial family meal, and of being well fed, not so much with calories, as with the loving concern that cooking symbolizes, even spiritualizes. "Food offered is love offered everywhere." I never cease to marvel, in work I've done with old people, that they can't remember what they said or did five minutes ago, but get them started on childhood recollections, and the anecdotes pour forth. Sedation, senility, seem to have no power over the impact of youthful impressions that have to do with food.

The old adage about never trying new recipes for a party is a warning I ignore. That's just when I'm inspired to try something new. Like Apicius (though I hope not to come to his sad end*), the only thing I'd rather do than go to a party, is to give one. The spreading of the festive board yanks one out of the doldrums, and is a remedy for many ills. But one thing is imperative: if you want to have fun and feel like a guest at your own party, be a good Boy Scout — "Be Prepared." If you so much as pull out an ice tray, or pour cream in a pitcher after guests arrive, you are not company-ready. This book attempts to show you how to be just that, and nearly every recipe is geared to easy entertaining with foods that can be prepared way ahead of time, a necessity in this servantless age. Lots more about this in the Household Hints section in the last part of the book.

Which brings me to a basic test I have for all the recipes that have

* When Apicius became too broke to entertain, he poisoned himself.

gone into this book. Each must fulfill the happy trilogy of 1) good, 2) good for you, 3) easy to prepare.

Everyone's idea of goodness is not the same. I can only go by what I think is good, and that family and guests have affirmed by their enthusiasm. Every recipe given here I have cooked many times, and in numerous instances am indebted to friends who have shared their cooking secrets, and enriched my precious portfolio of favorite dishes. Good food can only come from the hands of a good cook who is, above all, zealous — no bones in the stew, no fat or gristle in sandwich or salad, no strings of egg in a custard, no bits of shell in crabmeat, no sand in the spinach, no core in the applesauce, no limp crackers, no grease on the soup. The list is long, but you get the idea. It's all the little things, well attended to, that separate an artful cook from a slapdash provider.

As for requirement ※ 2, "good for you," I learned the necessity of this, a long time ago, when my husband brought his boss home for dinner. I was a bride, and, coming from New England, decided to prepare a typical meal of my own region, a boiled dinner of corned beef and cabbage. Also it was cheap, in those days, and The Depression was in full swing. The food turned out surprisingly well for a neophyte, but the boss was on a rigid diet and couldn't eat a bit of it. I had to fix him a poached egg on toast. This proved a bitter and never-forgotten lesson. So, my advice to all young homemakers: If your husband's boss is coming for dinner, chances are he has incipient ulcers, or he wouldn't be boss. Feed him as you would a baby, and all will be well. So many meals, prepared for company, assault the digestive system, and it isn't the best hospitality if guests leave your table furtively chewing Tums. The fact that five million people per year are hospitalized in the United States with digestive ailments would suggest that it's high time for better cooking methods and simpler fare, guests or not. A baby may eat most of the foods in this book, and so may grandma. There is an emphasis on basic, non-processed foods, and on some so-called health foods, but stopping short of food faddism. The frying pan is relegated to the back of the cupboard, with double boiler and blender competing for first place. Extensive use of the oven, which is recommended, may be a bit more costly, but one can pay the heating bill with the money saved on palliatives for indigestion. Most sauces, gravies, soups, and stews are not thickened by the roux method, but taste as good, are made faster, and are good for you.

*3, "easy to prepare", is a fetish with me. Though I stand in awe and admiration of French cuisine, the average housewife has neither time nor strength to fulfill its requirements. So most of my recipes are neither French nor fancy. There is concentration on dishes that go straight from stove to table. The recipes are arranged so that every step is the logical and easy one, in the sequence in which one really does things, and in a manner to save time and dishes. Read on — the proof of the pudding may be found in the pages ahead.

> "Now, good digestion wait on appetite,
> And health on both!"
> Shakespeare

Virginia Williams Bentley
Danville, Vermont

Beverages ~ Appetizers ~ Sandwiches

Plaque over faucet reads:

"Praised be my Lord
for our sister water,
who is very serviceable
unto us, and humble,
and precious, and clean."   — St. Francis

Ice-cold, crystal-clear water, running by gravity from a spring ¼ mile back in the woods, is one of the wonders of Bentley Farm. It has blessed the place since it was built in 1840, as has the cast-iron sink into which it gushes. If anyone thinks an iron sink is outmoded, let him consider its flexibility. It will accomodate three dishpans at once, leaving ample room for one person to be peeling vegetables, another washing his hands, and a child reaching for a drink of water. Try to find a modern sink that is equally accomodating. The only problem is the helpful city visitor who insists upon using scouring powder. It takes a few days to teach that the sink responds brilliantly only to a quick swipe with baby oil and a paper towel. It is kept sanitary with a bit of kerosene.

Sink rests in a large island of butcher-block maple. For those who pity me because of such primitive equipment, there's a modern dishwasher on the left, not visible in this drawing.

4

About Beverages

"So then because thou art lukewarm, and neither cold nor hot, I will spue thee out of my mouth," says the Bible. The intent was metaphorical, and I trust I may be forgiven if I use the quotation literally. By all means serve cold drinks cold and hot ones hot. (This applies to solid food also!)

As for alcoholic and non-alcoholic drinks, of which a few of my favorites follow, don't bother to serve an alcoholic beverage unless it has some authority. There is nothing more deadly than an insipid drink, a passport to a dull evening. Better to serve plain fruit juice, with guests alerted rather than disappointed. Neither is it smart nor kind to load a guest's drink. Learn to walk the tightrope of hospitality with discretion.

Probably the best rule that any host can follow is to keep the cocktail hour before dinner to what it is called — an hour. A book could be written on the pitfalls that await the unwary, the lack of common sense and sophistication that is indicated by endless imbibing before a lovely meal.

Non-drinkers are the ones who are noticeable in this day and age, an about-face from earlier times. By all means treat them with unobtrusive consideration. My abstaining friends complain (rightfully) that hosts often make a stir about bringing forth bright-colored juices, making those on the wagon feel both conspicuous and embarrassed. Ginger ale, apple juice, non-alcoholic white wines, are good things to have on hand and may be served in the same glasses as the alcoholic drinks. So no one suffers sensations of segregation.

Always have plenty of ice ready in the drink-serving area. Nothing is more disconcerting than the scramble for ice trays at the last minute. A pitcher of water, a lemon, a sharp knife, mixing spoon, cocktail olives and onions, dark and light Vermouth, a cocktail shaker, bottled mixes, necessary glasses — all should be lined up. And, depending on your circumstances, so should the alcoholic beverages you plan to make available. For the single woman hostess, it is smart to let guests help themselves. If there is a man in the house who enjoys mixing drinks, the situation is different.

Charles Dickens could be called both the ideal guest and host. Dickens loved a good drink and the happy conviviality it induces, but he never overdrank. As for his role as host, Longfellow, his devoted friend, wrote, "No witch at her incantations could be more rapt in her task than Dickens was as he stooped over the drink he was mixing."

One of the best touches there is, when it comes to serving a drink, be it cocktail or highball, is to slice a thin piece of rind off a lemon (so thin that none of the bitter white pulp is included), twist the peel with your fingers until it emits that lovely, fresh oil of lemon, and rub it firmly all around the edge of the drinking glass. Drop the twisted peel in the drink or not, as you prefer. One both tastes and inhales that pungent gift of nature that is balm to the soul. Research seems to suggest that it was a lemon (once called a Persian apple) with which Eve tempted Adam.

Ice Wreath for the Punch Bowl

(This is fun to make, and an aesthetic and gustatory delight as well.)

Take a ring mold that is the proper size for your punch bowl, pour about an inch of water in it and freeze it. Make a design of flowers and/or leaves (upside down) on the ice. Keep in mind that wreath will be reversed when turned out of mold. Carefully add a little more water (something for the flowers to freeze into but not to float around in). Freeze again. Lastly, fill mold with ice cold water and freeze, though its safer to add water and freeze in stages.

The finished wreath may be removed from the mold, when thoroughly frozen, and kept in a plastic bag in your freezer, all ready to top a bowl of cold punch.

The first time I saw one of these wreaths was at a wedding reception, and the flowers were the same variety that the bridesmaids carried, an enchanting extension of the wedding theme.

My favorite flowers (for ease of handling, and the fact that they are edible) are small chrysanthemums in winter, and daisies or marigolds in summer. Mint leaves, sage leaves, sprigs of rosemary — all lend the green touch as well as a pleasant taste. Edible flowers are numerous: roses, nasturtiums, violets, borage, and lavender, to name a few. Or make a bright fruit ring with strawberries with hulls left on. Thin slices of lemon stuck with cloves and alternated with mint leaves have eye and taste appeal. The variations are limitless. Use your ingenuity.

Of course you may eliminate all fussing with a frozen wreath and just float flowers on the punch.

Plain Old-Fashioned Lemonade
(Makes one quart, which serves 4 people)

½ cup real lemon juice (2 lemons*)

½ cup sugar
} Mix together.

3 cups water, stirred into above. Pour over ice, and there you are.

     So easy to make, delicious, thirst-quenching, yet few people make it any more. Or, if they do, they use the canned, frozen juice which is bitter, or the awful unidentifiable fluid that comes out of a plastic lemon. Real lemons are loaded with vitamin C, are a remedy for colds, fevers, jaundice, pulmonary, and skin ailments. One old treatise claims lemons "cleanse the blood", whatever that means, but it sounds great. Serve just as directed. Don't doctor it up with any imaginative flourishes.

Hot Toddy

For winter colds or flu: Put the juice of one lemon in a tall glass or mug. Sweeten with honey, to taste. Add 3 ounces of best bourbon or rye whiskey. Fill with boiling water. Stir and drink. Proceed directly to a warm bed. Better than an antibiotic.

* Approximately 2 lemons, depending on size and juiciness. Buy heaviest lemons for quality.

Blender Punch
(for the children — or for your fanciest tea party)

This consists of any fruit juices you may have in the house, fresh or canned, plus some whole fruits, fresh or canned or frozen, blended in a blender. I have never made it the same way twice, for different ingredients are at hand, depending on the season. However, I nearly always blend in a banana or two for the excellent flavor it imparts, and I sweeten the punch, to taste, with maple syrup or honey. (Honey mixes in better if blended with a little hot water). I always add just a touch of rum, and sometimes a drop or 2 of vanilla, but not so you would notice it. A few drops of lemon extract add zip. Pineapple juice is a necessity, and, lacking juice, blend a can of crushed pineapple. Canned or stewed apricots, pears, or peaches blend beautifully, and so will that little left-over dish of applesauce residing in the refrigerator, or left-over jelly or jam. Fresh apples, strawberries, blueberries, raspberries, and cherries, to mention only a few, may be incorporated into a delicious fruit punch, thanks to the miracle of a modern blender. I usually start with lemon and/or orange juice as a base, and go on from there, improvising, tasting, diluting with some water. Tea may be used as a base also. Adding a bottle of ginger ale to any punch, at the last minute, adds sparkle. And be lavish with ice.

Having a pitcher of homemade fruit punch in the refrigerator will woo children (and grownups) away from the harmful, oversweet, commercial soft drinks.

Rhubarb Punch (Serves 40) (a spring tonic)

2 quarts finely cut fresh rhubarb } Bring to a boil and simmer, covered,
2 cups water   } for 10 minutes. Cool. Blend in blender.

2 cups water   }
3½ cups sugar   } Simmer, covered, for 10 minutes. Strain out the
2 cinnamon sticks } spices, and add the liquid to blended rhubarb.
24 whole cloves   }

2 cups orange juice }
1 cup lemon juice   } Add this to rhubarb-spice mixture. Pour into
1 cup lime juice   } a punch bowl over plenty of ice. Test for sweetness.
1 teaspoon vanilla } Float sprigs of fresh spearmint on top of punch,
6 cups cold water   } if you have it.

Rosemary Punch (Serves 30) (good for the memory)

2 (20-ounce) cans unsweetened pineapple juice   } Combine 1 can pineapple juice with
2 tablespoons dried rosemary leaves or   } rosemary. Bring to boil, covered.
        6 tablespoons chopped fresh rosemary   } Remove from heat and let steep at
                                                   } least 10 minutes. Strain out rosemary.

dash of salt   }
2½ cups sugar   } Stir this into above decoction, along with the other can of
1½ cups lemon juice } pineapple juice. Cool. Pour over plenty of ice in punch
1 quart water   } bowl. Float thin slices of lemon on punch.

These are two unusual and utterly delicious punches for summer teas or weddings.

Switchel
The Yankee Haymakers' Drink

In the old days, no farmer went out haying without a jug of switchel for thirst quenching and energy boosting. Most people have never heard of it today, Madison Avenue having taken over even the Vermont hayfields. Packages of colored granules, representing zero nourishment, are now mixed with good spring water, more's the pity. Perhaps, with modern interest in more healthful foods, there may be a return to this great libation. Some vending machine outfit could make a fortune turning out switchel, rather than the inferior coffee and soft drinks that are undermining the nation's health.

In a gallon container put:

1½ cups of sweetening (maple syrup, honey, brown sugar, molasses — one or any combination of these sweets. But for the right taste there needs to be some molasses.

1 cup of cider vinegar (In the event you can get it, or prefer it, boiled cider may be substituted. Bottles of this brown brew were once in every New England preserving closet. It is now available commercially.)

1 tablespoon ground ginger
pinch of salt
2 beaten eggs (optional)
1 cup raw oatmeal (optional)
cold water, to fill container.

Shake with might and main. Chill.

Oatmeal was added on many farms, but all old recipes do not call for it. The elders I have talked with in Northern Vermont recall the oatmeal and how good it tasted after soaking in the sour-sweet liquid. One old man said, "When we were children we all competed to eat the oatmeal that settled in the bottom of the jug." My husband said oatmeal was included in the switchel of Nova Scotia, and was nostalgic about the drink.

Work out the combination that tastes best to you. It may be made in smaller quantities, of course, but a gallon of switchel disappeared, like dew before the sun, with a thirsty group in a summer hayfield.

Orange Juice Frappé

This is what I used to call it when my small son was recovering from a childhood illness and I wanted to get the most reviving nourishment into him. Put the juice of 2 fresh oranges into the blender with one raw egg. Blend thoroughly, and serve over ice in a tall glass. (You might want to add a little honey.)

This will take anyone healthfully through a busy morning who may be too lazy or hurried or diet-conscious to cook a decent breakfast.

~~~~~~~~~~

Cough Syrup

Mix fresh lemon juice and honey, half and half. Take a teaspoonful when seized with a coughing spell.

My son used to take a little bottle of this in his pocket to school, when a cold had passed the infectious stage, but a cough lingered on. I suspect he made it linger, he was so fond of the treatment.

Vodka Punch (for 35 people)

(This has authority, so watch it. But who wants a watery punch? Someone said, "That's not a punch, it's a right cross.")

1 half gallon (2 quarts) 100 proof vodka
10 ten-ounce bottles of Bitter Lemon
} Pour this over ice in a punch bowl, and serve. Multiply measurements for a larger crowd.

1 cup vodka
1 ten-ounce bottle Bitter Lemon
} If punch bowl runs low, and you don't want to add a large quantity, keep refreshing the bowl in this proportion, then nothing will be wasted.

Of all the punches I have served, this is not only the easiest, but also the most popular with everyone concerned. I no longer labor over complicated concoctions that call for a little bit of everything, including a headache the next day.

Have a punch bowl of lemonade at the other end of the table for non-drinkers. The bowls will look alike, but the resemblance stops there. As the party wanes, you will find yourself pouring any left-over lemonade into the vodka bowl! This is a great tapering-off technique, and so efficient.

There are times when it is too complex to set up a bar that offers every sort of drink for a crowd. This is when I serve Vodka Punch.

Holiday Eggnog (makes over a gallon)
(Concoct this at least 2 weeks ahead of time.)

<u>1 dozen eggs</u> — Bring to room temperature. Separate, putting whites into large beater bowl, yolks into any handy receptacle. Beat <u>whites</u> until stiff, while adding slowly :

<u>½ cup sugar</u> — Then tenderly transfer the stiff whites to bowl or kettle that will hold more than a gallon.

Now pour the <u>12 egg yolks</u> into beater bowl. Beat them long and well, adding during the beating :

<u>1 cup sugar</u> and ½ teaspoon salt — When yolks are pale and fluffy, pour them onto whites, folding in carefully.

To the egg mixture add :

<u>1 pint heavy cream</u> (2 cups)
<u>1 pint light cream</u>
<u>1 quart whole milk</u>
<u>1 quart best bourbon whiskey</u>
<u>1 cup dark rum</u>

Keep stirring as these ingredients are added.

Ladle this mixture (sampling the while) into 6 of the best-looking quart liquor or wine bottles that you decided were too decorative to throw away. You will need a <u>funnel</u> for this. Close the tops, and store in a cool place to age. As foam subsides, use one of the bottles to fill the others thoroughly. Give bottles a good shaking at this time, and <u>always shake well before serving</u>. Decorate the bottles for the most welcome of holiday gifts. Or hoard for a holiday punch bowl. Ladle into small cups. Sprinkle with <u>nutmeg</u>, and be of good cheer.

Singapore Sling

When I was in Singapore in March, 1969, we went to the villa of a Mr. Smith, a place of great charm and exotic gardens, on the Straits of Jahore, the northeast shore of Singapore Island. We were led to a lighted, flower-bedecked pavilion, out over the water, and were served Singapore Slings faster than one can say the words. The container was half a coconut shell, with four white blossoms floating on the potent drink, which was sipped through a straw. It was out of this world, as were our surroundings. Mr. Smith kindly gave me the recipe. <u>For one serving:</u>

Into a cocktail shaker put <u>1 jigger (1½ ounces) of gin</u>, <u>1 jigger of cherry brandy</u>, <u>1 jigger of Lemon Squash</u>*, <u>a generous dash of Benedictine</u>. Shake enthusiastically with <u>plenty of ice</u>. A very authoritative potation.

As most of us don't have coconut shells knocking about, serve in large tumblers, with a straw, and float some of our edible, temperate-climate flowers thereon (see page 6). It's a case of please <u>do</u> eat the daisies. A fun drink for a small party, but lacking lackeys, not suitable for a crowd.

The Singapore Sling originated at Raffles Hotel, where Mr. Smith once worked, and the hotel was named for the man who founded Singapore Island.

* Lemon Squash is not readily available in the U.S. Substitute <u>lemon juice</u> and <u>water</u> (half and half), sweetened slightly.

Irish Coffee (one serving)

Into Irish coffee glasses, or tall glasses or mugs, put:

{ 1½ teaspoons sugar
{ 1 jigger (1½ ounces) Irish whiskey

Then almost fill each glass with....

strong, hot coffee (or Sanka) (If you prefer instant coffee, make it in proportion
of 1½ teaspoons to 1 measuring cup of boiling water)

a spoonful of slightly whipped cream, as topping on coffee. The cream should
be thickened but not stiff. ½ cup cream is ample for 4 servings.

This is dessert and coffee all in one. Never gild the lily by
serving anything else with it.

~~~~~~~~~~~~~~~~~~~

Cardamom Coffee (serves 6)

Into an after-dinner coffee pot put 2 tablespoons of instant
coffee (or Sanka), and ¼ teaspoon ground cardamom, and 2 cups boiling
water. Stir. Allow to rest a few minutes to develop the bouquet. Serve in
demitasse cups with sugar only. No cream. A strong brew, much loved in the
Middle East, where coffee without cardamom is unthinkable.

~~~~~~~~~~~~~~~~~~~

Coriander Coffee

Crush coriander seeds, one at a time, in smallest mortar and
pestle. Place one crushed seed in each coffee cup. Fill cup with hot
coffee (of a normal strength brew). Serve with sugar only.
Both of these coffees are reputed to be digestives and love potions.

~~~~~~~~~~~~~~~~~~~

About Appetizers

If you are having a large cocktail party, it matters not how many appetizers grace the buffet table, but have contrasting foods, tastes, textures, colors, and easily handled fare. Letitia Baldrige, one-time secretary to Claire Booth Luce, says a lot in this reminiscence: "One night I attended a party.... and became engaged in conversation with a man by the buffet. We had both been trying to eat the same type of hors d'oeuvre — an open-faced sandwich with asparagus tips on it. We both simultaneously lost several of our asparagus pieces on the floor..... This resulted in mutual embarrassment, and then mutual mirth. He asked me if I knew of a school where diplomats could be taught how to eat complicated hors d'oeuvres without spilling..."

I would have told him to train the cook, not the diplomat. All the appetizers in this book are geared to painless consumption.

A lesson, not soon forgotten, was when I served a large Roquefort cheese, which crumbled alarmingly, and crisp crackers that sprayed crumbs far and wide, to a good-sized group. At 3 A.M. I was still scrubbing up ground-in cheese, and vacuuming rugs.

See page 22 for Roquefort appetizers that anchor the cheese, and page 34 for asparagus sandwiches that won't dive to the floor.

Never put anything gooey on crackers ahead of time. Mush prevails if you do. Bread that has been painted with butter, cut into desired shape, placed on cookie sheet, and lightly browned in a slow oven, is the ideal base for many a soft spread. A favorite trick is to slice uncooked "brown and serve" hard rolls for this purpose. No need to take the time and waste the bread involved in cutting rounds out of regular sliced bread with a cookie cutter.

When appetizers are served before a dinner party, there is no sense in preparing an imposing, exhausting and appetite-inhibiting array. Have only one or two, and those contrasting. One hot, one cold; one "spread," with toast or crackers, one finger green; one fruit, one cheese.

Serving just finger greens as an appetizer before dinner is a fine way of dispensing with the salad course at dinner. Suggested greens are carrots, celery, radishes, cucumber, turnip, cauliflower, cherry tomatoes, raw mushrooms. These can be cut into all sorts of interesting shapes, easy to eat with fingers. Serve with or without a dip. (See dips on page 26 and Parsley Spread, page 25.) The diet-conscious appreciate this sort of prelude to a meal.

Fruit and cheese, or fruit and meat, make fine cocktail snacks. Suggested fruits are melon balls, fresh pineapple wedges, slices of pear or apple, cherries in a bowl with stems on. Hard or semi-hard unprocessed cheese, whole, or cut into dainty slices or cubes, may surround the fruit, or alternate slices of fruit and cheese in an attractive pattern. Small cubes or slices of ham, chicken, cold roast beef (have horseradish handy), cubes of roast lamb (have vinegar-mint sauce for dipping), go well with fruit in season. Just be sure not to repeat the same meat, fruit or cheese at table. Supply toothpicks for spearing when necessary.

Keep in mind that most sandwiches (pages 34 – 44) make tempting appetizers, so long as they are not sweet. Either open-faced, or closed and cut into dainty fingers, the most mundane sandwich may be transformed into an hors d'oeuvre.

It is difficult to indicate, in all appetizer recipes, how many people can be served, for so much depends on circumstances. If appetizers are to be served before a meal, they are eaten in different quantity than at a cocktail party. Also, there is no way of knowing how many other canapés may be served along with one particular recipe, or how generously a mixture will be spread. Are the partakers young and voracious, or old and finicky? You are the judge.

Chicken Liver Paté

1 pound fresh chicken livers, placed in saucepan, covered with cold water.

2 chicken bouillon cubes, crumbled over liver. Bring to boil, and simmer, covered, for 20 minutes. Drain off water, and put livers through food grinder, using smallest fixture on grinder. (Remove the little stringy-tendony bit from each liver before grinding.)

½ cup soft butter (1 stick) placed in dish that catches the ground, warm liver.

1 medium onion, put through grinder.

½ teaspoon salt
1 teaspoon dry mustard
¼ teaspoon ground cloves
¼ teaspoon nutmeg
3 dashes cayenne pepper

Stir all this thoroughly into above liver mixture. It is all ready to serve, smoothed into a pretty bowl, and garnished with chopped parsley. Or divide into small ramekins and freeze. Serve with thin slices of Danish Beer Bread (page 204), or any good rye or pumpernickel. Butter bread or not, as you prefer. Sweet butter is best. Serve the paté at room temperature, or for a Danish touch, serve it hot.

Stuffed Eggs make great appetizers. See page 123.

See Horseradish Mousse on page 148.

Liverwurst Mold

1 can Campbell's Consommé

1 envelope (tablespoon) plain gelatin, soaked in ¼ cup of the cold consommé.
Bring the rest of consommé to a boil and pour over the soaked
gelatin, stirring until thoroughly dissolved. Pour ⅓ of this into
lightly oiled (not buttered) decorative mold and place in refrigerator
for quick jelling.

1 pound best liverwurst mixed with · · · · ·   } Spread this in the mold
2 tablespoons grated onion   when consommé in mold
6 tablespoons sherry and ⅓ of warm consommé   has jelled. Chill these
                                                        2 layers a while.

Lastly, pour the remaining ⅓ of consommé on top. Chill.
Unmold when ready to serve. Garnish with parsley. Serve
with crackers, or Melba toast, or rye bread.

Mushroom and Onion Canapé

Use the recipe for Mushroom and Onion Sauce (page 314).
The only change is to chop the mushrooms and onions finer than for
sauce. As some canapés are supposed to be salty, you may want to add
one more bouillon cube. Taste test, to be sure.

I try to keep this on hand, frozen, in ramekins. It is best served
hot, I believe. But may be served cold also. You can't lose. Serve with
homemade Melba toast. Prepare for addiction.

Bess Piqula's Party Meat Balls
(Will serve 20 as appetizer, 8 people as a supper dish.)

2 pounds ground beef
½ cup bread crumbs
¼ cup milk, poured over crumbs ⎫ Mix well. Form into small balls.
1 egg, beaten
salt and pepper, to taste

½ of a 14-ounce bottle of tomato ketchup ⎫ Mix together and heat in fairly large pan.
½ of an 8 ounce jar of grape jelly ⎭ Add the meatballs carefully. Cover, and simmer 20 to 30 minutes.

A delicious sour-sweet dish. Just the ticket for your favorite chafing dish, or casserole resting on a candle warmer. May be kept warm for ages with no harm to flavor. Keep a supply frozen in freezer-to-stove-to-table dishes. Serve with toothpicks for spearing.

Piping Pigs   (for 12 people)
1 package best hot dogs (1 pound or 10 hot dogs) cut into bite-sized pieces
1 cup prepared mustard ⎫ mix thoroughly and pour over hot dogs that
1 cup red currant jelly ⎭ have been placed in stove-to-table dish.

Place in 300° oven and bake until bubbling hot, covered. (½ hour).
Serve in same manner as the meat balls, above.

Dried Beef Rolls

Spread slices of <u>dried beef</u> with <u>cottage cheese</u> or <u>cream cheese</u>, or a combination of both, and roll up each slice, as one does a jelly roll. (The cheese should be brought to room temperature and beaten with a spoon, and perhaps softened further with a little <u>cream</u> or <u>milk</u>. It must spread easily, or the thin slices of beef tear.) These make a superb appetizer, may be rolled and chilled way ahead of time. Easily eaten with fingers.

If you can find a butcher who will slice dried beef for you while you watch, you are in luck. Otherwise you must fall back on the packaged or bottled variety. This is sometimes so torn that it is not possible to salvage whole slices for rolling. Be not downhearted, just chop it up fine, with a chef's knife (or put through a grinder), mix the meat with cheese, roll into little balls. Then roll the balls in chopped parsley. You can't lose; attractive and appetizing either way.

Neepie's Appetizer

Wrap <u>pitted dates</u> in a <u>bacon</u> covering, and secure with a <u>toothpick</u>. Place in baking pan, and spoon commercial (or your own) <u>barbecue sauce</u> over the wrapped dates. Bake in preheated <u>375°</u> oven until bacon is cooked. Drain on paper towels. When ready to serve, reheat in stove-to-table dish.

Bet's Cheese Spread

8 ounces of cream cheese
4 ounces of Roquefort or bleu cheese
1 teaspoon garlic salt or onion salt
1 tablespoon chopped pimento
1 tablespoon chopped green pepper

Mix together thoroughly. Place in a pretty little bowl. Serve with crisp crackers. Or make in quantity, filling small ramekins and freezing for that smug feeling of being ready for a party, or unexpected guests. For the extra-festive touch, roll this recipe into a ball, roll the ball in chopped nuts, stick a sprig of holly in the top, or whatever you want as a symbol of the season. Surround with crackers. It looks good — is good.

Roquefort Crisps

Cream together Roquefort cheese, cream cheese, and butter, in about equal proportions (or bleu cheese and butter, half and half). Spread on thin pieces of bread (slices of unbaked Pepperidge hard rolls are perfect for this), place on cookie sheet. Bake in preheated 350° oven until lightly browned. Watch! Best served hot, but they'll be eaten, gratefully, cold also.

The secret of easy mixing of above recipes is to have everything room-temperature soft.

Sesame Herb Toast (3 or 4 dozen appetizers)

¼ pound (1 stick) soft butter
1 tablespoon flour
} cream together

1 egg, beaten
3 tablespoons sesame seeds
¼ teaspoon marjoram
¼ teaspoon basil
¼ teaspoon rosemary
1 tablespoon freeze-dried chives

Mix and work into above butter and flour. (If fresh herbs are available, increase amounts and chop fine.) Spread on thin slices of bread. (I use unbaked Pepperidge hard rolls, which produce a dainty little round slice.) Place on cookie sheet and bake in preheated 325° oven until slightly brown (about 15 minutes, but watch). Excellent canapé, and also good with soup.

Cheese Balls (makes about 24)

1 five-ounce jar of sharp, processed, spreading cheese
3 tablespoons soft butter
} creamed together

¾ cup flour
½ teaspoon salt
¼ teaspoon paprika

Add to above. Mix well. Pinch off small pieces of dough. Roll into ¾ inch balls. Place on buttered cookie sheet. Bake in preheated 400° oven for about 10 minutes. Serve hot. May also be served cold, and I have made them by the hundreds for large parties. They freeze well.

Brown Canapés

Mix <u>chili sauce</u> and grated <u>Cheddar cheese</u>, half and half. Spread on small pieces of <u>bread</u>, being sure that every bit of bread is covered, and then cover with a piece of <u>bacon</u>. Line up on a cookie sheet, hours in advance of cooking. Bake in preheated <u>375°</u> oven until bacon crisps a bit and bread browns on the bottom. Serve at once, or place on oven-to-table plates or platters and reheat a few at a time, so there are always hot canapés to pass. (You may use the store variety grated American or Cheddar cheese. And, in a pinch, you may substitute ketchup for chili sauce, but the results won't be as good.)

This is the most durable appetizer recipe I own, and the most consistently met with cheers. Mrs. Gabriel Brown of Easton, Pennsylvania, an inspired hostess, gave it to me in 1930.

~~~~~~~~~~~

Mrs. Joseph W. Downs' Hot Appetizer Mix
(No home should be without it.)

<u>¾ pound very sharp Cheddar cheese</u>
<u>½ pound raw bacon</u>
<u>1 small green pepper</u>
<u>1 very small onion</u>

- - - - - - - -

<u>Triscuits</u> are a must.

Put all this through grinder, using medium blade. Mix well. Spread on Triscuits. Place under preheated broiler (on a cookie sheet). Broiler should be on low heat. Broil about <u>5 minutes</u>, but watch it diligently. Bacon should cook and cheese bubble. This mix keeps a year in freezer, 3 weeks in refrigerator. Mrs. Downs says it makes a good toasted sandwich for lunch, too.

~~~~~~~~~~~

Marion Wing's Parsley Spread

(Unbelievably good and good for you. Horses fed parsley run faster. So will you.)

LARGE bunch of parsley, well washed, well dried, stems discarded. Chop fine.
mayonnaise or salad dressing, mixed with chopped parsley in sufficient quantity
        to be nicely spreadable, no more.
salt and freshly ground pepper, to taste
a modest amount of chopped fresh chives, or freeze dried chives or grated onion (just
        a touch). Mix well. Place in small bowl. Best served with
        Wheat Thins, but Melba toast or Triscuits will do, or any cracker.
A French chef's knife, and the ability to use it, is imperative for this best of
recipes. The finer the parsley is chopped, the better. It reduces greatly. I'm
almost never without this when my garden is yielding great masses of parsley,
both curly and Italian. (The latter has slightly better flavor, I think, but probably
comparisons are odious concerning this blessed herb.)
        This makes an excellent spread for dainty tea sandwiches. Or
try thick slathers of it with white meat of chicken to make a luncheon sandwich that will prove memorable.
        Serve it with finger greens instead of crackers, for the diet-
conscious.

═══════════════

Shirley Kenney's Version of Parsley Spread

1 pint mayonnaise, ½ pint sour cream, 1 large red onion, grated
Load this with chopped parsley. Salt and pepper, to taste.
Richer and more oniony than above, but I should have called it a
vision (of loveliness) rather than a version. Enough for large group.

═══════════════

Avocado Cocktail Dip

1 ripe avocado, peeled and stoned
1 cream cheese (4 ounces) brought to room temperature
2 tablespoons lemon juice
1 teaspoon onion juice
½ teaspoon garlic salt
½ teaspoon Worcestershire Sauce
pimento strips for garnish

Mash together until thoroughly blended. Pile into a pretty serving bowl. Garnish with pimento. Colorful and fine dip to serve with finger greens or the cracker of your choice.

Wing Dip

Mix cream cheese and Bovril. Could anything be simpler? Try it!

Yale Club Cocktail Dip

Using sour cream, cream cheese, cottage cheese, one of them, two, or all — as a base — mix in some horseradish and plenty of chopped watercress.

Melba Toast

Paint thin slices of bread with a little melted butter. (You may skip the butter, but it gives a better flavor.) Cut into squares, fingers, circles, or triangles. Place on cookie sheet and dry out slowly, slowly, in 300° oven until pale tan and crisp. Commercial Melba toast tastes like cardboard. It has a tendency to stick in one's throat, and can quite successfully cancel the goodness of your best cocktail spread.

Black Caviar (The classic way to serve this greatest hors d'oeuvre)

If you can acquire and/or afford fresh black caviar, you know what it feels like to be a king. Otherwise, buy the canned variety that is really black caviar (not fish eggs dyed black!). You will, at least, feel like a member of the royal entourage.

chilled caviar
Melba toast
sweet butter (optional)
chopped onion
chopped hard-boiled egg white
chopped hard-boiled egg yolk
wedges of lemon

Serve all these things in separate dishes of suitable sizes. Let guests butter their own toast (if they want butter), pile on the caviar, egg, onion, and squeeze of lemon. It takes skill to eat without spilling, so is best served when there are few people, and these gathered around a table. Best to provide individual butter plates. The balancing act is worth the delight of eating. See "Caviar, My Way" for greater economy and ease of handling.

Sardine Canapés

Buy the best boneless sardines and drain them thoroughly. Make toast, and butter it, and cut it like this: On each elongated triangle of toast place a sardine, the tail at the pointed end. Just before serving, squeeze lemon juice generously over all.

Caviar Canapés ~ My Way

hard-boiled eggs (1 egg to 4 people) put through potato ricer or mashed fine.

mayonnaise

dry mustard, just a touch

grated onion, judicious amount

lemon juice

salt, be careful, as caviar is salty

pepper, freshly ground

black caviar (let others serve red)

parsley

Stir all this into eggs. Be careful to keep eggs firm, not runny. This calls for a light hand with the seasonings. Spread this mixture on rounds of buttered and dried-out bread. Put a dab of caviar on the egg (the amount determined by your pocketbook). Place on serving tray. Decorate with parsley. There will be no left-overs.

With this way of serving caviar there is no fuss, and no muss to clean up afterwards. It is also more saving of worth-its-weight-in-gold caviar.

Crabmeat Cocktail Spread

1 cup plain yogurt

¼ cup chili sauce (or ketchup)

1 Tablespoon lemon juice

1 teaspoon celery seed

garlic salt, to taste

chopped parsley, fresh, the more the merrier

1 can king crabmeat, drained and shredded fine (about 7½ ounces)

Mix all together and serve with well-crisped Wheat Thins.

(Served on lettuce, this also makes a fine luncheon salad.)

Hot Seafood Spread

1 tablespoon butter, melted in frying pan

2 stalks celery) chop fine and cook in butter, above, slowly, and until juices
½ green pepper) dry out a bit.

1 Tablespoon lemon juice sprinkled over the following fish:

1   6½-ounce can shrimp, cut small) Let this soak in the lemon juice
1   6½-ounce can crabmeat, flaked fine) while celery and pepper cook.

¾ cup mayonnaise -----------) mix with the fish. Then stir everything
1 tablespoon Worcestershire Sauce) into the cooked celery and pepper.
pepper, freshly ground, to taste) Place in buttered baking dish.

6 saltines, crushed fine ------------------) mix and use as a
¼ cup grated cheese (Parmesan or store cheese)) topping. Dot with
) butter. Bake in preheated
350° oven about ½ hour. Watch it. Serve hot with
Melba toast. Let guests help themselves. Brace yourself for rave notices.
This may be made hours, or a day ahead, refrigerated, then heated
as guests approach. (Also makes a good luncheon dish served
in scallop shells or ramekins.)

See Codfish Cakes on page 114. They make superb appetizers.

Dell's Tuna Canapés

<u>1 can of white tuna fish</u>, the best, drained and chopped fine

<u>Mayonnaise</u>
<u>dry mustard</u>, a dash
<u>lemon juice</u>
<u>grated onion</u>
<u>celery</u>, finely chopped
<u>salt and pepper</u>

Mix all this into tuna fish, according to taste. Be careful not to make it runny. Spread generously on buttered toast. Cut each slice into 4 squares. Garnish each square with an olive circle. (This recipe may be stretched by adding chopped hard-boiled egg.)

<u>pimento-stuffed olives</u>, cut in circles, as one cuts a loaf of bread
<u>buttered toast</u>

I have never forgotten how delicious these canapés were when served at Dell Davis' gracious home at Fairfield Beach, Connecticut, many years ago.

This recipe is equally good for a luncheon sandwich or salad.

If you should make this (or any spread) too runny, crush crackers or Melba toast with mortar and pestle and add the crumbs to the mixture until it assumes the correct consistency. This isn't recommended as a practice, just to meet an occasional emergency.

Tuna canapés are not exotic, or even very original, but still they are the sort of uncomplicated thing that people seem to like better than a lot of gourmet surprises (maybe I should say "shocks").

About Sandwiches

Only since the American Revolution have sandwiches, as we know them, been around. Or so the story goes. And, indirectly, they helped us win the war, because John Montague, the 4th earl of Sandwich, and first lord of the admiralty, spent a lot of time at the gaming table instead of tending to business. Desiring to eat in an informal fashion, while gambling, he requested that slices of bread with various fillings be brought to him. This convenience food, since then, has borne his name. He allowed the British navy to fall into decay. We won the fight. Sandwiches may have been an innovation according to British custom, but actually man, throughout the ages, has used breadstuff as a plate upon which to place his food. One sees it still in the Middle East, Africa, and Mexico, for example.

A sandwich is as good as the bread that encloses it, and the filling within. Use various types of bread, homemade if possible. Spread butter to the very corners, heap it with filling that is neither too moist nor too dry, season it well. Be generous.

A few years ago I gave a wedding reception for a friend, in buffet-supper fashion, the food being of things easily balanced on a plate. Among other things, there were several hot dishes, plus stuffed eggs, plus ham and turkey sandwiches that I wanted to be particularly delicious. The sandwiches were to be made with small potato rolls (page 207). All went well with the ham, for I roasted it myself, mixed some of the pan drippings (skimmed of fat) with mayonnaise, mustard, brown sugar, and a little ground clove, and spread this on the split, small, tender, flat, buttered rolls, and then added the sliced ham. Delicious. Not having time or strength, I let the grocer talk me into buying sliced white meat of turkey, commercially roasted. I should have known better. Cardboard would have been as flavorful.

In desperation I rushed to town, bought a small roasting chicken, baked it until golden, and the pan drippings crusty. Pouring off all fat, I made a very concentrated gravy salted with chicken bouillon cubes. The meat of the chicken was ground up and added to the strong gravy. I spread this excellent-tasting emulsion generously on the buttered rolls, folded the cardboard turkey slices thickly thereon, and the day was saved.

For another wedding I was asked to supply recipes for three different tea sandwiches. The woman who was to make them in quantity did a test run, a week in advance, and asked me to sample them. Something was seriously wrong and I had to say so. They seemed to stick to the roof of my mouth, and lacked the deliciousness that should have been theirs. Then she said, "I didn't want to waste butter on samples. These are made with oleomargarine, but for the event I'll use butter." She did, and the buttered sandwiches at the wedding were a success. The difference between the two batches would easily demolish any defense by oleo fanciers.

A sandwich may furnish a hearty meal, or be the daintiest little sliver at a tea party, depending on the technique of preparation. For a tea party, I like non-sweet sandwiches best; then the tea cakes and candies are more of a treat. Three kinds of sandwiches are ample, and it adds to their appeal if each is presented in different guise: one open-faced and round; one a three-decker type, sliced thin —— so easy to make and looks so fancy; one a sandwich finger, square, or triangle, which is simply a normal closed sandwich cut into tiny, bite-sized pieces.

Remember that some sandwiches make good appetizers, and some appetizers make fine sandwiches. So, refer back to the appetizers, as well as ahead to the sandwich alphabet. (Incidentally, the alphabet was developed for my radio program, at the Time of school opening in the fall, to help mothers produce sandwich variety for the lunch box.)

Many sandwiches freeze well, ready for everything from school lunch box, to picnic, to cocktail-hour appetizer. Just be sure not to freeze a sandwich containing <u>tomatoes</u> or <u>lettuce</u> or <u>hard-boiled eggs</u>. Wrap sandwiches separately for freezing, and thaw them in their wrappers. Never refreeze a thawed sandwich.

Always keep a dish of <u>soft butter</u> in a cupboard, not the refrigerator, ready for action.

Never, never allow anything containing <u>mayonnaise</u> to remain long at room temperature. Food poisoning from warm mayonnaise is all too common. Once a bottle of mayonnaise is opened, always keep it refrigerated.

The Naughty Earl of Sandwich

Sandwich Alphabet

Almond-chicken — To one cup chopped chicken add ¼ cup chopped, toasted almonds, ½ cup chopped celery. Bind with mayonnaise. Season to taste with grated lemon peel, lemon juice, salt, paprika.

Apple butter with cream cheese, and/or with sliced, chopped, or deviled ham.

Asparagus, the best canned asparagus tips. Or cook your own. These to be rolled up in slices of bread from which crusts are removed. (The bread must be the cotton-boughten kind I ordinarily disdain.) Roll over the bread slices firmly with a rolling pin, to make them more pliable. Butter the bread, then spread with mayonnaise to which a little lemon juice has been added. Place a spear of asparagus on one end of bread. Salt it if necessary, and then roll up the asparagus snugly in the bread. Secure the roll with a tooth pick at each end. Then cut the roll in half. One of the best treats there is, whether it finds its way into a child's lunch box, or the fanciest collation for diplomats.

Banana bread spread with butter and cream cheese.

Banana, mashed and spread on dark bread that has been buttered and generously spread with peanut butter.

Baked beans, cold, mashed, spread on buttered brown bread and touched with tomato ketchup.

Beef — Cold roast beef makes the king of sandwiches. Trim meat of all fat and gristle. Butter the bread, add a bit of cold gravy or jellied pan drippings, a touch of horseradish, salt, pepper.

B.L.T. meaning bacon, lettuce, and tomato—an all-time favorite. Put these three things between slices of buttered toast well spread with mayonnaise. Season with salt, pepper, and be sure to put a sprinkling of sugar on the tomato.

Celery and nuts chopped fine, bound with mayonnaise, on whole wheat bread.

<u>Cheese</u>!~ This opens a Pandora's box of possibilities, all good, none evil. It may be plain or toasted, combined with all sorts of meat, especially ham. An endless array of cheese awaits one at supermarket or cheese specialty shop. A loaf, a jug, and cheese comprises the French working man's lunch. Why not yours?

<u>Cheeseburger</u>~ Pan broil hamburgers (page 83) allowing ¼ pound meat per serving, undercooking them somewhat. Place on bottom half of hamburg bun that has been buttered and slightly toasted. Place a slice of your favorite cheese on the meat. Slide under broiler until cheese puffs and bubbles and browns slightly. Transfer to plate and put buttered and toasted top of bun beside the cheeseburger. Let the diner choose or refuse such embellishments as ketchup, onion and/or relish.

<u>Chicken</u> may be made of slices of meat on buttered bread, with a generous spreading of mayonnaise, salt, pepper, a leaf of lettuce, or parsley spread (page 25). Or sometimes skip the greens and slather some cold chicken gravy on the buttered bread, and salt the chicken with a crumbled chicken bouillon cube. This latter treatment desirable for sandwiches that are to be frozen. A <u>chicken salad sandwich</u> is made with finely chopped chicken bound together with mayonnaise, seasoned with chicken bouillon cube, a touch of lemon juice and onion juice, and chopped celery, and perhaps some chopped green pepper and pimento. Sometimes a dash of curry is good. The finer the occasion, the finer the filling should be chopped. For tea sandwiches, I put everything through the grinder and produce a fine tasting emulsion that serves well for a 3-decker type sandwich that looks so dainty and tempting when sliced. Use 2 slices of white bread, and

have the middle slice of dark bread for eye appeal. Cream cheese
will stretch this mixture and improve its adhering qualities.

<u>Club Sandwich</u> ⌣ Between either 2 or 3 slices of buttered toast spread
with mayonnaise, arrange lettuce leaves, sliced tomatoes that are
salted, peppered and slightly sugared, slices of chicken, and strips
of crisp bacon. Steady the structure with toothpicks and cut into
4 triangles. ⊠ The three-decker is traditional but not compulsory.

<u>Cold Cuts</u> ⌣ Take your choice. The mind boggles at the array available.

<u>Corned Beef</u> on buttered rye bread, with a dash of horseradish.

<u>Crabmeat</u>, fresh or canned, is perfect sandwich material, provided that
the stiff little tendons it harbors are conscientiously removed.
Sprinkle the picked-over crabmeat with lemon juice, add a bit
of onion juice, chopped celery, green pepper (if you like it), a
dash of Worcestershire Sauce, paprika, salt, pepper, and stir
all together with mayonnaise. Taste test. You are the judge
of seasonings. This makes a whole meal if served in a
buttered and oven-toasted hot dog roll, with or without lettuce.
Or it can be the basis of delicate tea sandwiches, in which case
the finer chopped the better.

<u>Cucumber</u> needs nothing but buttered bread, mayonnaise, salt, pepper. It lends
itself perfectly to little round open sandwiches. Score the cucumber skin
by dragging a fork down the length of it. Slice. Place on rounds of bread.
A pinch of paprika adds color. One of my favorites. Crunchy, refreshing.

<u>Date and peanut butter</u> ⌣ Chop dates fine and mix with soft butter.
Spread this mixture generously on one slice of white bread. Top with
another slice of bread which has a thick layer of peanut butter on top
of it. This middle slice should be of dark bread, but not one bit necessary.

Slap on another slice of white bread. Press together firmly. Wrap, refrigerate. When ready to serve, trim off crusts with a sharp, serrated knife. Cut the 3-decker sandwich in half, or even in thirds. Then slice very thin and you have the most decorative tea sandwiches, with negligible effort. All 3-deckers are made this way. The fillings depend on your imagination. It needn't be a tea party. Serve for cocktails as well. There's no better method of transforming the mundane.

Dried beef ⁓ Chop the beef fine and mix with softened cream cheese, or cottage cheese. A touch of horseradish is good but optional.

Egg salad sandwich ⁓ Chopped, hard-boiled eggs may be lightly seasoned with just mayonnaise and salt and pepper. But for adults a little more zip is needed. See stuffed eggs (page 123) for seasoning ideas. Some chopped ham and/or chopped pickles added to eggs lends interest. Lettuce in an egg sandwich is usually a welcome addition.

Frankfurters ⁓ Who needs directions for these? Well, some do. Buy the best and simmer them in water for a few minutes. This removes some of the fat while making them plump and juicy. They may be broiled or roasted or fried after this, but it's not necessary. Place in a buttered roll that has been slightly crisped in oven. Serve with mustard, ketchup, chopped onion, relish, or whatever suits your fancy. Leftover frankfurters, chopped and mixed with a bit of mayonnaise and chopped pickles make tasty sandwiches. They add zest to an egg sandwich.

Fluffernutters are difficult to recommend, but children find them

38

enslaving. They are simply sandwiches made of half marsh-mallow fluff and half peanut butter. There is no accounting for taste, but small fry find them as festive as spun sugar at a fair.

Flapjacks left over from breakfast may be spread with butter along with jam, brown sugar, or maple sugar, rolled up like a jelly roll and secured with a toothpick.

Grape jelly, plain, with cream cheese, or made into a nourishing conserve by the addition of raisins and chopped nuts.

Ginger, crystallized, cut into small pieces and mixed with cream cheese. Especially good on banana or apricot bread. Recommended chiefly for the tea party department.

Ham — Plain slices of ham on buttered bread with mustard, mayonnaise, perhaps lettuce. Ham and cheese, plain, or toasted. When you are down to bits and pieces of left-over ham, put it through the grinder, moisten with mayonnaise, and add the finely chopped sweet green pickle that comes all prepared, or lacking that, put some whole sweet pickles through the grinder along with the ham. Ham nearly always calls for some mustard, also rye bread. A touch of the jelled pan drippings from a home-baked ham adds authority to a sandwich.

Hamburger — Read all about it on pages 83 and 84.

India relish with cream cheese on rye bread or pumpernickel.

Jelly and jam, plain, on buttered bread, or with cream cheese, or with peanut butter.

Kidney beans, the canned variety, drained, mashed, and seasoned with a little chopped celery, grated onion, chopped gherkins, some mayonnaise, a bit of tomato ketchup, salt to taste, and a touch of dried or fresh savory (the bean herb). Spread on dark bread that has been buttered. Chopped hard-boiled eggs go well with the mixture, but are optional. Likewise lettuce.

Kosher corned beef on rye or dark pumpernickel, with plenty of mustard. If you add butter it is not kosher. Save the butter for the regular tinned corned beef. Always serve a dill pickle with either type of sandwich.

Lamb ⁓ Lovely slices of cold roast lamb on buttered bread, moistened with its own gravy, with plenty of salt and freshly ground pepper, makes a sandwich so plain, so good, that it is heresy to doctor it up with another thing. We never had lamb sandwiches that my husband didn't reminisce about how good they tasted in his boyhood. Hunting in the wintry woods of Nova Scotia, he would take the slightly frozen sandwiches from his knapsack; they had a special charm, washed down with warm, sweet tea from a thermos.

L is for lettuce which adds so much to many a sandwich, and can even stand on its own, with a bit of mayonnaise.

Liverwurst ⁓ Mash liverwurst and cream cheese together. Season with a little onion juice and sherry until of proper spreading consistency. Use salt and pepper to taste. Rye or pumpernickel bread goes best with it.

Lobster roll ⁓ Mix small pieces of lobster meat with lemon juice, mayonnaise, prepared mustard, cayenne pepper, salt, and freshly ground black pepper — all to suit your taste. Chopped celery stretches and also enhances the precious lobster, likewise chopped hard-boiled egg. A bit of grated onion helps. Heap this mixture into a buttered and toasted hot dog roll. As with crab, this may all be chopped ever so fine and emerge in tea-sandwich form.

Marmalade, plain, or with cream cheese, or with chopped ham, or with grated carrot, or transformed into a conserve by adding nuts and raisins.

Meat loaf, cold, sliced, makes an excellent sandwich, plain, or with lettuce and mayonnaise, or a touch of tomato ketchup, or a little of the tomato sauce you may have left over from serving the meat loaf hot.

Nut bread with cream cheese. Nuts of any kind, chopped, mixed with cream cheese and spread on the bread of your choice, as is, or with jelly added.

Onion ⌒ Slice a sweet onion very thin. Arrange the rings on buttered bread. Add a bit of mayonnaise, salt, pepper. Wonderful, but for bovine digestions only, though it won't leave you with a bovine breath. Chew some parsley and all will be well. Reputed to induce sleep!

Olive and cream cheese ⌒ Chop pimento-stuffed olives fine. Mix with cream cheese. Or buy the commercial olive butter spread that has been on the market for years, and deserves to be. Use plain or with cream cheese, as you see fit.

Peanut butter sandwiches are a national cult, thanks to George Washington Carver. Peanut butter always reminds me of a small boy who traveled with our group in the Middle East. The unusual food of the region not only made him unhappy, but downright sick. Looking pale and shaken from days of tummy upset, he said to his mother, "If only I could have a peanut butter sandwich I'd get well." There was no such thing in the length and breadth of the lands we traveled. Poor kid. Anyway, he managed to survive the deprivation. There are the plain peanut butter devotees and also those addicted to the addition of jelly. The peanut butter — jelly enthusiasts claim these sandwiches are also good toasted.

<u>Pimento cheese</u> makes a tasty sandwich. You may manufacture your own by adding chopped pimento to cream cheese.

<u>Pizza sandwich</u> ⌒ Great for a quickie lunch. Split English muffins apart with a fork. Toast lightly and butter. Place pieces of fresh or canned tomatoes on each half, along with thin rings of onion. Sprinkle with salt, pepper, and a touch of dried or fresh oregano. Top with a slice of mozzarella cheese. (Preparation thus far may be accomplished way in advance of meal.) Just before serving, place under broiler until cheese melts and browns slightly. Ever so good.

<u>Poor Boy</u>, which is another name for a "Submarine" or "Hero" sandwich. A small loaf of French bread is cut in half lengthwise and spread with butter. The jaw-breaking sandwich may contain many things, according to personal preference: slices of salami, cheese, ham, tomato, onion, green pepper. It must include some mustard. There seem to be no hard and fast rules.

<u>Pork</u>, cold, left-over, on buttered bread, with a touch of its own gravy, or a thin coating of apple sauce. Plenty of salt and pepper.

Quince jelly — Who has that these days?! Unique in flavor. Make a plain sandwich, or add cream cheese. Its haunting taste should not be masked in any way.

Radish — Slice radishes very thin and arrange generously on well-buttered bread. Add salt and pepper to taste. Apply a bit of mayonnaise if you want, but not traditional. A European standby that we are prone to ignore, unfortunately.

Sardine — See page 27.

Swiss Cheese, plain or with sliced ham, and always some mustard.

Shrimp — Season as with Tuna (page 30) or as with the crabmeat or lobster in this alphabet. Be sure to add a touch of ketchup or chili sauce along with other seasonings.

Tomato — A tomato sandwich is one of the best, whether served with lettuce or without. Be sure to put a little sugar on the tomato, along with salt and pepper and mayonnaise or salad dressing. Butter the bread well to prevent soaking. Don't freeze!

Tongue is best on rye bread and needs a touch of mustard. Tongue goes nicely with Gruyère cheese.

Tuna — See page 30. Sliced tomatoes are sometimes a happy addition to a tunafish sandwich. So is lettuce.

Turkey — Do all the things with turkey that have been suggested for chicken. A hot turkey sandwich is a pleasant aftermath to a roast turkey dinner. Place bread or toast on a warm plate. Heap on the sliced turkey. Ladle piping hot giblet gravy over all. Be sure there's some stuffing alongside, and some cranberry jelly.

Underwood's Deviled Ham or Chicken or Liverwurst Spread ~ All are delicious. No picnic was complete without deviled ham sandwiches when I was a child. They were served as lovely little triangles, rich with filling and trimmed of crusts. To have one of these in one hand, and a hard-boiled egg in the other, spelled pure joy. I seem to smell pine needles as I write this. Pine groves were de rigeur for picnics in those days.

Veal and venison, cold, sliced and arranged on buttered bread coated with the gravy of whichever meat you are using. Salt and pepper. If its a venison sandwich, be sure to make a currant jelly sandwich also. Venison and currant jelly are soul mates. A few drops of sherry in the venison gravy will give another proper touch.

Walnut and cream cheese ~ Chop walnuts fine before mixing with the cheese. Jelly may be added, and guava jelly is especially good.

Watercress ~ Watercress sandwiches, for greatest appeal, should be rolled as with asparagus. Be sure to let the fluffy leaves of the watercress protrude becomingly from each end of sandwich roll. There are never, never any left-overs.

Western ~ Brown just a touch of chopped onion in a little butter. Beat an egg, plus 1 tablespoon of water, very lightly with a fork; then add a little chopped ham. Pour the egg-ham mixture over the onion. Cook just long enough to make it possible to turn the egg. Cook only a second on the reversed side. Slide between slices of buttered bread or bun. Skip the onion and you have an Eastern sandwich.

X=tra good Survival Sandwiches — When the gas works blew up in Easton, Pennsylvania back in the 1940's (I think), it was enough of a disaster for the Red Cross to move in and set up a field kitchen. And what did they serve? Hearty sandwiches made of peanut butter, grated carrots, and raisins. All the elements of a good meal are contained in this really delicious sandwich. It has been a family favorite ever since. Try it. The ingredients are practically always in everyone's kitchen, a cinch to make, and no need to feel guilty about the kids not being properly nourished, because they are.

Yankee Pot Roast — See page 88.   And while we are on the Y's, remember that yogurt is sometimes a fine substitute for mayonnaise, or may be mixed with it to stretch it and add interesting flavor.

Zoo Sandwiches — Small children will eat almost anything placed on an animal-shaped piece of bread. Get out the cookie cutters and line up a Noah's ark procession of sandwiches. Great birthday party fare for the juvenile set.

Zwieback is a favorite of many children, especially if it is homemade. Simply spread bread with a little butter and a mixture of cinnamon and sugar. Cut into fingers. Place on cookie sheet and dry out in 300° oven until crisp. Good for grown-up teas as well.

Soup

Chicken Soup (page 49) for Two, Before The Franklin Stove

"In January / it's so nice
while slipping / on the sliding ice
To sip hot chicken soup / with rice.
Sipping once / Sipping Twice
sipping chicken soup / with rice."

—Maurice Sendak

About Soup

Better that a bride should have a <u>large</u> <u>stockpot</u> of enamelware or stainless steel, than a silver tea service (if she can't have both). So many people don't make soup simply because they never get around to buying the proper kettle to make it in.

Though I have suggested* that certain soups can be brewed in about 4 hours, I must admit that I am more inclined to put everything in the soup kettle before retiring at night, having the heat beneath the stockpot at a simmering temperature, and forgetting it until morning. I figure that it takes about half the night for the cold fluid to come to a simmer, and the other half to draw forth a good broth.

This brings up the subject of <u>skimming</u> the broth, usually recommended by the experts. I certainly don't get up at night to skim soup. Should I do any sleepwalking, I'd be more liable to <u>stir</u> the potage, so as to spread the seasonings. In the morning, the brew is cooled somewhat for easier handling, strained first through a colander, and again through 2 fine strainers (one placed inside the other). There is nothing objectionable left in the broth.

This leads to the subject of <u>clarifying</u> soup — again an activity I leave to the professionals, the zealots, the untiring. Most definitive cookbooks will tell you how to clarify, if you are so inclined. To me, it is in a class with ice carving, and not suited to the average American home. Furthermore, I can't see that such extremes of perfectionism improve the flavor.

As for <u>flavoring</u> soups, I've tried to be as specific as is practicable. In the long run you will work out the seasonings that suit you best. There need be no slavish adherence to "1 onion stuck with 4 cloves" or "6 peppercorns". A dash of this and a sprinkling of that, is the general rule with soups, and in all my years of presiding over the stockpot, every brew is a little different than the one before. Like snowflakes, there are no two exactly alike.

* (in recipes that follow)

In using <u>canned chicken broth</u> it is wise to put the cans in the refrigerator for a while before opening. This solidifies the fat that is present, and makes it easy to lift out in one cold blob.

Depth of <u>flavor</u> and firm <u>jelling</u> is better achieved by stewing meat and bones, etc., in some broth of their own ilk, as well as in just water. For this, one may often turn to canned broths, lacking a homemade stock. Once in a while, if a soup or stew seems too innocuous, I toss in a package of Lipton's Onion Soup. This will put the breath of life into the blandest dish. It is usually not necessary, — just a hint.

I speak of the deliciousness of <u>pan juices</u> from cooked meat all through this book. There's a double reward to saving them: first, they give flavor supreme to many a dish; second, boiling some water in a roasting pan, and scraping up the goodness with a spoon, is the easiest way there is of cleaning the pan.

"Beautiful Soup, so rich and green,
Waiting in a hot tureen!
Who for such dainties would not stoop?
Soup of the evening, beautiful Soup!
Soup of the evening, beautiful Soup!
    Beau — ootiful Soo - oop!
    Beau — ootiful Soo - oop!
Soo — oop of the e-e-evening,
    Beautiful beautiful Soup!"
                    Lewis Carroll

Chicken Soup and/or Broth

Often called "Jewish penicillin," and for a good reason. Sick or well, it is one of life's great sustainers. Keep some on hand most of the time, in refrigerator or freezer. It is almost as basic as bread or milk, water or fire. Sam Levenson reminisces nostalgically about his mother's ability in making chicken soup, and her faith in its curative powers. He claims she brought two live hens home from market one day for the purpose of making a large kettle of broth. Before she could set about the task, one hen became ill. Nothing daunted, she made soup of the healthy chicken, fed it to the sick one, and cured it! We no longer have to kill and pluck and clean a chicken for the soup kettle. It comes, mostly packaged, but completely ready, in many different ways. Depending on circumstances, I do one of 4 things:

1) Buy a whole good-sized fowl, if I can get it. The chicken world suffers from our youth-oriented society, so that when the poor things begin to put on some age and flavor, they are consigned to the axe. So one settles for the most mature bird the butcher has.

2) Buy chicken parts, just breasts, for instance, if I want to make a fancy chicken salad.

3) Buy the very inexpensive "waste" chicken parts — the backs, wing tips, necks, that are often available. This makes a potful of the finest broth, but doesn't yield much of any meat worth saving.

4) Use left-over carcasses of roast chicken.

The procedure is about the same for all 4 variations. Place the chicken in a stewing kettle and cover with cold water, or, better still, with chicken broth (canned or homemade), which gives the broth the greatest authority. Into the kettle toss all or some of the following, according to your taste: a cut-up onion or 2 (don't bother to peel), a carrot or 2 (washed but not peeled), a couple of stalks of celery, leaves and all, a tiny piece of a bay leaf, parsley, a touch of thyme, a touch of allspice, a few peppercorns, 1 or 2 whole cloves. Cover the kettle, bring slowly to a simmer, and allow to bubble along, barely boiling, until chicken is falling-apart tender. About ½ hour before chicken is fully cooked, add salt or several chicken bouillon cubes. I prefer the latter, for it makes the broth more chickeny. Stir a couple of times during cooking to distribute the seasonings. When cooking chicken meat for later use, it must be removed from heat when satisfactorily tender. When you are only interested in the broth, simmer longer — at least 3 or 4 hours. Remove from heat, uncover, and allow to cool a bit, for safer handling. Then place a large colander over a large kettle and pour everything from soup kettle into colander. When all broth has drained into kettle beneath the colander, rinse the soup kettle of any debris, place 2 fine strainers (one within the other) across the soup kettle and pour broth through the strainers. They will catch the last smidgen of sediment. I'd rather wash strainers than cheesecloth. Also, I don't trouble to tie up little bags of bouquet garni. What for? The last fleck of everything is removed in this final straining, which saves time and work. Cordon Bleu would flunk me, but my soup tastes great.

Refrigerate broth or soup always, until it jells and all fat can be removed from the surface with ease. There is no way to over-emphasize the importance of this step. Plan on 2 days to make an expert soup.

Concerning variation #4 above (soup made from left-over

roast chicken — or any sort of cooked chicken or roast turkey), this is more of a slightly thick soup than a clear broth. For in addition to, or instead of, the seasonings named, one adds left-over gravy, creamed onions, mashed potatoes, almost anything the refrigerator yields. The stuffing in the birds imparts a particularly good flavor to this type of broth.

As for the chicken meat available in variations 1, 2, and 4 (page 49), as soon as it is cool enough to handle, separate it from all bone, skin, gristle, with the utmost care. You want pure pieces of meat, nothing else. If you lean on the side of wasting a little meat, in throwing aside the skin and gristle, you are on the right track, and to salve your conscience, remember that most of the good of the bird is in the broth, not the meat. Refrigerate meat at once — and there you are, ready for all sorts of wonderful dishes: chicken salads, sandwiches, shortcake (page 74), creamed chicken, or meat ready to add to whatever sort of soup you decide to concoct. For busy weekends, with guests in the house, a generous pot of broth and a platter of chicken meat have reassuring potential.

As for the golden, jellied broth, it may be served cold, with a wedge of lemon, as prelude to a summer luncheon, or hot, as a sure-fire pick-me-up, any hour of the day or night. Serve plain, hot broth in cups, as a signal that the cocktail hour is over, and dinner awaits. It's a happy way of taking care of that transition stage. Another inspired time to serve hot broth is at a morning coffee. Have coffee at one end of the table, and broth at the other, in your best urn. Even coffee buffs lean toward this elixer of life. Or for lunch or dinner, serve chicken soup with rice (as touted in picture and verse on page 46). Simply add rice to broth, and simmer until rice is done. Or make Greek Soup (page 105), and the gods from Olympus might abandon their high perch and join you. Or make Queen Victoria's Favorite Soup (page 60).

With the thicker broth made from left-over chicken or turkey bones, add some rice and chopped onion, and when rice is nearly cooked, add some fresh chopped vegetables: carrots, celery, a little tomato, peas, whatever you have. Cook them only to crisp-doneness, and lastly add the cut-up meat you have gleaned from the initial soup-pot routine.* This soup should follow a roast chicken dinner, or Thanksgiving Turkey, as surely as night follows day. Nothing is wasted, and a soup is created that is unobtainable in cans.

~~~~~~~~~~~~~~~~

There are 3 optional additions that may be made to any chicken broth or soup:

    1) garlic, either fresh or powdered

    2) basil, just a touch ~ Fresh or dried, this herb imparts a haunting aroma.

    3) cracked veal bones, added to the chicken parts, develop flavor and nutrition.

~~~~~~~~~~~~~~~~

*This would be some of the well-stewed meat that is left on the bones. Or the meat could be that which is salvaged from a cold roasted bird before stewing its carcass. Or it could be a bit of both.

Beef Broth or Soup or Stew

This is made from meat and bones purchased especially for soup making, or from left-over beef roasts or steaks containing bones, or from all of these things. The routine is exactly the same as with chicken soup. Many of the seasonings are the same, though with beef broth I add a parsnip, a turnip, a touch of marjoram, which I would not use with chicken. In addition to this I toss in a bouquet garni (1 bay leaf, a pinch of thyme, a few sprigs of parsley — which I don't wrap in cheese cloth), a carrot, a couple of onions, some celery stalks or tops, a few peppercorns and whole cloves, maybe a bit of garlic or garlic salt, left-over beef gravy or pan drippings or vegetable waters or left-over vegetables that might be around. Beef bouillon cubes or powder, and a can or 2 of consommé or beef bouillon may be added. Add cold water to cover all this and place on low heat which slowly, slowly draws all the good out of meat, bones, vegetables. After the brew comes to a boil it should simmer along for at least 4 hours. It seems that the slower the heat and the longer the time allowed, the better is the finished product. Add salt toward end of cooking.

Careful straining, long chilling so that all fat may be lifted off, the conscientious cutting up of the meat (if you plan to use it), the willingness to take 2 days to complete the process, all add up to a perfect product. Again, as with chicken or lamb, you are blessed with a sturdy broth and tender meat, ready for many variations: just broth, or a vegetable soup, or by thickening the broth and adding meat and vegetables, you have a fine stew or meat pie.

Fresh-purchased bones and meat, for beef broth, may be treated in 2 ways: 1) Simply put them in a kettle, as is, and simmer slowly with seasonings of your choice until meat is tender. 2) Put bones and meat into hot oven until they brown a little. Then proceed as directed above. This makes a browner and more flavorful broth. But in no case do I brown the meat or vegetables in fat, as is usually directed. This makes a more digestible broth, and, to me, tastes just as good. Bones are no longer given away, but, considering the nourishment they impart, neither are they expensive. So buy lots of them, and here's hoping you have a good-natured butcher who will cut them into small pieces (the better to leach out their nutrients). May your butcher also be helpful concerning the cheap cuts of beef that make the best soups and stews.

My husband used to say, "Make something easy. Make stew;" not only because he loved it, but because I never was able to convince him that there was far more work to turning out a good stew than a roast of beef. It has been my experience that the things that are easiest to serve, and appear effortless, are just the opposite, and as deceptive as an iceberg.

There is such a thing as quick beef stews (see pages 59 and 93), so don't despair if you are not up to the 2-day production.

See <u>Lamb Broth</u> and <u>Greek Soup</u> on page 105. See <u>Scotch Broth</u> on page 107.

Don't throw out <u>parsley stems</u>. Toss them in the soup kettle as professional chefs do.

Beef Tea (1 pint)

<u>1 pound best round steak</u>, trimmed of fat, ground, and placed in quart jar.
<u>2 cups cold water</u>, poured over beef, covered, and allowed to stand for <u>1 or 2 hours</u>, at room temperature, to draw juices. Then place jar in a deep pan of cold water. Heat slowly to just below the boiling point and cook that way for <u>2 hours</u>. Strain out the meat, and add to the tea ---

<u>½ teaspoon salt</u>   If you serve the broth at once, get rid of all traces of fat by dragging pieces of paper towel over the top. Or chill broth in refrigerator, and then the hardened bits of fat are easily removed. Reheat over hot, <u>not boiling</u>, water.

The sick simply pick up their beds and walk, shortly after drinking this. A friend, feeling frail, will love you forever if you come bearing this gift. What to do with the mound of leached-out meat? Give it to the dog, who'll love it.   Or put it in a hash for humans. Most of the nourishment is in the tea, but the hash will taste good.

Sparrow Broth
          Once upon a Time, there was a little girl named Ruth Sassaman, who lived in Milford, New Jersey. Whenever she was sick abed, her father would go out and shoot a sparrow or two. Her mother would make a broth from these tiny birds, and feed it to the sick child. Ruth claims this always made her recover at once. Did the sparrow broth really possess such healing powers, or was it the loving concern revealed in going to so much trouble, that wrought the change? Probably both.

Basic Soup (Serves 4)
(To be served very hot or icy cold)

2 potatoes }
2 onions } peeled and cut up }
generous piece of butter }
1 cup water - - - - - - - - - }

Boil together in fairly large pot until vegetables are tender. Do not drain. Cool slightly, blend in blender, and pour back into cookpot.

1 can chicken broth (10¾ ounces), or equivalent of homemade broth, poured into blender.

1 large bunch parsley, or dandelion greens, or watercress, or a good handful of any sort of garden lettuce or spinach or chard or beet greens; or a 10 ounce package of frozen broccoli or cauliflower, or asparagus (or equivalent fresh-grown), slightly cooked, and put into blender with the chicken broth, along with some salt, freshly ground pepper, a pinch of sage, or curry powder (but not to be noticed), a slight sprinkle of Worcestershire Sauce. Blend well and pour into the cookpot.

2 cups of milk, or two cups of light cream, or half milk, half cream are now stirred into the pot and tasted for seasoning. At this point you either heat or chill the completed soup. Garnish, when served, with chopped chives or dill or parsley. Have croutons if served hot.

So here are 10 soups, all on one page. Your garden or imagination may suggest more. Deliciousness is guaranteed. A great way to get greens into people who think they don't like them.

Cold Borsch (Serves 4)

1 can Campbell's Consommé
1 can (1 pound) beets, juice and all
1 medium-sized onion
juice of 1 lemon
salt, to taste (be generous)
- - - - - - - -
sour cream, for garnish

Blend thoroughly in blender. Chill well before serving in soup plates, with a topping of sour cream. Melba toast goes well with this.

Hot Borsch
Simply heat above recipe for a winter soup.

(See page 153 for Borsch salad.)

I bless the day I stumbled on this beet recipe. So will you!

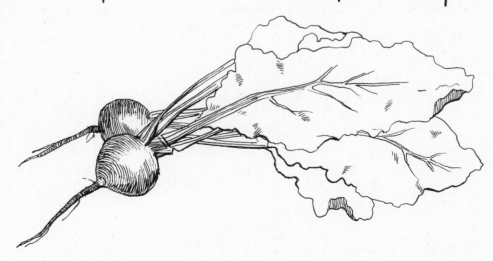

Swiss Soup (Serves 4)

2 tablespoons butter, melted in top of double boiler
2 tablespoons flour, stirred into butter
1 cup milk ⎫ Add this slowly, while stirring constantly,
1 can Campbell's Consommé ⎬ to above roux.
1 teaspoon Maggi seasoning, added to above.

Keep on stirring and cooking, until absolutely
smooth. It is ready to serve after 10 minutes of
cooking over boiling water. Or hold and reheat
at your convenience. A great hit for a winter luncheon.
Serve with cheese crackers, or tiny toasted cheese sandwiches.

Carol Ayers of Easton, Pennsylvania, gave me this
recipe. Her Quaker mother said to her, back in the 30's, "If thee is going
to be married, thee is going to cooking school." Which she did. This
put her way ahead of the other brides in the area, and we all stood in awe
of her culinary prowess. This soup, one of many marvelous things
Carol served, stands out in memory.

Ruth Allard's Hamburg Vegetable Soup (Serves 10)

1 pound best hamburger
1 onion, chopped
1 green pepper, chopped
} Brown together, in butter, in pan of sufficient size to hold whole recipe.

2 cans Campbell's Tomato Soup
6 cans water
1 package frozen mixed vegetables
salt, pepper, Worcestershire Sauce, sugar, to taste
} Add all this to above, when it has browned somewhat. Simmer until vegetables are cooked, but not mushy. Should you desire a thicker soup, add rice or noodles or macaroni or spaghetti, at the same time, or ahead of the vegetables, according to package directions. A whole hearty meal in minutes. Ruth's family are so fond of this that she makes it in quantity and freezes it in coffee cans. A boon to the wife with an outside job, just so long as she remembers to remove it from freezer in the morning. With hard bread, a green salad, and dessert, the family have fared well. Likewise a gang of unexpected guests.

My Own Hamburg Soup (for one or many)

Brown best-grade hamburger and onion in a bit of butter, add a can of Campbell's Consommé (bouillon cubes, or powder, or a can of chicken broth). Toss into the simmering pot some cubed potato, carrots (cut fine), and small pieces of anything your refrigerator holds: turnips, parsnips, peas, tomatoes, summer squash, zucchini — one or all of them. The last few seconds of cooking, add a handful of celery for flavor and crunch, and some chopped parsley. Test for saltiness, and add a bit of pepper and sugar.

Queen Victoria's Favorite Soup (Serves 6 to 8)

(Adapted from The Congregational Church Cook Book, Westford, Vermont ~ 1909)

1 quart chicken broth
1 onion, finely chopped (or blended in blender with a cup of the cold broth)
1 cup diced celery
1 tablespoon butter
Salt and pepper, to taste

} Simmer together for 15 minutes in kettle of sufficient size to hold entire recipe.

2 hard-boiled eggs, put through a ricer (or chopped very fine)
½ cup cracker crumbs
1 cup cooked white meat of chicken, chopped fine
2 cups light cream
½ teaspoon powdered sage (or 1 tablespoon chopped fresh sage)

} Mix these ingredients together in a bowl, and let soak until above broth has cooked the required length of time. Then stir this mixture into above broth. Bring to a boil, stirring the while. Correct salt.

Serve in hot soup bowls. Garnish with ....
chopped parsley

A fine luncheon or supper dish. I like it served with dainty ham-and-lettuce sandwiches, and a fruit dessert.

The Queen grew plumper and plumper. I fear this was just a preamble to even heartier courses. So watch it.

Corn Chowder (Serves 4)

1 potato, cut in small cubes
1 onion, chopped fine
1 cup water (Water and onion may be blended in blender if you lack the ambition to chop.)

Simmer in saucepan until potatoes are tender.

2 cups milk
2 tablespoons butter
1 regular can* cream style corn
Salt and freshly ground pepper, to taste

Stir into above when potatoes are done. Bring just to a boil, no more. Remove from heat.

1 egg, beaten — To this beaten egg, add a little of the hot chowder. Then stir well and return to the sauce pan of chowder. Reheat for a second, but don't boil. Ladle into soup plates and garnish with . . . . .

4 slices of bacon, that have been cut into small pieces with scissors, baked until crisp, and drained on paper towel.

Serve with crisp saltines, or lightly buttered chowder crackers that have been slowly oven-heated until they acquire a healthy tan.

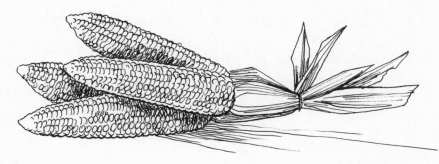

*(around one pound)

Clam Chowder (New England) (4 moderate, 2 opulent servings)

(As Bets Allright makes it, true to memories of Martha's Vineyard.)

1 piece fat salt pork (about 2"x 3"x 1") cut into small cubes, fried slowly until crisp and golden, then drained on paper towel.

2 onions, chopped fine ~ Pour off most of fat from pork scrap pan, and slightly brown the onions in remaining fat. (Pan should be of size to hold all recipe ingredients.)

2 large or 3 medium potatoes, cut into small cubes and added to cooked onions. Add water to just submerge potato and onion. Simmer gently until potatoes are tender.

1 can clams, juice and all, added to above. (Use either Geisha brand whole baby clams (10 ounces), or Snow's chopped clams (8 ounces). Allow all this to cool, unless you plan to serve immediately. In either event add:

dried dill weed*, a pinch, or more if you have fresh dill to chop.

salt and freshly ground pepper, to taste.

2 cups milk } When ready to serve add this to above and heat slowly to
1 tablespoon butter } just below boiling point, no more. At the same time heat the pork scraps. (I do this in the oven.)

Ladle chowder into hot bowls, sprinkle with paprika.

Sprinkle crisp pork cubes on each serving. If they sizzle when they hit the soup you will deserve honorable mention.

Toasted chowder crackers or saltines are the suitable accompaniment.

* You may substitute thyme.

Lobster Chowder (Serves 4)

1 cup water

1 medium onion, peeled and quartered } blended in blender

2 medium potatoes, cubed and cooked with above until potatoes are tender

2 cups lobster, fresh boiled, frozen or canned, cut in pieces

1 teaspoon salt

1/4 teaspoon pepper, freshly ground — } added to above when potatoes are tender, and brought to a boil.

2 cups whole milk

1 small Tin (1 cup) evaporated milk

butter, the size of an egg } added to above and held, as is, until Time to eat. Then bring just to boil, (no more!) and serve.

Serve with real chowder crackers which have been split, buttered, and baked slowly on cookie sheet until slightly browned. (Encourage guests to break crackers into chowder. They are difficult to cut with soup spoon.) This is nearly a meal in itself. I always serve it with sparkling cold glasses of beer, and for dessert some fresh fruit and cheese. Great for Sunday night supper or a luncheon. I happen to like this chowder better than lobster stew. Don't doctor it up with anything but the best lobster. It has a clean, breezy, salt water Taste that smacks of the freshness of the Atlantic.

This is a recipe from Lunenburg, Nova Scotia, home of the famed schooner, Bluenose.

Did you know that lobster is one of nature's most digestible foods?

Oyster Soup   (Serves 4)

2 tablespoons butter
2 teaspoons finely chopped onion   } Cook together over boiling water in covered top part of double boiler until onion is soft. (About 15 minutes)

2 tablespoons flour, well blended into above.
1 quart rich milk, scalded, and stirred into above until completely lump-free.
1 stalk celery, finely chopped
3 soda crackers, crushed (I use saltines)   } Add to above and cook over boiling water 5 more minutes.

16 oysters, cut apart with scissors, leaving bellies intact, but snipping the hard parts fine. Add this to above after its 5 minutes of cooking. Add salt to taste.
Now place top of double boiler over direct heat and allow to come just to a boil, stirring every second! Serve at once.

I like the above soup better than oyster stew, and, according to Dr. Sara Jordan*, it is more digestible. The double boiler method is the secret; those with squeamish digestions take note.

*Dr. Jordan was one of the great gastroenterology specialists of the world, practicing at Boston's Lahey Clinic.

Crab Madrilène (Serves 6)

2 thirteen-ounce cans consommé Madrilène
6 ounces of canned crabmeat, drained, flaked, and
        any tendons removed } Bring to a boil, remove from heat, and add . . . .
salt, pepper, just a touch, if your taste demands
4 tablespoons sherry ~ Pour into hot soup cups, and on each serving place . . . . .
a slice of lemon, chopped parsley

~~~~~~~~~~~~~~~~

Quick Chicken Corn Chowder (Serves 6 to 8)

1 can (10½ ounces) cream of chicken soup
2 soup cans milk } Mix thoroughly and heat in saucepan.

1 can (10½ ounces) condensed chicken noodle soup
1 can (1 pound) cream-style corn
1 cup diced cooked chicken } Add to above, and heat, but do not boil. It is ready to serve at once. You may thin with milk or water if you care to.

~~~~~~~~~~~~~~~~

Popcorn scattered on a bowl of soup makes it particularly appealing to children.

~~~~~~~~~~~~~~~~

Moppets go for this birthday special: Press a piece of cream cheese onto a cracker or small piece of toast. Into the cheese poke a tiny candle. Float this little raft on the soup bowl. Light the candle and serve.

~~~~~~~~~~~~~~~~

Farina Balls for Soup

1 cup cold milk
¼ cup farina (or quick-cooking Cream of Wheat) } Mix together in saucepan. Bring to a boil while stirring constantly. Then remove from heat.

½ tablespoon butter
¼ teaspoon salt
⅛ teaspoon paprika
nutmeg, a touch
1 egg, beaten
} Stir all this vigorously into above as soon as it has been removed from heat. Drop this batter by the teaspoonful into a simmering broth (chicken or beef). Cover, and cook 2 minutes. Serve at once. A whole, simple meal, and a soothing one.

Croutons

When thinking of soup, one thinks of croutons, and here is the simple way of making them, as well as the digestible way. (Fried croutons, loaded with garlic, are for bovine digestions.) Take any left-over bread and cut into small cubes. Put cubes in a baking dish, with a generous piece of butter. Bake in slow (325°) oven until golden brown, stirring a few times, so that the butter coats all the cubes. That's all. Your kitchen will smell like baking bread. Soup will be properly enhanced. A great way to make use of left-over bread. Keep croutons in deep freeze for future use. I like to heat croutons in small Corning Ware dishes, a stove-to-table work saver. If you want a garlic flavor to croutons, shake on a bit of garlic salt or powder before baking.

Bird ~ Beast ~ Fish

68

Platter warming,
trout frying (page 108),
hamburger pan-broiling (page 83),
on the wood-burning stove.

About Bird ~ Beast ~ Fish

Buy the best !

Don't panic about holding roasts out of the oven for some time. They carve better as a result of this rest period. If plates, gravy, vegetables are piping hot, the meat need not be.

Remember that meats continue to cook after removal from oven. So allow for this, especially if you like your beef rare.

Fruit and meat go well together. Who wants pork without applesauce, or turkey without cranberry, or ham without pineapple? There is a long list of other fruits that are equally good with the main course: baked bananas, raisin sauce, baked fruit compotes, fruits in jelly, to name a few. There are many suggestions throughout this book. Of course if one serves a fruit cup to start or end the meal, or a fruit salad, it is not necessary to have more fruit with the meat. I can scarcely think of any bird, beast, or fish that is not improved by a splash of lemon.

Always preheat oven.

There are only a few recipes that call for the frying of meat, because fried foods are less digestible and more work.

When serving roast lamb ask your butcher to leave the caul on. It makes for juicier meat.

Always butter a roasting pan. It pays off when you wash the pan, it adds flavor, and helps prevent meat from sticking to pan. You are probably wondering why I don't recommend the use of a rack in a roasting pan. I've never used one in my life. If I use anything, it's a rack of raw onions to set the roast upon. This does wonders for the gravy, and the flavor of the meat generally. Also, I always shake a bit of flour on the buttered pan _and_ the meat. This browned flour adds great taste appeal to meat and gravy.

Even if you skip making gravy, _save_ the pan drippings! To see someone soak a beautiful, encrusted roasting pan with soap and water, and pour all down the drain is enough to make any conscientious cook burst into tears. When time permits, add some water to the pan and bring to a boil, stirring and scraping all the while. Strain this glorious essence into a dish, and refrigerate. Remove the layer of fat and use the jelly beneath to enrich a soup or stew, to spread on a sandwich, or whatever. It is worth its weight in gold, a seasoning impossible to purchase in any cubed or powdered form.

Directions for making gravy by the blender method will be found on page 103. This is a recipe for lamb gravy, but the same principles apply to all gravies. Gravy made this way is practically fat-free and digestible, which cannot be said of the roux method. When making chicken or turkey gravy, one would omit the Worcestershire Sauce and lemon called for in lamb gravy. I season gravy from roasting a bird, with chicken bouillon cubes, any giblet broth that may be left, potato water, or onion water, if I have any. Perhaps I use a can of chicken broth as another seasoned liquid with which to boil and scrape up pan drippings. All this develops a tasty and nutrition-laden gravy, practically guaranteed to turn finicky eaters into trenchermen.

With beef gravy, season with beef bouillon cubes or powder, or Bovril or a can of beef bouillon, and maybe a few dashes of Worcestershire, or Maggi, or Kitchen Bouquet. Keep tasting until you are satisfied. Good gravy can _make_ a meal, or it can spell disaster in the form of a greasy, tasteless paste.

If you are having company, make the gravy ahead! The only price you pay is washing an extra pan. Switch your nearly-done roast to a new pan. Use the old one for gravy making. Pour the completed gravy into a double boiler and keep hot endlessly.* Hide the two roasting pans until the next day if your energy level is running low or you are pressed for time. Most hostesses look red-faced and harried making gravy at the last moment. Who wants that?

I always make gravy with flour, not cornstarch. I like the flavor better, and flour maintains its thickening power. Using the blender to mix the flour and liquid for a gravy is indispensable for ease, as well as smooth, lump-free results.

If you prefer a shiny gravy, made at the last moment, use cornstarch, but remember that cornstarch is doubly thickening in its action, and if kept heating for any length of time, begins to thin out. For one pint (2 cups) one would use 2 tablespoons of cornstarch, whereas with flour one uses 4 tablespoons to a pint of liquid.

Or be European, and don't thicken gravy at all. Just scrape up the crusty pan residue (having poured off fat!) with water, vegetable water and/or wine. Season to taste and serve.

Remember that bird, beast, or fish — being protein — responds best to slow cooking, low heat.

When making hamburgs, hot dogs, tuna rolls, crabmeat rolls, or whatever, be sure to paint bread with a little butter and heat in oven until slightly browned. This added care makes all the difference. Cold, cottony buns are an abomination too often encountered.

★ If you are equipped with an attractive double boiler, serve directly therefrom.

How To Roast A Bird (chicken or turkey)

(Allow 1 pound per person.)

There is no need to make a career of this, as most cookbooks would have us do. Simply place the bird in a buttered roasting pan, hold it on its head (I mean where its head <u>was</u>) by one leg, and pour some prepared stuffing directly from the bag into the bird cavity. Give the bird a quick massage with butter. Salt it. Sprinkle flour over bird and pan. Toss it into a preheated <u>325°</u> oven, <u>uncovered</u>, breast up. Yes, a little of the stuffing will fall into the pan, but that makes the gravy taste better.

Put the giblets and neck into a saucepan. Cover with water. Add a chicken bouillon cube or two. Allow to simmer away until giblets are tender. (The liver may be lifted out with a slotted spoon after ½ hour of simmering; the gizzard and heart need longer cooking; the neck needs the longest. But I must admit that I often let it all cook for several hours. The giblet gravy tastes just as good.) With a bulb baster, squirt some of this giblet broth onto the chicken. As the roasting pan dries out, baste bird with more of the giblet water, or just some hot water and butter, mixed. Once in a while, baste the bird with pan juices, and at some point be sure to squirt some of these juices into the bird cavity to moisten the stuffing.

When the legs or wings of the bird move easily, and are about to fall off, the creature is done — brown, crisp, and to a turn. Don't serve slippery chicken! If limbs are tough to manipulate, and the joints are pink, the bird is seriously undercooked. I'm probably in the overcooked category, but would rather be. Never test doneness of bird by attacking it with a fork. Out pour the precious juices if you do. If breast seems to be getting too brown, lay a piece of foil over it.

It is difficult to give the exact time for roasting a bird, for we are talking of everything from a small chicken to a large turkey. And they differ in age and tenderness. Directions are sometimes given on the wrapping, but take these with a grain of salt and <u>add</u> to the recommended time.   An average 5-pound roasting chicken I bake for <u>3 hours</u>, at least, and always at <u>325°</u>.   A large turkey may take <u>8 hours</u>, and I refer to completely <u>thawed</u> birds.   Experience is the best teacher, but don't let lack of experience deter you from barging right ahead. It is more relaxing to have bird cooked well in advance of meal. Don't try to <u>keep</u> it hot. That will dry it out. Put it back in the oven for a bit, just before serving, if you must.

The pan juices need to be nicely dried out, so there is just brown crust on the bottom of pan, topped with fat only. This fat should be poured off completely. Then proceed from there with gravy making, as directed on pages 70   and 103 . Giblets should be carefully peeled of gristle, tendons and such, and then the clear meat chopped fine, along with the meat salvaged from the chicken neck. Have this ready to toss into the completed gravy.

There are more advantages to dispensing with the trussing and sewing up of a bird than time-saving. The wings and legs get browner and more deliciously edible that way. If the bird's position, after roasting, appears a bit impolite, judicious use of parsley will make the sprawling limbs look clothed and lovely.

For a Thanksgiving turkey I fuss a little more, adding chopped celery and onion to the stuffing, chestnuts, and perhaps some mushrooms browned in butter. The stuffing may be moistened with a can of chicken broth, and/or some water brought to a boil with some butter in it. Be careful not to add too much liquid or it makes the dressing soggy.　　　The above speedy method of just pouring stuffing from package into bird is for hurried days, and it encourages one to serve roast chicken and turkey often, birds being one of the more economical meats these days, not to mention their delectableness.

　　　Don't throw away the bones and carcass when roast is reduced to that. See page 49-52 concerning its reincarnation into a nourishing soup.

Chicken à la King (Serves 6)

1 cup chicken broth
1 cup cream, or rich milk
4 tablespoons flour
1 chicken bouillon cube

Blend together in blender. Pour into top of double boiler, over boiling water, and stir until thickened and smooth. Stir in some salt and pepper, to taste, and a generous piece of butter.

2 heaping cups cut-up cooked chicken
¼ cup finely chopped pimento
¼ cup finely chopped green pepper
some sliced sautéed mushrooms (optional)

Add to above. Heat thoroughly, but do not stir any more than is absolutely necessary, so that chicken pieces may remain intact.

2 egg yolks, 3 tablespoons sherry, beaten together, and stirred gently into above just before serving.

Chicken Shortcake (Very popular in Vermont.)

Make a gravy of good chicken stock (pages 49-52) in the proportion of 1 cup stock to 2 tablespoons flour. Add cut-up stewed chicken meat. Season with salt, pepper, butter. Pour in between and on top of split and buttered baking powder biscuits (page 218).

Chicken Superbe (Serves 8 or more)

8 chicken breasts, halved, boned (boning optional)
½ pound dried chipped beef
bacon, sufficient to cover each piece of chicken
1 pint sour cream — — — — — ⎱ mixed together
2 cans cream of mushroom soup ⎰

Butter a good-sized shallow casserole dish. Spread dried beef over the bottom of dish. Arrange chicken pieces neatly on the beef. Top each piece of chicken with bacon. Pour cream-and-soup mixture over all. Cover dish with foil. Bake in preheated 300° oven for 2 hours. Remove foil and bake another hour until nicely browned on top.

Superb is the word for it! Good with rice. This is a rich dish. Keep the rest of the meal simple and non-creamy.

Do not add salt or pepper to Chicken Superbe. The beef, bacon, and soup are sufficient seasoning.

Scalloped Chicken (Serves 12)

1 five pound chicken (or equivalent thereof in chicken parts) stewed slowly until tender

1 quart of broth from the stewed chicken

5 eggs

1 loaf of bread

Seasonings To Taste : crumbled chicken bouillon cubes, grated onion or onion powder or onion flakes, a dash of thyme and Bell's Poultry Seasoning (Careful, these last two seasonings should not be noticeable.)

After chicken is cooked, strain out the broth. Cut up chicken carefully, disposing of all bone and fat and skin.

Break bread into small pieces and wet with hot broth from which fat has been removed. (I keep broth in refrigerator overnight, then skim off fat and reheat broth.)

Add beaten eggs and seasonings to soaked bread. Stir well. Fold in cut-up chicken. Taste test. If not salty enough, crumble in more chicken bouillon cubes — not salt. This is the secret of making the chicken more "chickeny." Place in a shallow buttered baking dish. Dot with butter. (This may be done a day ahead — ready for a party.) Bake at 325° until slightly browned, about one hour. Don't over cook. Eggs could separate.

(see next page)

This was a favorite dish at church suppers at The old Greenwich Presbyterian Church of Bloomsbury, New Jersey. People came from miles around to partake of it.

One refinement: (Not in the original old recipe but an improvement, I believe, if you want to take the Time.) Put the broken or cubed bread into the oven in a baking dish. Dot bread generously with butter. Bake slowly, stirring occasionally, until golden brown. Then pour hot broth over it and proceed as directed.

Great for buffet meals, and a delectable concoction That stretches one chicken a long, long way.

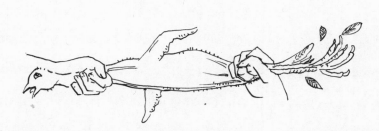

Treasure Island Chicken (Serves 4 to 6)

(This recipe received many awards in some sort of country-wide cooking contest. Well deserved, too!)

4 chicken breasts, boned, halved, and placed skin side up, and neatly tucked into place in a buttered, shallow, stove-to-table baking dish. Now steal a little melted butter (below), and paint the chicken with it. Sprinkle chicken with

½ teaspoon salt, and place in preheated **375°** oven, uncovered, and bake **30 minutes** (or longer, if chicken juices are not pretty well dried up).

½ stick butter (¼ cup), melted in pan large enough to contain ingredients that follow

3 tablespoons flour
3 tablespoons sugar
½ teaspoon salt
¼ teaspoon dry mustard
½ teaspoon cinnamon
⅛ teaspoon ginger
1½ cups orange juice

Mix these dry ingredients together and stir them into melted butter (above). Then, stirring constantly, add the orange juice (below) slowly, until you have a thick, smooth sauce. Pour this heavenly sauce over the partially cooked chicken and bake **40 minutes** more. If chicken is not brown enough on top, turn on the broiler for a few minutes, watching carefully.

If cooking this for company, and I want to be totally ready, I cook the chicken in the morning for the prescribed 30 minutes, pour the sauce over it and let it cool off and marinate. The last 40 minutes of cooking is done after guests arrive. I usually serve it with boiled rice to which pineapple chunks have been added. Most butchers will graciously bone the chicken. Otherwise I serve the breasts split, with the bone in.

Christmas 1977 – Delicious

Poulet Chasseur* (Serves 6)

2 cut-up frying chickens, browned quickly in butter and then placed in buttered casserole

salt and pepper, to taste } sprinkled over browned chicken
juice of 1 lemon

½ pound mushrooms, cut small and browned in butter in same pan in which chicken was browned

½ teaspoon garlic salt
⅛ teaspoon pepper
2 onions, chopped fine
1 cup dry white wine
} Add these ingredients to browned mushrooms and allow to simmer until reduced by ½

chicken (home-made)
1 cup ~~roast beef~~ gravy, leftover, canned, packaged, or made with beef bouillon cube }

1 tablespoon Tomato sauce
1 tablespoon Cognac —no
½ teaspoon dried Tarragon) —no
½ teaspoon dried parsley } triple amount if fresh
} added to reduced mushroom mixture. Pour all of this over the chicken in casserole. Bake, covered, in preheated 350° oven for 1 hour or more.

Excellent company dish. The longer it waits, the more it mellows.
    This was the main dish at a state dinner for the President of Pakistan, served at Mt. Vernon during the first year of President Kennedy's administration. The chef chose it because it could be prepared in the White House kitchens, endure transportation to Mt. Vernon, and still retain its goodness.

*Adapted from a Poppy Cannon recipe.

March '98 - Made for Maria & boys.
Served w/ rice - Used too much soup.

Dell's Chicken

Use a half broiler per person, or cut-up chicken parts, or split breasts. Arrange them in a buttered, shallow baking dish, skin side up. Spread completely and generously with cream of chicken soup (I use Campbell's). That's all! Place in preheated 350° oven and bake until nice and crusty-brown on top. This takes over an hour, and sometimes 2 hours if there is a lot of chicken exuding juices. The pan juices should be fairly well evaporated, so all is crunchy, not watery. I know of no more effortless, easy, and elegant way to serve chicken. Well, the recipe that follows could compete. Take your pick.

Lemon Chicken

Place chicken in buttered dish, as directed above. Use a pastry brush to paint chicken all over exposed surfaces with melted butter. Anoint lavishly with lemon juice (the real thing, please). Salt well. Bake at 375° for an hour or more, until crisp. Simple, and simply delicious. Lemon is the reason.

For a brunch:

Buy chicken wings only, with tip of wing removed (save for soup), and the rest of the wing cut apart at joint. The butcher will oblige. Line up the cute little sections in a stove-to-table shallow pan. Season as for "Lemon Chicken" and cook to a crisp. People eat them by hand, bones and all, if sufficiently cooked.

For a picnic:

Treat drumsticks in the same manner as above. Chill and put into picnic basket. (Have plenty of tomato, lettuce, and mayonnaise sandwiches.) Prepare to overeat.

Roast Partridge

One bird will serve 2 people, but if the bird shooting proves lucky, give each person a whole partridge.

After the birds have hung by their necks for as many days as please you, have been cleaned and skinned (to pluck 1 partridge takes hours and isn't worth the trouble), soak the cute things (along with their giblets) for a few hours in cold, salted water. If they are really "high," soak in water that has a tablespoon or 2 of baking soda dissolved therein.

Take the livers, hearts, gizzards, and (if you are serving just breasts, as some people do), all the rest of the birds' anatomies (which have been washed under running water after the soaking) and place in a pan with an onion or 2 stuck with cloves, a bit of bay leaf, and sufficient chicken bouillon cubes for saltiness. Add water. Simmer, covered, until all is tender. Drain, and reserve the fine broth. Put the giblets (trimmed of any weird arteries or gristle), and whatever meat you can glean, through a food grinder (small blade). Mix plenty of butter into this precious paté, and spread on toast triangles. Set aside, ready for last-minute heating. They are placed around the cooked birds, constituting one of the best parts of a partridge dinner.

In a buttered roasting pan (stove-to-table kind, if possible) arrange washed and dried partridge. Give each a going-over with generously buttered hands. Stuff each with 1 onion and 2 peeled and cored apple quarters which have been sprinkled with thyme (fresh or dried). Sprinkle all with flour and salt and slide into 300° oven for 3 hours. Yes, 3 hours. You are welcome to eat tough, bloody partridge if that is your preference. But try my way just once. The secret is slow cooking, frequent basting. Use the giblet broth, to which the juice of a lemon and a good chunk of butter has been added, for basting. Keep anointing the birds with this broth (hot) until used up. Baste and baste. About the last half hour of baking, remove pan from oven and paint partridge with honey or maple syrup. Return to a 325° oven, and bake until birds are nicely glazed, which doesn't take long. Watch!

Surround partridge with hot, paté-covered toast triangles. Make all pretty with parsley. I like to round out this feast with wild rice, winter squash, creamed onions, and a 3-way dish of crisp celery, fat stuffed olives and thyme jelly. You may be able to think up even better accompaniments.

Partridge Pie (1 bird serves 3 or 4 people.)

This is one of the eating delights of the hunting season. Best to save the senior citizen birds for a pie, using the young ones for roasting. In a pinch I've stretched a partridge pie by adding a few chicken breasts to the stewing pot, but if game is plentiful, such an emergency measure is not called for.

Simmer the prepared birds (pages 49, 50) slowly in canned chicken broth, for extra richness, or just plain water. Along with the liquid, add a bay leaf, a sprinkling of thyme, a carrot or 2, a celery stalk or 2, an onion or 2, a few cloves, and, in place of salt — chicken bouillon cubes. When the partridge are falling-apart tender (depending on their age), strain off the broth and chill it. Cut up the meat in nice-sized pieces, and refrigerate until you make the pie. This is usually a 2-day process, one to stew the birds, two to manufacture the pie. Nothing difficult, just relaxingly slow-paced due to planning ahead.

Make a sauce with the partridge broth (skimmed of any fat) in the proportion of 2 tablespoons flour to 1 cup broth (blender method, page 103). To the thickened broth add some butter, any salt or pepper that might be needed, and a dash of sherry. Keep tasting. Pour this elegant gravy into a buttered casserole. Add the cut-up partridge and some under-cooked vegetables: peas, carrots, little onions, celery (sliced and browned mushrooms are optional). Don't overwhelm with vegetables. Stir carefully together. Cover, and, about 1 hour before dinner, place in 350° oven and heat until bubbling hot, no more. Remove from oven, uncover, and top with a parsley biscuit crust (page 218) that is all cooked and ready. This crust may be just the size of the casserole, covering pie completely, or it may consist of drop biscuits nicely spaced on top, or you may have gone to the trouble to bake biscuit letters that spell out a greeting for some special event.

Be sure to serve extra parsley biscuits on the side, with plenty of butter and some thyme jelly, if possible. (Quick Relish, page 307, goes well with partridge pie.) This meal produces brain recordings that play back beautiful music for a lifetime.

How to Cook a Hamburger

More people ruin a hamburger than any other well-known food. They must work out hidden resentments on the meat, because the first step is usually to pound the meat mercilessly into hard round cakes. This is the first mistake. The second is to add a lot of flavorings and onion to good fresh meat. The third heresy is to fry the meat in a a pan of hot fat, all the while pounding and pressing the meat with a spatula, making it even tougher. Of course, it is difficult to completely ruin good meat, no matter how badly it is treated.

But try it my way once and see if you're not a convert. Having told you what _not_ to do, here are the few simple rules to follow to turn a plain old hamburger into a delicacy:

First: Pan broil it. That means taking a heavy frying pan and heating it thoroughly and salting it. Thats it, SALT it only. No butter, no fat. While pan heats, go on to the second step.

Second: Use freshly ground meat with practically no fat in it. I use the best round steak.

Third: Using a knife, cut the meat gently into slices. Even so tenderly pick up the slice and coax it into a rounded shape. No banging or thumping, please. With the meat cake practically falling apart, but not quite, put it into the hot frying pan where the salt has just commenced to jump a bit. The salt keeps the meat from sticking to the pan, and also flavors it. Brown the meat cake on one side, then carefully turn it over and brown on the other, but never, never whack or press it with the spatula. If a few pieces of meat crumble off into the pan, so much the better. They taste delicious. When cooked to your satisfaction, remove from the pan and place on a buttered and warmed-to-slight-crispness hamburger roll.

Then and only then, douse it with all the condiments and onion you want. There are people who like just plain meat taste, and this is what you get. A piece of tenderloin steak is no more delicious than a hamburger cooked this way. And it is so digestible.

Try meat cooked this way, not to put in a hamburg roll, but to have with potatoes and other vegetables for dinner. After meat cakes are cooked, remove them to a platter. Pour water, a bit of Worcestershire Sauce, a dab of butter into the hot pan, and scrape up all the bits until it forms a nice, brown, water gravy. Pour this over the meat. As tasty as steak, cheaper, and good for everyone, from baby, to grandma, to ulcer patient. It's not fried. It's pan broiled.

~~~~~~~~~~~~~~~~~~~~~~

Favorite Shish Kebab

beef, cubed in about 1-inch squares (tenderloin or sirloin).
hot dogs, cut in about 1-inch lengths
bacon, cut into 1-inch lengths

Have equal parts of each and alternate on skewers until they are full. Roast over open fire on a rack, turning on all sides until cooked to your satisfaction. Or broil in oven. To give yourself a rest, let diners skewer their own meat from 3 platters of ingredients. 'Shish' means skewer. 'Kebab' means roast meat — Armenian words.

~~~~~~~~~~~~~~~~~~~~~~

Martha's Company Casserole (Serves 10 or 12)

<u>3 pounds best round steak</u>, ground. Heat and generously <u>salt</u> a large frying pan. (No fat!) Put in the meat and brown slightly.

<u>2 eight-ounce cans best tomato sauce</u>, stirred into the cooked meat.

<u>1 twelve-ounce package medium noodles</u>, cooked in salted water and drained.

<u>2 tablespoons butter</u>, stirred into hot noodles.

<u>1 pint (2 cups) cottage cheese</u>

<u>1 eight-ounce package cream cheese</u>

<u>1 cup sour cream</u>

<u>1 heaping tablespoon chopped green pepper</u>

<u>⅓ cup chopped scallions</u> (or grated regular onion)

} thoroughly mixed together

Butter a large casserole. Put in a layer of ½ of the noodles, then a layer of all of the cheese mixture, then the rest of the noodles. Top with meat layer, smoothing it over nicely. It is ready for oven now — or hours later. Bake, uncovered, at <u>350°</u> until bubbly and a bit brown on top. This takes a good hour or more. May be held hot indefinitely. Good heated next day. Freezes well.

Don't let the "square" name of this dish turn you off. It is one of the better culinary delights. Ideal for large buffets. Betty Parks of Fitchburg, Massachusetts, gave me this recipe. I have shared it with more people than any other recipe in this collection. So I guess you'd call it the winner in a popularity contest. Who on earth Martha was, is lost in the mists of time.

Martha Hebb's Lazy Casserole (4 generous servings)

2 pounds beef cut into 2-inch chunks (chuck or round)

½ ⅛ cup red dinner wine

1 onion, sliced

1 cup sliced mushrooms   } Place in a buttered casserole.

¼ cup fine, dry bread crumbs

¼ cup flour

1 can consommé (beef, 10½ ounces) } Blend together in blender. Add to above. Mix well. Add . . . . .

salt and pepper, to taste. Cover, bake in 300° oven for 3 or 4 hours, or until meat is tender. Tastes somewhat like Boeuf Bourguignon, but without any of the effort that dish involves. Serve with noodles. *added ½ can crm of mushrm soup when done.*

Lucille Parker's Easy Beef Stroganoff

1 pound round steak, ground

1 package Lipton's Onion Soup   } Brown beef, and mushrooms (if you use them), in a bit of butter in frying pan. Then mix in the dry onion soup, cover, and let simmer on

1 pint sour cream

¼ pound fresh mushrooms, sliced (or 2 small cans)
      (The mushrooms are optional.)

low heat for about 10 minutes. Mix in sour cream. Heat. Serve with rice or noodles.

The above two recipes are as delicious as they are work-free. The lazy casserole is the ideal dish to cook by itself all afternoon while you are gone. The easy stroganoff is my standby when unexpected guests appear — a cinch to concoct at the last minute.

Did not like— Different
Sauce too thin.
Too much trouble!

87

Pennsylvania Dutch Meat Balls (Serves 12)

3 pounds ground beef (or part beef, liver, veal, or pork, mixed in
           any combination you prefer.)

3 slices bread, soaked in water, wrung out, crumbled, and
           added to meat

3 eggs
1 onion, peeled and quartered
2 teaspoons salt
1 teaspoon paprika
2 thin shavings of lemon peel
juice of ½ lemon
2 teaspoons Worcestershire Sauce
parsley, several sprigs, added to blender
     at the last second and barely
     chopped, not emulsified

Whirl all this together in blender and pour over meat. Mix all together thoroughly with hands. Then roll the whole lot into nice 2-inch balls. Drop them gently into simmering broth below. Simmer a good 15 minutes.

2 cans Campbell's Consommé, diluted to make 6 cups, and brought
     to a simmer in kettle of sufficient size to hold all the meat balls.
     (Half consommé, half chicken broth is likewise acceptable.)
Remove cooked meat balls from broth with slotted spoon and place in buttered casserole. Measure broth, allow to cool somewhat. For every cup of broth use 2 tablespoons flour. Blend together in blender. Return to kettle and, stirring constantly, bring to a boil and stir until you have a nice smooth gravy. Stir in nearly ¼ pound butter, some capers, *No* or chopped pickles, or more lemon juice. Taste test it. Pour this elegant sauce over meat balls. Your casserole is ready for

No

reheating, covered, in <u>350°</u> oven, which may be delayed for a full day if you want to be forehanded. Serve with noodles tossed with either croutons or poppy seeds, and a green salad that contains some tomatoes.

Party or not, I make this large batch of meat balls which are excellent heated up as left-overs. They freeze well, also.

~~~~~~~~~~~~~

<u>Parker's Yankee Pot Roast</u> (Serves 8)

Buy a whole <u>eye of the round</u> of beef. If need be, cut in half to better fit the heavy kettle you cook it in. A Dutch oven is ideal, but any pot with a tight cover will do. Heat the pot well, and then put in the beef (fat side <u>down</u> to begin with) to sear. As it browns, add <u>salt</u> and <u>pepper</u> and a dusting of <u>flour</u>. Keep turning to brown on all sides. Add <u>2 chopped onions</u> toward last of browning, so that they, too, brown slightly. Don't let them burn or get dark. Now slide a rack under the meat so it won't scorch in long cooking. Add <u>1 cup water</u>. Cover. Simmer slowly <u>4 or 5 hours</u>, or until absolutely tender. Check once in a while to see if a bit more water is needed. Remove meat to a warm platter. Make gravy of pan juices by adding <u>1 quart of water</u> that has been blended in blender with <u>8 tablespoons of flour</u>. Pour this flour-water slowly into hot pan juices, stirring constantly. Correct <u>salt</u> and <u>pepper</u>, and add a few dashes of <u>Worcestershire Sauce</u>. Allow gravy to simmer about <u>10 minutes</u> so the flour cooks. Don't doctor up the gravy with another thing. You want that inimitable, old-fashioned, good beef taste. You also want left-overs. So don't flinch at the whole eye, even though you are only four people.

~~~~~~~~~~~~~

American Schoolash* (Serves 6)

2 cups uncooked elbow macaroni   Cook according to package
directions. Drain and set aside.

1 pound ground beef   } Brown together in butter in
1 medium onion, chopped fine } large skillet.

2 cans cream of tomato soup } Add this and the cooked macaroni
1 small can tomato paste } to meat when it is browned.

Salt, To Taste.   Allow everything to simmer a while to improve
flavor. It is ready to serve. Or you may want
to make it a day ahead and reheat in double boiler.
Serve with a green salad, crusty bread, and a fruit dessert.

~~~~~~~~~~~~~~~~~~~

   Margaret Ide says this is the favorite of the
Danville, Vermont, hot lunch program. Kids who turn up
their noses at many fine dishes, never fail to sail into this. The
minute she tried to embellish it with more onion, celery, bean sprouts,
green pepper, or whatever, the young people carefully picked out
all the vegetables, or refused to eat it at all.

~~~~~~~~~~~~~~~~~~~

* generally known as American Chop Suey

Lobscouse (Serves 10)
(As Gladys Elviken makes it.)

3 pounds round steak, trimmed of fat, cubed } Place in large kettle.
salt pork, about the size of 2 sticks of butter, } Just cover with
cut into small pieces, rind discarded } water, no more.
Bring to boil and
simmer 3 hours.

6 onions, cut up } added to above after the 3 hours
10 medium potatoes, cut in chunks } of cooking. Simmer 2 more
hours. Careful about scorching!*

pepper, freshly ground, added last. Test for saltiness. The
salt pork may prove sufficient.

Serve right from the kettle you cooked it in. It is supposed to be cooked almost dry of liquid. The onions and salt pork seem to disappear in the cooking. Don't let the plainness of the recipe tempt you into trying to brown the meat, adding herbs, or colorful dashes of this and that, or you will ruin it. The honest simplicity of the dish is its chief charm. Serve it with a bright tossed salad and crusty bread.

This hearty sailor's dish from the days of clipper ships, with a name whose origins are unknown, is elegant fare. It is also the easiest main course recipe, for a crowd, contained in this whole cookbook. Having 10, 20, 30 for supper? Dish up Lobscouse.

* I have an old metal rack I place on the burner to prevent the kettle from coming in direct contact with the heat.

Michigan Church Supper (Serves 6 to 8)
(by Miriam Lusk)

<u>2 pounds best ground beef</u>, browned in a bit of butter in a skillet.
When browned, drain off any fat.

<u>4 large potatoes</u>, peeled and cut into thin slices or small pieces.

drain on paper bag.

<u>1 can cream of mushroom soup</u>
1 ¼ cups milk
1 cup Sour cream
1 teaspoon salt
<u>Freshly ground pepper</u>

Mix together well. This is the sauce.

In a good-sized buttered baking dish put a layer of ⅓ of the potatoes, then ½ the meat, ⅓ the potatoes, remaining meat, and top with the last of the potatoes. (3 layers of potato, 2 of meat) Pour above sauce over all. Top the dish with generous slices of <u>cheese</u> (I use Vermont store cheese (cheddar), but you may want to use another kind.)

<u>corn flakes</u>, crushed, and sprinkled over cheese.

Place in preheated <u>350°</u> oven for <u>at least 1 hour</u>. Be sure potatoes are thoroughly cooked. Do not cover.

Miriam claims that of the myriad ways of making a ground beef casserole, this is her favorite. She's one of the better judges in such matters.

*not bad — but family did not like. Very bland.
Maybe needs more seasonings & tomatoe
with meat.*

Sybarites' Meat Loaf   (serves 8)
(As prepared by Emma Lou)

2 pounds high-grade beef, ground
½ pound good bulk sausage
   (I like McKenzie's, but its not available everywhere)
1 small can Sell's Liver Paté
   (or Underwood's liverwurst spread or
   ¼ pound of regular liverwurst)

        } Place in good-sized mixing bowl.

1 egg, not beaten
1 teaspoon Worcestershire Sauce
1 tablespoon Kitchen Bouquet
1 tablespoon prepared mustard
salt and freshly ground pepper, to taste

        } Toss all this onto above meat.

Now wash your hands, and go to work mixing this all together diligently. Don't be squeamish. Thorough blending is only accomplished with bare hands. Spoons and beaters are useless. Have a large bread pan beside you, slightly buttered, and plop this well-mixed mass therein. Don't pound and press it into the pan, as is the usual practice. Be gentle. Bake in preheated 350° oven for at least an hour. Another 20 minutes or so won't hurt it. Use judgment. Tip out onto hot platter with its succulent juices. This recipe takes meat loaf out of the mundane class. Serve with honest-to-goodness fluffy mashed potatoes (page 173) and plain buttered carrots (page 182). Scalloped tomatoes (page 193) or creamed onions (page 188) would also make the perfect accompaniment. This meat loaf, sliced cold, makes excellent sandwiches.

Ginger's Stew (Serves 4 generously)

1 pound lean beef, cubed, dredged with flour and browned
rapidly in butter and olive oil (half and half).
(You may substitute corn oil or any good vegetable oil.)

Salt and pepper, added to meat as it browns.

1 cup red wine) Pour onto well-browned meat and keep stirring,
3 cups water) so as to pick up all the nice residue in pan.

2 onions, chopped
Parsley, chopped, the more the merrier
Thyme, a pinch (if fresh, several pinches)
1 bay leaf

> Add to above and simmer until meat is tender. (This all depends on meat — anywhere from 2 to 5 hours.)

4 medium-sized potatoes, peeled and quartered
4 carrots, cut small

> Remove bay leaf from meat and add these vegetables 3/4 hour before serving time.

4 stalks celery, cut small, and added to stew 15 minutes before
serving time.

+ peas

Serve with crusty bread and green salad. (Stew is served in
soup plates or bowls.)

This is the French way of making a stew, a
happy departure from our thickened variety. Ginger, my
niece, namesake, and illustrator of this book, lived in France,
picked up the cooking habits of that country, and frowns on
pasty stews.

Cantarella Spaghetti Sauce   (Serves 4)

1 large can Italian peeled tomatoes
1 tablespoon dried oregano
    (or 3 or 4 tablespoons chopped fresh)
1 clove garlic
1 bay leaf
1 tablespoon sugar
touch of freshly ground pepper
(no salt, please!)

Combine. Cook over high heat for 15 minutes, stirring often.

1½ tablespoons pure olive oil, added to above after it has cooked for 15 minutes. Lower heat and simmer 10 minutes more. Fish out the garlic and bay leaf and it is ready to serve.

While the above sauce is on the boil, there is just enough time to bring salted water to a boil in a large kettle for cooking spaghetti. Drain when cooked the shortest time indicated on box. Put into warm bowl. Add some butter and stir around to coat the spaghetti. Pour sauce over top and serve.

Accompany this with a platter of little, browned meat balls, a dish of grated Parmesan cheese, a green salad. This is the way it is done in Italy.

I buy best ground beef, salt slightly, roll into small balls, with buttered hands. Arrange balls in shallow stove-to-table baking dish, sprinkle with flour. Bake at 375° until browned. Takes about ½ hour. (1 pound ground beef for 4 people.)

<u>Creamed Chipped Beef</u> (Serves 4)
(Kindness of Ruth Sassaman)

<u>1 package chipped beef</u> (Also called <u>dried</u> or <u>smoked beef</u>. A
package runs around 3 ounces. If you can get it freshly
sliced, which is preferable, ask for ¼ pound.)
<u>butter</u>, several dabs
<u>4 Tablespoons flour</u>
<u>2 cups milk</u>
<u>4 hard-boiled eggs</u>, cut up

Separate and tear slices of beef and drop in frying
pan with butter. Sprinkle on the flour. Cook slowly, stirring
now and then until slightly browned. Pour milk slowly into
pan, stirring constantly. Add eggs, a dash of ~~pepper~~, and
serve at once, on toast, or with a baked potato.

Equally good for breakfast, brunch, lunch, or
supper. For large brunches I make this well ahead of time
and transfer to double boiler to reheat at serving time.

Boeuf Bourguignon (Serves 12)

(Favorite for a gang at a buffet supper and well worth the effort)

⅛ pound of butter and ⅓ cup salad oil, well heated in large frying pan.

6 pounds round steak, trimmed of fat and cut into 2-inch squares. Add beef, a little at a time, to hot fat. Brown quickly, and keep transferring to a large, buttered casserole. Keep reducing juices, so meat will brown, not boil.

2 carrots and 2 onions, cut fine, and browned slightly in frying pan after meat is done. Add to casserole.

½ pound bacon, cut up small with scissors, covered with water, simmered 10 minutes, drained, cooked in frying pan, then added to casserole.

4 tablespoons flour, 2 teaspoons salt, ½ teaspoon pepper, 1 teaspoon thyme, 1 thoroughly crumbled bay leaf, ½ teaspoon garlic powder, mixed, and sprinkled over contents of casserole. Now, with your bare hands, do a complete and thorough mixing job.

2 tablespoons tomato paste, 2 cups Burgundy or Chianti wine, 2 cups canned beef consommé (use one can and increase with water to make 2 cups), combined and poured over all. Cover. Bake in 325° oven 4 hours or more, until meat is very tender. Stir around in juices now and then.

1 pound fresh mushrooms, sliced and browned in above much-used pan, adding more butter if necessary.

12 or more small boiled onions, (I use canned variety and cook them to tenderness and drain). Spread mushrooms and onions over top of completed casserole. You may serve at once, or chill and reheat 24 hours later. It improves with waiting. Garnish with parsley. Serve with noodles or rice or crusty bread and sweet butter, a green vegetable, a tossed salad maybe, though I prefer raw finger greens. The seasonings of the Bourguignon are so delicious that I like them to give their subtle emphasis, rather than the salad dressing. The choice is yours.

Roast Tenderloin of Beef (Serves 6)
(Effortless; so, expensive)

Order 1 whole tenderloin of beef. Butter a shallow pan and place meat therein. With your hands, rub some soft butter all over it. Dust it nicely with flour. Sprinkle it with plenty of onion salt and freshly ground pepper. Be sure to let it come to room temperature before baking. This is important. Place in a preheated 325° oven. Let it roast for exactly 1 hour, not a minute more or less, and no peeking during the process. That's all there is to it. Place on platter or carving board at once. Let it sit and cool for a bit. It will carve better. It should be a perfect pink all through.

A better meal you will never have. There is no waste. Because it is not fatty, and because gravy would be de trop, have something gloriously rich with it like the Vegetable Casserole on page 194. Pour Mushroom and Onion Sauce (page 314) over the meat if you want to.

When I go out to dinner and see how much even a poor meal costs these days, I think to myself, "We could have stayed home and gorged on roast tenderloin and saved money." My husband has always said, "The worst meal at home is better than the best meal out." Which reminds me of the remark of the head chef at the Madrid Hilton. I was interviewing him in connection with my radio program, and asked what his favorite meal was. He replied, "Any old thing at home, alone with my wife, that she cooks."

Ida Gershoy's Viennese Goulash (Serves 6)

4 tablespoons butter
4 medium onions, chopped
} put these in deep pan and brown the onions slightly

2 pounds best veal, cut into 2-inch chunks
1 Tablespoon paprika
Salt and freshly ground pepper, to taste
} add to above and stir around until meat is slightly browned. This takes time, for meat exudes a lot of moisture.

1 large tomato, peeled, and cut small
1 green pepper, chopped
2 tablespoons water
} add to browned meat. Cover tightly and simmer gently for 1 to 1½ hours, or until meat is tender. Remove from heat.

When ready to serve add
½ bottle of capers with ½ bottle of caper juice and
½ pint (1 cup) sour cream
Heat and serve with noodles tossed with butter and loaded with chopped parsley.

Play Viennese waltz records, softly, in the background. You will feel like dancing.

Baked Ham

At the risk of sounding boastful, I'm forced to admit that people often say my baked ham tastes better than theirs. The secret is simple. I bake it longer, lots longer. Don't believe the claims of "completely cooked" on the wrapping of a ham (unless you like slippery ham). I've been known to bake a large one for 8 hours in a 300° oven. The water and juices pour out of it, and the weight is greatly reduced. It is not the economical thing to do, but it surely produces results if your aim is tender deliciousness. At the very last, I remove any offensive skin, score the fat, stick with cloves, and apply a glaze (page 315). I usually serve it with raisin sauce (page 316), sweet potatoes in some form, a green vegetable, a crunchy salad, and custard for dessert; or a corn custard (page 185) with the ham, and a light fruit dessert.

A hot ham dinner is followed through the week with cold ham, ham sandwiches, chopped ham in scrambled eggs, ham soufflé, — the variations are endless. Last of all, I boil the meaty bone and come up with dried bean, split pea, or lentil soup. If you will chill the pan juices from baking a ham, remove the fat, and save the good jelly, it will enrich the soup. A little of the jelly, mixed with mayonnaise, and spread on a ham sandwich, makes the hammiest treat imaginable.

Try baking bacon, on foil (spread in a pan) in 350° oven. Tastes better, better for you, no pan to wash.

Easy Boiled Dinner

Depending on number of people, have ⅓ or ½ a leg of ham. Or use one of the small rolls of ham that look like over-sized hot dogs. Place in a large kettle, cover with water, and simmer about 3 hours, or until falling-apart tender. During last hour of cooking add a potato and an onion per person. You may also add cut-up turnip, if you like it. During last ½ hour of cooking add a carrot per person, a parsnip per person (optional), and a wedge of cabbage per person (optional). The ham seasons all to perfection. (Increase vegetable amounts for hearty eaters.) When ready to serve, remove everything from the steaming kettle and arrange on big platter. Beautify with parsley. This is about as good and effortless a meal as there is. I dress it up with Mary Stone's Mustard Sauce* and Betty Lilly's Baked Pineapple (page 306). Skip dessert. Oh happy day.

Save the precious pot liquor! Make Senate Bean Soup** from it another day.

* page 52, Let Herbs Do It by Virginia W. Bentley, Houghton Mifflin Co. Boston
** page 11, ibid.
1973

Baked Ham Slices (Serves 6) (Esther Klarén's recipe)

<u>2 slices of ham</u>, each slice about 1 inch thick ⌐ Pour hot water over ham, and allow to soak for a good <u>2 hours</u>. Drain well. Place in slightly buttered baking dish (a shallow stove-to-table dish if you have one).

<u>whole cloves</u> ⌐ Use plenty of them, pressing into the ham, about 1½ inches apart, until well studded.

<u>orange marmalade</u> ⌐ Spread it generously over the ham. Bake in preheated <u>350°</u> oven for <u>1½ hours</u>.

This dish emerges from the oven tender, brown, spicy, juicy, just sweet enough. Serve with a yam or sweet potato casserole (page 178) and plain boiled spinach (page 191), being sure to include the garnish of hard-boiled eggs which go so happily with ham, and vinegar (in a cruet) which supplies the sour touch in juxtaposition to sweet ham and potatoes. This is the perfect color-taste-texture-contrast meal.

~~~~~~~~~~~~~~~~~~~~~

Ham Casserole (Serves 6 to 8)

<u>1 pound ham</u>
<u>1½ pounds pork</u>
} Make a date with your butcher to grind this together <u>twice</u>. (Butchers have to be fussy about grinding pork.)

<u>2 eggs</u>, beaten
<u>1 cup cracker crumbs</u>
<u>1 small onion</u>, grated
<u>freshly ground pepper</u>, a touch of salt
<u>1 (16-ounce) can tomatoes</u>
<u>1 (16-ounce) can sweetened crushed pineapple</u>

} Stir together, add the above ground meat to this mixture, then blend all together thoroughly with your hands. Transfer to buttered baking dish. Bake, uncovered, in 325° oven for at least <u>3 hours</u>, and more if your judgement dictates. Serve directly from baking dish.

~~~~~~~~~~~~~~~~~~~~~

Noodles Alfrédo (Serves 4 to 6)

<u>1 generous lump of butter</u>, heated in large frying pan.

<u>1 onion</u> finely chopped, and cooked <u>slowly</u> in butter until transparent

<u>2 cups chopped cooked ham</u> (you may substitute chicken) added to above
and stirred around for a minute or two.

<u>1 twelve-ounce package medium-sized noodles</u> cooked al dente,
drained, stirred into above, along with

<u>more butter</u>, and

<u>1 cup cream</u> and

<u>Parmesan cheese</u>, grated — a very generous sprinkling

Toss all this energetically, with a large fork and spoon, until well mixed and piping hot. It only takes minutes to produce this great Italian dish. Served most often for luncheon, with a green salad. A good Sunday supper dish, too.

At the original Alfrédo's in Rome (there are three of that name as I write this) the noodles are tossed with a large gold fork and spoon, presented to Alfrédo by Mary Pickford and Douglas Fairbanks. My sister, who has traveled the Rome route some twenty five times, always makes a bee line for Alfrédo's, to partake of this delectable concoction, even though Alfrédo himself has gone to his reward. She gave me this recipe, and manages to enjoy it in my Vermont kitchen, tossed without benefit of golden utensils.

Roast Lamb

(Plus suggestions to make the left-overs as delicious as the original roast)

Get the very best leg of spring lamb your butcher can provide. Rinse under running water, dry, and place in a buttered roasting pan on a bed of two cut-up onions. (Forget a rack. The onions make an edible one.) Squeeze the juice of ½ lemon over lamb. Dust with flour, garlic salt, regular salt, freshly ground pepper, and 1 teaspoon dried rosemary pulverized with mortar and pestle. (Double amount chopped, fresh rosemary if you have it.) Place, uncovered, in preheated 325° oven and roast 3 or 4 hours, depending on youthfulness of lamb. (I like it crisp and well done. If you are a pink lamb buff, cut down roasting time.) If I think of it, I baste lamb with pan juices. However, lamb seems to thrive on neglect, which makes it a relaxing company meat. A good half-hour before lamb is done, shift it to another pan, and make the gravy before company arrives. Keep on roasting the lamb.

Lamb Gravy   (1 quart plus)

Pour off all the fat from the roasting pan, leaving only the crisp onions and wonderful brown residue. (Fatty gravy is an inexcusable abomination.) Hopefully you have saved potato water from preparing potatoes ahead of time. Measure this, or plain water, or a combination of both, to make one quart. Pour half of this into the roasting pan and let it simmer away on medium high burner while you scrape and stir, scrape and stir, until you have a lovely brown liquid. Pour the remaining potato water in the blender. Add 8 scant tablespoons flour and blend to total smoothness. Pour this slowly into bubbling liquid in roasting pan, stirring constantly until thickened. Add water if thinner consistency is desired. Correct seasoning with salt, pepper, Worcestershire Sauce, and maybe a touch of lemon juice. Pour gravy, as is, or strained, if you want to remove onions, into a double boiler (gravy scorches easily!) and keep on cooking over boiling water until time to serve.

You may have as little or as much gravy as you want. Just keep the proportions of 2 tablespoons flour for each cup of liquid. Left-over gravy is ever so useful, so plan to have some. Always cook gravy made with flour at least 10 minutes to take away the raw flour taste, and as much longer as is convenient — another reason for early gravy making.

Concerning the roast of lamb: when cooked to satisfaction, remove from oven and let it sit for any length of time. It carves better if it has rested a bit. No need to panic and call everyone to the table just because the meat is finished. Hot plates, hot gravy, will compensate for the meat being somewhat cooled.

~~~~~~~~~~~~~~~~~~~~~~~~~~~~~~~~~~

So you have some left-over roast lamb in your refrigerator. Lucky you. The most obvious thing to do with it is to make cold lamb sandwiches with just plain bread and butter and salt and freshly ground pepper, the whole moistened with some of that good, cold gravy — just enough so sandwich isn't too dry.

Another thing that has been done since time immemorial is to make a Shepherd's Pie. This is simply cut-up pieces of lamb mixed into the left-over gravy, placed in a buttered casserole, topped with mashed potatoes and baked, uncovered, in 350° oven until potatoes are slightly browned. Children love it, as any hot school lunch supervisor will testify. If you fancy it up (as I sometimes do) with slightly cooked peas, onions, celery, carrots, green pepper, or whatever, the kids carefully pick it all out, I've been told. So check your age group, and be guided thereby. Most children are of plain meat-and-potato persuasion. Men too! So it is probably best to serve vegetables on the side.

You still have some bones and scraps left, so its time to make:

Basic Lamb Broth

Put lamb bones, discarded scraps, and left-over gravy into a soup kettle with 2 or 3 quarts of water, any left-over vegetables that stand around in worrisome array in the refrigerator, even a few pieces of stale bread. Be sure to throw in a couple of onions cut in half (no need to peel them), a few stalks of celery — tops and all, a couple of carrots — washed but not scraped, 1 bay leaf, a little parsley (fresh or dried), a pinch of thyme and rosemary, salt, a few peppercorns. Bring this seeming mess slowly to a simmer, and let it bubble away, covered, for 3 or 4 hours, extracting all the good from its many ingredients. Place a colander over a large kettle and into it pour entire contents of soup kettle. Allow it to drip and cool until manageable. Throw away colander contents and strain the broth through a fine strainer (or through cheese cloth) into a convenient receptacle for refrigeration. Chill over night. Fat will harden on top and every bit of it can be removed easily, and discarded, when you are ready to turn the elegant lamb broth, that lies beneath the fat, into Greek Soup or Lamb Curry or Scotch Broth.

Greek Soup (Serves 6)

6 cups lamb broth
⅓ cup real rice, stirred into above and simmered ½ hour
2 egg yolks ⎱ well beaten together
juice of 1 lemon ⎰

Add 1 cup of hot, cooked soup very gradually to egg-lemon mixture, stirring constantly. Then pour this back into the rest of the soup, still stirring. Heat for a minute, but do not boil! Correct for salt. Serve at once. A life sustainer. (May also be made with chicken broth.)

Curry of Lamb

Assuming you have left-over roast lamb (I've been known to roast 2 legs so as to have plenty of meat for a lamb curry party), cut all the meat from the bone. Eliminate every last bit of fat and gristle, tossing such scraps into the soup kettle, and cut up nice, clear, bite-sized pieces of the cold lamb. Wrap in waxed paper and keep in refrigerator until broth is ready. (broth, page 105)

Figuring on 1 cup of broth plus 2 tablespoons flour plus ½ teaspoon curry to each person, blend the 3 ingredients, in proper amount, in blender until smooth. Pour into adequate-sized double boiler and stir busily over boiling water until thick and smooth. Correct seasoning with salt and pepper. Add cut-up lamb from refrigerator, heat thoroughly, but cease stirring, for you do not want to break up the meat. Your lamb curry is ready to serve directly from double boiler.

Serve it over boiled rice, and have an imposing array of small dishes, each holding a different garnish, to sprinkle over all, according to taste. Let everyone help himself. This is fun. In tiny dishes, with an after-dinner coffee spoon in each, put: 1) extra curry, 2) shredded coconut, 3) chopped peanuts, 4) crumbled bacon, 5) chopped parsley, 6) raisins, 7) currants, 8) orange marmalade, 9) finely chopped lemon peel, 10) chopped hard-boiled egg, 11) Major Grey's Chutney, or the homemade variety, 12) chopped crystallized ginger, 13) chopped green and/or black olives, 14) chopped scallions and/or onions, 15) watermelon pickle, 16) mashed banana, 17) guava jelly, 18) candied orange peel, 19) mustard pickle, 20) a larger dish of pineapple chunks, 21) radishes, 22) cherry tomatoes, 23) celery sticks, 24) carrot straws, 25) cucumber sticks. Serve a few, or all of these. There are no hard and fast rules. The possibilities of dressing up a lamb curry are nearly endless, and they transform left-over lamb into an exotic buffet meal. The great bowl of steaming rice with its satellites of colorful little dishes is a delight to behold as well as to eat. A fat-free meal, incidentally.

Scotch Broth (Serves 6)

Put 2 quarts of lamb broth (page 105) in a kettle. Stir in ⅓ cup of barley. Cover, simmer 2 hours, making sure barley doesn't stick to bottom of pan. Then add 2 onions, 2 carrots, 3 stalks celery — all finely chopped, a few frozen peas for color (easily stolen from one of those boxes in your freezer), a bit of left-over lamb cut up fine. Simmer until vegetables are just tender, but still a bit crisp. Check for needed salt and pepper and maybe a dash of Worcestershire Sauce. Don't hesitate to add water to soup if need be. Serve in soup plates for an energizing repast that would bring joy to the heart of any Scotsman.

Speaking of a Scotsman, the price of a leg of lamb might make him turn pale, but the good that can be wrung out of it, as indicated in these recipes, would bring the color back to his cheeks.

Back at the turn of the century, Aunt Helen's father was walking home from his office at the Fairbanks-Morse Scale Works in St. Johnsbury, Vermont, when he met the butcher just walking away from his horse and wagon (from which he peddled good meat to the citizens of the town). He was carrying a leg of lamb into the Patterson home on Main Street. The butcher said, "Hello, Mr. Patterson. Nice day. I have your wife's leg under my arm."

Brook Trout

Put a frying pan on to heat, large enough to hold your catch. Put in plenty of honest-to-goodness _butter_ and a bit of _corn oil_ to keep butter from getting too brown. Now take a paper bag and shake into it some _pancake flour_*, _salt_ and fresh ground _pepper_. Shake to mix. Then drop the trout in the bag and shake back and forth, gently, until trout are well coated. When butter is bubbling hot, put the fish in the pan and cook them _slowly_ until crisp and brown on both sides. (About 20 minutes, more or less, depending on size of fish.) Transfer to a warm platter. Surround with wedges of _lemon_, _parsley_ and crisp _bacon_, and then feast like a king.

The pancake flour trick I learned from one of our best local fishermen, Leslie Vondle. The bit of leavening agent in it makes the coating on the fish a tiny bit puffy and more crisp than regular flour.

Another trick I learned from Leslie, when it comes to freezing trout, is to freeze them in water in a bread pan. In this way they do not become dehydrated. If the trout had jumped from brook to pan, they could not taste fresher.

Some purists insist that trout should be rolled in corn meal before frying. I admit that trout and corn meal have an affinity for one another, but I have another way of having them meet: Serve Johnny Cake (page 221) with them for breakfast.

If you have a fresh catch and want to keep in refrigerator overnight to serve for breakfast, _keep them in water_.

(See next page)

---

* Lacking pancake flour — just use regular flour with a bit of baking powder mixed in.

If the trout are served for lunch or dinner, cook exactly as directed above. But be sure to serve with them good mealy boiled potatoes bathed in plenty of butter and chopped chives. Fresh asparagus or new peas would be the perfect accompaniment. Then, in Pennsylvania Dutch country (and they know good food!) there would be side dishes of crunchy Pocono Pickles (page 300). For dessert in trout season: Rhubarb Pie (page 276), of course.

"Serenely full, the epicure would say,'Fate cannot harm me, — I have dined today.'"

Sydney Smith

If trout are truly fresh, they are liable to try to take one last swim in the frying pan and curl up. To prevent this, make 2 or 3 little cuts in the backbone, from the inside, while "dressing them out".

Merrymount Lobster (Serves about 8)

3 cups cut-up lobster, frozen, canned, or fresh

1 Tablespoon lemon juice, sprinkled over lobster
2 eggs, slightly beaten, and poured over lobster
2 cups light cream ⎫
1 cup soft bread crumbs ⎬ brought just to a boil,
2 Tablespoons butter ⎭ stirred together well,
                      and poured over lobster

1 heaping teaspoon prepared mustard ⎫
dash of cayenne pepper   ⎬ stirred care-
black pepper, freshly ground (about ¼ teaspoon) ⎬ fully into
salt, to taste (Be careful. Lobster may be salty.) ⎭ lobster mixture

      Pour all this into buttered casserole dish
and top with
1 cup buttered cracker crumbs (Saltines)*

      The dish is now ready to hold all day in refrigerator
or bake at once. Bake, uncovered, in preheated 350° oven
until crumbs are brown and lobster bubbly, no more. About
½ hour. Excellent for large buffets. Easily eaten from plate on
lap. Not runny, as is lobster Newburg.

* I use mortar and pestle to crush crackers, place crackers in pan with piece of
butter, heat in oven until butter melts, stir well, and place on casserole.

Steamed Salmon Loaf (Serves 4 or 5)

3 egg yolks
½ cup milk } slightly beaten together in bowl large enough to hold entire recipe

½ cup bread crumbs
1 teaspoon Bell's poultry seasoning
 (Lacking this, ground sage will do.)

1 Tablespoon chopped parsley
Salt and pepper, to taste (use sparingly)
4 Tablespoons melted butter

} mixed together, and added to egg and milk above

1 tall can red salmon, the best, please, cleaned of all bone and skin, broken into pieces and stirred into above. (At this point the mixture may be held in refrigerator until 1 hour before serving time, if it suits your schedule better.)

3 egg whites, beaten stiff and folded gently into whole mixture.
   Pour into well-buttered mold with tight cover. Steam in covered kettle of gently boiling water (that reaches about half way up the side of the mold) 1 hour or more; it matters little how much more. (I use a melon mold, but any tin with tight cover will suffice.) Serve with Egg Sauce* (page 311).

   In New England, we must have salmon for Fourth of July. Lacking this king of the fish world in fresh form, this loaf is no mean substitute. Another Independence Day tradition is new peas and new boiled potatoes, a combination that really rings the Liberty Bell. Pity those who have never had this taste sensation.

* Alleged to be the way Abigail Adams made it.

Shrimp Newburg (Serves 4)

<u>1 pound cooked and de-veined shrimp</u>

<u>1 cup milk</u>
<u>2 Tablespoons flour</u>
<u>½ teaspoon dry mustard</u>

} whirl this in blender, then pour into top of double boiler, place over boiling water, and stir constantly until thickened and smooth.

<u>2 tablespoons butter</u>
<u>3 Tablespoons tomato ketchup</u>
<u>Scant tablespoon Worcestershire Sauce</u>
<u>salt</u>, <u>pepper</u>, <u>cayenne</u>, to taste

} Stir into thickened Sauce above.

Lastly, stir in the shrimp and let them heat thoroughly! At this point you may serve at once, or chill and hold all day, reheating over boiling water at mealtime. Just before serving stir in
<u>2 tablespoons sherry</u>

Serve over rice. A great shrimp recipe.

Eppie Lasell's Scalloped Scallops (Serves 3 or 4)

<u>1 pint small bay or cape scallops</u>, well washed and patted dry with paper towel

<u>½ cup (¼ pound) butter</u>, melted

<u>1 cup cracker crumbs</u>
<u>½ cup bread crumbs</u> } stirred into above melted butter

<u>¾ cup light cream</u>
<u>1 Tablespoon sherry</u> } mixed

<u>Salt</u> and <u>freshly ground pepper</u>, to taste

Butter an appropriate-sized casserole dish. Place in it a layer of scallops, then crumbs, then scallops, then crumbs. (Salt and pepper the scallops very lightly as you put them in.) Pour the cream and sherry over all. Dot with butter (optional). Bake in preheated 400° oven, uncovered, for <u>25 minutes</u>.

Be sure to have a touch of lemon with whatever accompanies this dish — such as lemon on asparagus or broccoli, or some lemon juice and a bit of grated lemon rind to enhance the dressing of a tossed green salad.

<u>Codfish Cakes</u> (Serves 10 to 12 for dinner fare) " 25 for cocktails)

<u>1 wooden box best dried cod</u> (1 pound net)
<u>8 large potatoes</u>, peeled and cut in quarters
<u>2 eggs</u>, beaten
<u>pepper</u>, freshly ground
<u>butter</u>, a generous piece

Freshen cod by soaking in plenty of cold water for at least 1 hour. Pour off water. Cut cod into pieces with scissors, add potatoes, cover generously with more water and boil until potatoes are tender. Drain, remove any skin or bones from fish, mash potatoes and fish enthusiastically until fluffy and lump-free, stir in beaten eggs, plenty of pepper, and the butter until well incorporated. Taking up a spoonful at a time, drop gently into hot fat (sufficiently deep that fish cakes float.) (I use corn oil.) Cook until golden brown, turning them once in the fat. Drain on brown paper. They are ready to enjoy at once. However, as I do not like having the kitchen smelling of hot fat, and as deep frying involves some effort, I usually fry fish cakes in the morning, place them in a shallow, oven-proof serving dish, and set them aside until meal time, heating quickly in the oven at the last minute.

I have had long distance calls asking how I made these fish cakes, and a letter I treasure from a better cook than I who wrote, "If you don't put anything else in your cookbook, be sure to give the fishcake recipe. It makes me drool to think of them." These were always served for Saturday night supper in my New England home with <u>Baked Beans</u> (page 166) and <u>Boston Brown Bread</u> (page 217) — a sort of Holy Trinity. It was unthinkable to have one without the others. Ditto for Sunday morning breakfast, except that the deep-fried fishcakes always evaporated totally on Saturday night. Therefore, an extra bowl of prepared, but not yet fried, fish and potato mixture was ready in the ice box.* These were made into flat, round cakes, and browned in a bit of butter in a frying pan. There was no time for the deep fat routine with Sunday school, church, and Christian Endeavor to walk to at the other end of town.

    <u>Tomato and Apple Relish</u> (page 299) goes perfectly with baked beans. Lacking this, commercial ketchup will do. <u>Snow Pudding</u> (page 257) with <u>Custard Sauce</u> is the usual dessert, a necessary light touch, after the heavy but heavenly trinity.

    Cocktail parties were unknown in the New England of my childhood, but times have changed. So, for the finest hot canapés imaginable, make this recipe up into tiny round balls. Butter your hands and then roll them. More fun than mud pies. Deep fry as directed. Store in deep freeze in varying-sized freezer-to-stove-to-table dishes. Heat and serve (with toothpicks for spearing) at the last minute.

There are recipes for fishcakes that call for the addition of ¼ teaspoon of sage. Not a bad idea, though I've never tried it.

---

* Anyone who refers to an "<u>icebox</u>" is bound to be over fifty.

Scalloped Oysters (Serves 4)

1 pint of oysters, drained, reserving liquid

½ cup bread crumbs
1 cup cracker crumbs
½ cup melted butter } Mix together.

2 tablespoons oyster liquid
1 tablespoon cream (or milk) } Mix together.

salt, pepper, nutmeg

Butter a small baking dish and spread the bottom with ⅓ of the buttered crumbs. Distribute half of the oysters over the crumbs, and sprinkle with salt, pepper, ever so little nutmeg, and ½ the oyster liquid-cream mixture. Then more crumbs, the rest of the oysters, seasonings, liquid. Lastly, top with remaining crumbs. Bake ½ hour in preheated 450° oven. Warning: Should you want to double or triple this recipe, never have more than 2 layers of oysters, or the middle might be underdone. Use a larger, shallow dish. Take it easy with the nutmeg!

Scalloped oysters make an excellent main dish for a Sunday night supper. But in the old days in Newton Centre* (when we walked farther and ate more), they were one of countless hearty accompaniments to Christmas dinner. There is an heretical trend today to present the oysters in the turkey stuffing. Don't be misled. I have my grandmother's 1902 Fannie Farmer Cook Book. The Scalloped Oyster page is heavily stained. I compared that recipe with the one in my new 11th edition. It hasn't changed an iota in over 70 years. So, as this recipe obviously can't be improved upon, I've lifted it, lock, stock and barrel from Fannie's famous book, for the benefit of the benighted souls who have never tasted the genuine article.

* Called "Saints' Rest" by early settlers. The Baptists were especially fond of this Massachusetts town due to the baptizing facilities of Crystal Lake. Holes were often chopped in the ice for total immersion of those who "saw the light" in winter.

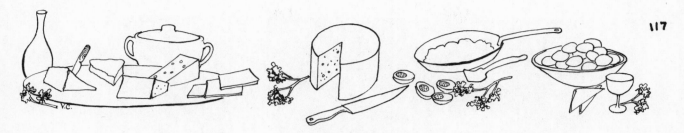

Egg ~ Cheese

Eggs in a Bennington Bowl   Vermont Cheddar Cheese
(resting on an old ox cart wheel hub)

"Have you any treasure
to compare with the egg?"

— Mary C. Ferris

"Many's the long night
I've dreamed of cheese....."

— Ben Gunn in Treasure Island

About Egg and Cheese

To break an egg, if it is whacked on a flat surface, rather than on the edge of bowl or pan, it is less liable to shatter and put chips of shell where they don't belong.

Should pieces of shell get into the egg, fish them out with eggshell as a scoop. It seems to have far better attraction-action for the elusive chips than spoon or fingers.

In separating eggs, if only the tiniest bit of yolk gets into the whites, the whites do not beat into airy peaks, as they should. So take care.

Cold eggs separate more easily than room-temperature ones. But for most baking it is best to have eggs at room temperature. So, resolve their temperament and temperature problem by separating ahead of use, and letting the separated eggs come to room temperature. This is being a bit of a zealot, but don't say I didn't tell you.

In all recipes involving beaten egg whites, beat the whites first, then the yolks. This saves the trouble of washing and drying (egg whites hate water) the beater if you reverse the process. Egg whites will remain cloud-like until you need them, unless you're a real slow-poke.

Now, this is hard to believe, but true. If you beat on the side of the bowl to jolt egg whites off the beater back into the bowl (an automatic gesture with most of us), it knocks some of the air out of the fluffy whites, the very thing to avoid. So make a practice of whacking the beater on your other hand, not the bowl. It is just as effective and your whites remain fluffier. (The same treatment goes for whipped cream. It remains more high and airy, and is less liable to whey.)

What to do with left-over whites of eggs you don't want to use right away? Freeze them. When thawed, they are as good as new. As for left-over yolks (which I never seem to have), there are conflicting views about freezing. Let's say they're almost as good.

To hardboil an egg is simple, but there are a few rules which, if not followed, yield a poor product. If a hard-boiled egg is rubbery, and the yolk has a greenish coating, it has been cooked too long and hard. See pages 121 and 123 for explicit directions.

Should you want to hard-boil eggs a day ahead of use, leave shells on while held in refrigerator, or eggs will toughen.

Even though hard-boiled eggs have been cooked correctly, and shells whacked, and immersed in cold water, they are often difficult to peel. Be consoled by the fact that the harder it is to remove the shell, the fresher the egg.

When frying eggs, shortly before they are done drop a teaspoon of water in the pan, and put a lid on the pan instantly for a few seconds. The hissing steam cooks the tops of the eggs, so they need not be flipped over, which often breaks the yolks.

To me, one of the hardest things to achieve is a perfect poached egg, yet a short-order cook in the lowliest diner can always turn out just that. If making just 1 egg, boiling water in a fairly deep pan can be swirled with a spoon, and the egg slipped into the swirl from a saucer. This keeps the egg white from spreading. Turn off heat, and let egg remain in water until done to your satisfaction. If cooking several eggs, it works best for me to bring water to boil in fairly wide, deep pan. Turn off heat. Slide in the eggs, one at a time, from a saucer, and allow eggs to remain in water until cooked to taste. Remove with slotted spoon. Salt the water before cooking.

No food plays a more important role in cooking than the egg, about the most basic ingredient there is. It is necessary to good health, is easily digested, and responds to slow treatment of short duration;

otherwise it gets tough, or falls apart in a shower of tears.

The _easiest method for hard-boiling eggs_ is to place eggs in cold water and bring to a boil. Remove from heat (but not from water), and keep them covered for at least ½ hour. They will be perfectly cooked. In fact you are free to forget them for hours. No clock-watching necessary.

Cheese is said to be the first man-made dairy product, and, like leavened bread, was discovered by happy chance. Some Arab, in the dim past, was jogging along on a camel (donkey? horse?) carrying milk, for sustenance, in a pouch made from the stomach of a suckling calf. Rennet and milk acted upon each other, and when the Arab stopped to eat, he not only had a thirst-quenching liquid, but a fine-tasting solid as well. From this discovery has evolved the only food in the world that can be served at all courses of a meal. A good rule, however, is to have it for only _one_ of the courses, the repetition of any food theme being taboo, to my way of thinking. If you have a cheese dish for a _main course_, or a cheese sauce or topping for vegetables, _don't_ serve it as an appetizer or a dessert. One can have too much, even of a good thing. Brillat-Savarin considered a meal without cheese somewhere on the menu, like a beautiful woman with one eye missing.

A knowledge of cheese in all its forms, like wine, can be a lifetime study. The main thing is to learn by the eating of it. A stunning array is available to almost everyone in this era of instant transportation from distant places.

Be sure to serve cheese at _room temperature_. There is

no more elegant _dessert_ than cheese served with fresh fruit; it is also effortless. With some fruit pies, especially apple, cheese is imperative. Don't forget to add cheese to a _salad_, either in the dressing (as with Roquefort or bleu cheese), or add hard, unprocessed cheese, in cubes, or julienne strips, to enliven and enrich a tossed green salad. Cream or cottage cheese, with any variety of fruit salad, is loved by all. For the quickest and most acceptable _appetizer_ extant, bring forth cheese and crisp crackers.

A large cheese that has been cut into, is inclined to dry out on the exposed surface. Rub a little _butter_ on this before refrigerating for future use. A cheese may be inclined to mold, so always wrap it in a _whiskey-soaked piece of cheese cloth_, and place all in a plastic bag. Refrigerate.

Grate your own _cheese_. It pays off in taste appeal. Goodness knows how long some of the commercially grated varieties have languished on the grocery shelves.

Every year friends send me a 5-pound wheel of excellent Roquefort cheese. For keeping purposes I cut the precious stuff into wedges, and wrap and _freeze_ them. They keep perfectly, and are ready in convenient-sized amounts.

Deviled or Stuffed Eggs
(Plan about 1½ eggs per person.)

eggs, placed in a pan of cold water, to cover, brought to boil and allowed to simmer for 12 to 15 minutes, covered. Pour water and eggs into sink at once. Whack each egg to break shell. Place eggs in pan of cold water. Remove shells. Cut eggs in half, lengthwise. Remove yolks and mash thoroughly in a bowl. If you have a lot of eggs, use potato ricer.

mayonnaise
salt
pepper
Worcestershire Sauce
tomato ketchup
dry mustard
curry powder, just a touch
paprika
Cayenne pepper

Add these seasonings to well-mashed egg yolks. Tasting as you go is the only possible rule. The mixture should be soft, but not runny. The ketchup and curry make these eggs exceptionally good, but use a light hand, especially with the curry. You want a what-is-it concoction with no evidence of the answer. Fill whites with this mixture and decorate with - - - - -

pimento stuffed olives, cut in thin slices, like a loaf of bread, and placed on each stuffed egg, one slice per egg half.

For a change of filling, follow above directions, but omit ketchup and curry and add finely chopped sweet or sour pickles. Skip the olive garnish and use a snip of parsley instead.

For consistent popularity, stuffed eggs steal the show.

Brud Bartow's Omelet (serves 2)

2 tablespoons butter, melted in hot omelet pan, to sizzling stage.
    Tip pan to spread butter all over bottom and sides.

3 eggs, slightly beaten
¼ teaspoon salt
¼ teaspoon Tabasco sauce
2 tablespoons beer

Stir into eggs, then pour into sizzling butter. Keep lifting with spatula, to let uncooked egg run under. When eggs are creamy, but not the least bit hard, slide onto warm platter, fold in half, cut in half, and serve. This is all done in less time than it takes to tell. Never try to make a large omelet, it doesn't work. Keep flipping out small ones until you have enough.

Extra Special French Toast (Serves 2 or 3)

4 slices bread (not fresh) placed in shallow dish
2 eggs, beaten
½ cup rich milk
2 tablespoons sherry
dash of salt

Mix and pour over bread. Coax bread into soaking up all the mixture on both sides of the slices. On preheated griddle, slightly buttered, gently brown the bread on both sides. Serve with butter and room-temperature maple syrup (not heated!). Some bacon, or sausage, or ham, should nestle alongside.

Baked Egg Crisps
(Great for a company breakfast.)

Generously <u>butter</u> a sufficient number of muffin tin sections. Cut crusts from the same number of slices of <u>bread</u>, and <u>butter</u> them. With a round cookie cutter, cut a hole in the center of each slice, slightly bigger than the bottoms of muffin tin: ⊡ Press the rounds into tins, allowing them to turn up a bit around the edges. (This holds eggs better.) Cut what is left of the bread into 4 pieces: ⊞, and fit each piece snugly around edge of tin, points up. Place in preheated <u>350° oven</u> and bake for <u>7 minutes</u>.

Remove from oven and put a raw egg into each section, breaking the egg into a teacup first. (Your aim will be better than straight from the shell.) <u>Salt</u> and <u>pepper</u> each egg, and sprinkle with grated <u>Parmesan</u> or <u>Cheddar cheese</u>. Return to oven for <u>10 minutes</u> (or more if you like eggs better done, but remember they keep on cooking somewhat after removal from oven).

Coax each cup of goodness from tins onto hot plates. Serve proudly, as is, or garnish with crisp <u>bacon</u>, fresh sliced <u>tomatoes</u>, <u>green pepper</u> rings. No need to make toast, for it already envelops the eggs.

～～～～～～

Eggs should always be at room temperature for proper timing of their cooking. (Ice-cold eggs take several minutes longer to cook.)

～～～～～～

Basque Potatoes (Serves 4 to 6) (by Ella Fifield)

1 tablespoon butter
1 tablespoon corn oil } Heat in heavy skillet.

4 boiled potatoes, cubed
1 small onion, chopped or grated } Place in hot fat and cook until delicately browned, turning occasionally.

4 eggs, slightly beaten, to which add ---
2 tablespoons chopped fresh parsley
salt and pepper, to taste
¼ teaspoon dried marjoram
¼ teaspoon dried thyme } Increase amount, if herbs fresh from garden. } Pour this egg mixture over all, when potatoes are nicely browned. Cook until eggs are just creamy, no more. Turn onto warm platter. Serve at once. A hearty breakfast, or fine fare for any meal.

Eggs in Ramekins

Butter ramekins or custard cups and fill ⅓ full of milk. Into each cup break a raw egg. Sprinkle with salt and pepper, and place a dab of butter on each egg. Put ramekins in a shallow pan and wait for breakfasters to appear, having a 350° oven in readiness. Bake for about 10 minutes. Remember that eggs cook somewhat after removal from oven. I find this an easy way to prepare eggs for a group.

Sue Boyer's Cheese Spoon Bread (Serves 4)

<u>2 cups milk</u>, brought to a boil in 2 quart saucepan.

<u>½ cup yellow corn meal</u>, poured slowly into hot milk while stirring <u>constantly</u>. Keep over heat until mixture is both thick and smooth. Remove from heat and add...

<u>2 tablespoons butter</u>
<u>1 teaspoon salt</u>   } Mix in thoroughly.
<u>¼ teaspoon baking powder</u>

<u>3 eggs</u>, separated.   Beat the <u>whites</u> until stiff, and <u>yolks</u> until thick and lemon-colored.
Stir a little of the hot cornmeal mixture into the yolks, and then return all to saucepan, mixing well. Then stir in ...
<u>¾ cup shredded Cheddar cheese</u>.   Slowly fold entire mixture gently into egg whites.   Turn into soufflé dish or casserole of sufficient size to allow for expansion. Bake in preheated <u>325°</u> oven about <u>45 minutes</u>. Serve at once.

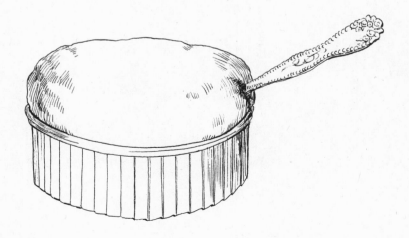

Puffed Egg and Cheese Bake (Serves 12)

12 slices of bread, crusts removed, buttered

12 slices packaged, processed, sliced cheese

> Make into 6 sandwiches, using 2 slices of cheese for each sandwich. Cut each sandwich into 4 squares. Place in buttered, shallow non-metal 9"x 14" baking dish.

5 eggs, beaten

3 cups milk

1 teaspoon prepared mustard

dash of Worcestershire Sauce

salt, pepper, paprika, to taste

> Combine and pour over sandwiches. Cover and refrigerate overnight. Uncover, and bake 1 hour in preheated 325° oven.

A good variation of above is to add sliced ham to the cheese sandwiches, and omit the Worcestershire, salt, and pepper. The ham gives sufficient verve.

Frannie Williams' Cheese Pudding (serves 4 to 6)

6 <u>slices bread</u>, <u>buttered</u>, crusts trimmed off, each slice cut into 4 fingers.

3 eggs, beaten

2½ cups milk

½ teaspoon salt

¼ teaspoon dry mustard

grated onion (just a little, about ⅓ of a medium onion)

2½ cups freshly grated Cheddar cheese

Add these ingredients to the beaten eggs, above.

<u>Butter</u> a non-metal, shallow baking dish. Line the bottom with half of the buttered bread fingers. Spoon half of egg mixture over the bread, then sprinkle on half of the cheese. Repeat, to make 2 layers. Bake, <u>uncovered</u>, in preheated <u>325°</u> oven for about <u>45 minutes</u>, or until puffy and light brown.

This may be baked the minute it is prepared, or fixed a day ahead and allowed to soak. It makes no difference in deliciousness of result. Equally suitable for breakfast, brunch, lunch, or supper. <u>Crisp bacon</u> garnishing the top, is a happy addition, but optional.

People really gather around when Frannie takes this to a church supper in Peacham, Vermont.

American Blintzes (Serves 6)
(Thanks to Fran Waterman)

1 egg, beaten
1½ cups cream-style cottage cheese } Mix together.
2 tablespoons sugar

12 slices of bread   Spread 6 slices with the above cottage cheese mix. Cover with the other 6. Place in shallow dish.

3 eggs, beaten)
½ cup milk } mix and pour over the sandwiches, moving them around until all egg is soaked up.
Salt, a dash)

Brown these sandwiches on both sides on well-buttered griddle. Serve with strawberry jam, the runny kind. (See page 303)

These sandwiches, with coffee or tea, make a quick and adequate breakfast, lunch, or supper.

Macaroni and Cheese (serves 4 to 6)
(by my speedy method)

<u>1 cup uncooked elbow macaroni</u>, cooked according to package directions, aldente, drained, put into buttered baking dish with about <u>1 tablespoon butter</u> extra, and mixed around until butter melts.

<u>1½ cups milk</u>
1 thin, <u>small slice of real onion</u>
<u>½ teaspoon salt</u>
<u>sprinkling pepper</u>, freshly ground
<u>¼ teaspoon dry mustard</u>
<u>2 tablespoons flour</u>
<u>½ pound Cheddar cheese</u>, cut into a few pieces so as to be manageable in blender.

Toss all of this into blender, in order given, and blend until you have one glorious emulsion. This only takes seconds. Pour over the macaroni.

✷ Instead of blender, cook onion w/ butter & add rest of ingred. & mix well.

<u>½ cup cracker</u>, or <u>bread</u>, or <u>cornflake</u> crumbs, or <u>sesame seeds</u>, or <u>wheat germ</u>, that has been heated with <u>1 tablespoon butter</u> and stirred around thoroughly.

Sprinkle over top of macaroni. Bake in pre-heated <u>350°</u> oven for about <u>40 minutes</u>, or until brown and bubbly.

For a meal-in-a-dish, place a layer of chopped ham or chicken in middle of macaroni. Good with a green salad, and crusty bread or rolls.

Blender Welsh Rabbit (Serves 6)

"Rabbit" or "rarebit," all the same. The better the cheese, the better the rabbit. Our Vermont Cheddar is Tops.

1 can evaporated milk (regular 13 ounce size), poured into blender.
1 pound Cheddar cheese, cut into fairly small pieces, added to milk
    and blended, a little at a time. As blender gets too full, keep
    pouring some of the mixture into top of a double boiler, until
    all cheese is fairly well blended.

2 eggs
½ cup beer
½ teaspoon dry mustard
½ teaspoon paprika
dash of cayenne pepper
1 teaspoon Worcestershire Sauce

Blend together in blender and add to double boiler. When guests are ready to sit down at the table, and not until then, place the mixture over boiling water, and stir constantly until all bits of cheese are melted, the mixture is hot, and starts to thicken. Remove from stove and hot water and serve at once over buttered toast. Garnish with crisp bacon, green pepper rings, and slices of tomato. This is a Sunday night favorite, served with tall glasses of cold beer. (Left-over rabbit makes fine sandwiches, cold, the next day.)

    No need to make toast at the last minute. Paint butter on 8 or 9 pieces of bread. Cut diagonally. Arrange on cookie sheet and dry out in a 300° oven until pale golden brown. At the same time bake 1 pound bacon. Drain on paper towel. Warm up toast and bacon in warming oven just before serving.

Greens ~ Grains ~ Vegetables

Green Salad Ensconced on Watering Trough at Bentley Farm

In the background, on the left, is maiden hair fern that springs up every year, unassisted, behind the wooden trough. At the right is woodbine that takes over in a burst of tropical splendor. There is icy spring water pouring into the trough on the right, but not visible.

As for the salad, there is every sort of garden lettuce in the bowl, plus tender sprigs of basil, dill, chives, rosemary, savory, anise, caraway, coriander, fennel, marjoram, mint, oregano, sage, tarragon, thyme. Radishes and hard-boiled eggs give color contrast and quality. When greens are ripe in the garden, it's a different combination every meal.

Possibilities are endless, limited only by supply or lack of imagination.

It takes longer to prepare fresh greens than almost any other kitchen operation, but rewards are great in the pleasure of eating, and in nutritional value. Every leaf must be washed and carefully dried. (A wet salad rates a failing grade.) I keep bath towels in the kitchen for this purpose, sometimes washing greens 24 hours ahead of a party, wrapping gently in towel and refrigerating. Or I swing washed greens in a French salad basket. Recently, I was presented with a salad drier that looks like a small washing machine, centrifugal force taking care of the dampness. It really works. After greens are washed and dried as well as possible, and torn into salad bowl (sometimes I use scissors for cutting, but wouldn't dare admit it to a zealous gourmet), I put bowl in refrigerator for a while to chill and crisp. The dressing is added at the last second before serving, and all is tossed well. Because the salad pictured here contained a medley of pungent herbs, I used Basic French Dressing (page 139).

If you have the basics in your kitchen, such as oil, vinegar, salt, pepper, mustard, etc. — why buy any of those miles of salad dressings at the supermarket? They are expensive, not as good as you can make yourself in minutes, and before long your refrigerator is overflowing with half-used bottles.

When it comes to salad greens in the winter months, avoid the ubiquitous iceberg lettuce, and try to get escarole, romaine, endive, chickory, watercress, Boston lettuce, young spinach— to name a few. Did you know that canaries fed iceberg lettuce will curl up their toes and die? They thrive on other varieties of lettuce. Iceberg won't kill you, but is less digestible than the above mentioned greens, and it also gets to be a bore.

When, in winter, the stores carry only cardboard-tasting tomatoes, substitute the best variety of canned tomatoes, well drained, in a salad. There's a fancy brand of tomato wedges that are quite satisfactory. (Save juice. Doctor with lemon juice and Worcestershire for a tomato juice cocktail.) Or another trick — if store tomatoes are firm, place in a sunny window to further ripen and redden them.

Some favorite salad combinations to place on lettuce, or toss are: 1) _avocado and grapefruit_, 2) _tomato and white grape_, 3) _canned artichoke hearts and canned mandarin oranges and avocado_, 4) _sweet onion rings and orange sections_, 5) _cooked asparagus, peas, green beans, lima beans, carrots_ — any one, all, or several, marinated in _Basic French Dressing_ (page 139) and tossed with _greens_ at last moment. _Croutons_ (page 66) and _hard-boiled egg_, chopped, go well with a vegetable salad, as do little pieces of _cheese_ and tiny strips of _ham_ and/or _chicken_. This is a fine way to make use of _left-over vegetables_, but be sure butter is washed off of them with hot water. Don't forget to add some _raw onion_, either chopped, rings, or just onion juice!

In making a molded salad, grease mold lightly with salad oil, such as corn oil that does not solidify under refrigeration. Your salad will turn out of the mold perfectly.

For quick and easy scraping of carrots ——

use a metal sponge.

When grating <u>carrots or onions</u>, leave the stems on. This gives you something to hold onto, and prevents grating your fingers.

When purchasing <u>celery</u>, try to get the great big stalks of the Pascal variety, instead of the celery hearts. It's about the only thing I know of that is cheaper but better. It is greener, crunchier, tastier, more vitamin-filled. The important thing is to scrape the strings off the big stalks, for more tempting eating. They may then be cut into small sticks. One stalk goes a long way. For texture, flavor, contrast, I put freshly chopped celery into many creamed dishes, at the last minute; and, of course into many salads. Celery is as standard in my refrigerator as milk, eggs, butter.

When it comes to <u>frozen vegetables</u>, and you need part of a package for something, simply cut through the package with a heavy chef's knife. Return what is left to the freezer, protected in a plastic bag.

<u>Squash</u>, the hard winter ones —— steam in a little water in a covered kettle until tender when tested with fork. Then peel, remove core, mash, and reheat. I used to resort to an axe, a cleaver, anything — and end up bleeding. This is a merciful discovery.

If you are a <u>fiddlehead</u> enthusiast, the edible ferns are bracken, cinnamon, interrupted, and ostrich. Ostrich are the best, and the least woolly. (see page 187)

Fresh garden corn, if not eaten immediately, is best husked as quickly as possible, and kept in plastic bag in refrigerator. I've been told that leaving the husks on after picking destroys the vitamins.

Most vegetables should be cooked in the tiniest bit of water, with a dab of butter, a bit of salt, and (except for string beans), a bit of sugar to bring out the flavor. Cover, and cook just long enough to be tender-crisp, not mushy. Never drain. It has been an American failing to drown vegetables in water, cook them to death, and then pour most of the vitamins down the drain. I often cook vegetables in the morning, in preparation for guests, cool them, uncovered, in their own juices, and reheat rapidly just before serving.

As for string beans, I remove stems, line the beans up on cutting board, and, with a French knife, reduce them, in seconds, to pieces no bigger than a pea. Cooked, as suggested above, they are done in minutes, and oh so good. (See page 180.)

For the easiest and best onion dish, wrap onions, skin and all, in a foil package. Toss in oven when you are baking potatoes. When cut open on one's plate, salted and buttered, they are as sweet and delicious as one could imagine. My sister says, "Put onion in everything but ice cream." I know an old lady in her nineties who is never sick and claims never to have had a cold. Her secret, she says, is a raw onion sandwich at bedtime, every night of her life! Strong medicine.

For low fat diets, try cooking vegetables with a bouillon cube instead of butter. For low salt diets, season with herbs.*

---

* See Let Herbs Do It ~ Virginia Bentley (Houghton Mifflin Co., Boston) 1973

Basic French Dressing
(Preparation Time: one minute)

¼ cup vinegar
¾ cup salad oil
1 teaspoon sugar
½ teaspoon salt
½ teaspoon garlic salt
½ teaspoon dry mustard
¼ teaspoon paprika
⅛ teaspoon freshly ground pepper

Put everything into appropriate-sized bottle and shake to mix. It is a good idea to keep this on hand in refrigerator at all times. A fine dressing as is — or it can be doctored up in any way you desire: with crumbled Roquefort or bleu cheese or chopped herbs in season or chili sauce or a bit of mayonnaise. The possibilities are limitless. No need to choose from those miles of dressings in the supermarket. Make your own variations with this as a base. But don't forget to use it in the simplicity of its basic form. It's a relief from too much "gourmet" everything.

Poppy Seed Salad Dressing (Carol Ayers)

2/3 cup vinegar
1 medium onion, cut in quarters
2 teaspoons salt
2 teaspoons dry mustard
1½ cups sugar

} blended in blender

1 cup corn oil (or salad oil of your choice) added
slowly, while still blending, to above.
Pour into glass jar.
3 Tablespoons poppy seed, stirred into above.

Keep in refrigerator, well covered.
If dressing separates, shake well before
serving. This makes any salad an event,
but I like it best embellishing these three
favorites: 1. avocado and grapefruit
2. Tomato and white grape
3. sweet onion rings and mandarin
orange sections

If you serve Poppy Seed Salad Dressing
at a party, have the recipe mimeographed.
Everyone will ask for it.

Cole Slaw Dressing

1 cup evaporated milk (1 small can)
½ teaspoon salt
¼ teaspoon freshly ground pepper
5 tablespoons sugar
} mixed in glass jar

5 tablespoons vinegar added slowly to
above while stirring constantly.
Keep chilled in refrigerator until mixed
with chopped cabbage. Cole slaw is
sometimes enhanced by the addition of
chopped celery, onion, shredded carrots —
either, all, or any one. A natural with
Baked Beans.* This dressing has a clean,
uncomplicated taste — a relief from
too much seasoning.

When washing fresh spinach which you are about
to cook, put aside a few prize leaves to give dark green emphasis
to a salad at another meal.

* See page 166

Bess Shipman's Dandelion Dressing (Serves 4 to 6)

Have 1 quart of dandelion greens well washed, drained, cut up with scissors, and chilled and ready in a plastic bag.

6 slices bacon, cut small with scissors and baked or fried until crisp. Drain off fat and put bacon aside on paper towel.

Wet ingredients:

2 eggs, beaten

1 cup water

¼ cup vinegar } added to eggs

Dry ingredients:

¼ cup sugar

½ teaspoon dry mustard

½ teaspoon salt

1 tablespoon flour } mixed in saucepan large enough for all ingredients

Pour wet ingredients slowly onto dry and stir well. This mixture may be prepared way ahead of the meal. When ready to serve, bring just to a boil, no more, stirring constantly. Pour over the greens. Now add the bacon. Toss well and serve at once. Sensational.

This is an old Pennsylvania Dutch recipe, not to be found, in just this form, in any cook book I have ever seen. I have named it for the good cook who shared this treasure with me many years ago. Never let anyone claim to dislike dandelion greens until tried in this fashion. Hard to say whether this is a vegetable or salad. It fills the bill for both. Dandelion is recognized as the most vitamin-filled wild plant that grows. It is supposed to cure everything. Lacking wild greens, or the cultivated kind, try this sauce over <u>curly endive</u> or <u>escarole</u>.

———————

<u>Dandelion</u> —— coming from the French <u>dent de lion</u> (lion's tooth). The leaves do have a tooth-like appearance. Be sure to pick this epicure's delight (and dooryard weed, so distressing to the lawn-proud) when it is young. See how to make dandelion soup on page 56.

———————

When I speak of vinegar, I mean the common variety of cider vinegar. When speaking of oil, except in a few rare instances, I mean corn oil. This seems to work best for me. I'm not in an area where I can get the best olive oil, or exotic wine vinegars, and probably wouldn't indulge too heavily if I could. At the corner store in our small village, I recently counted <u>36</u> different varieties of commercial oil and vinegar dressings, all of which could be reasonably duplicated out of basics, at home. For example, if I want Roquefort dressing, I put real Roquefort cheese in my homemade dressing. If I want tarragon flavor to vinegar, I simply pick tarragon from garden or herb shelf, instead of going out and buying a bottle of tarragon vinegar. Etc., etc., etc., until I, too, have 36 varieties, but not all those bottles to store.

———————

Catherine Beattie's Salad (Serves 12 or more)

2 packages Orange Jell-O
1 large can crushed pineapple
1 large can apricots, cut up } mixed

Drain the fruit and place in large, shallow glass bowl or a large Pyrex cake pan. Reserve 1 cup of juice for Topping. Mix the remaining juice with enough water to make 4 cups and bring This just to a boil. Pour hot juice over Jell-O and mix until dissolved. Pour Jell-O juice mixture over the fruit and refrigerate.

Topping

½ cup sugar
2 Tablespoons flour
1 egg, well beaten } mixed together in sauce pan.

Heat the 1 cup of reserved fruit juice and stir carefully into above mixture. Cook, stirring constantly, until Thickened, and remove from heat at once. Chill.
1 cup heavy cream, whipped, mixed into cold custard and spread over The jellied fruit.

Catherine says it is particularly good with ham. When she served this at a Vermont Farm Bureau Board Meeting There were cheers. Called a salad in New England, it might be a dessert elsewhere. Fruit with the meat course is a happy combination too often overlooked.

Corned Beef Salad (Serves 6)
(by Marion Gavel)

2 tablespoons (2 envelopes) plain gelatin ⎱ soaked together in
¼ cup cold water ⎰ good-sized bowl for a few minutes

1½ cups tomato juice, brought just to a boil and stirred into above until gelatin is dissolved

juice of ½ lemon ⎱ stirred into above and allowed to
½ teaspoon salt ⎰ cool but not to set

1 twelve-ounce can of corned beef, shredded with 2 forks
3 hard-boiled eggs, chopped
2 cups celery, chopped
½ cup cucumber, chopped
1 tablespoon chopped onion
1 cup mayonnaise

⎱ folded into above and poured into ring or loaf mold that has been lightly oiled.

Chill until set. Unmold. Garnish with lettuce. Have extra mayonnaise and horseradish for accompaniment. A winner, almost a whole meal, all ingredients of which are on hand all seasons of the year.

Bouillabaisse Salad* (Serves 6 to 8)
(reserve for royalty)

1 cup cut-up canned or fresh crabmeat, cartilage carefully removed ⎫
meat of 1 small lobster, canned, frozen or fresh, cut up ⎪
½ pound cooked, deveined shrimp, canned/fresh/frozen ⎭

Combine in bowl and sprinkle with

juice of ½ lemon

1 medium head Boston lettuce ⎫ washed, dried, torn, and
1 medium head romaine lettuce ⎬ placed in large bowl.
1 bunch watercress ⎭ Then spread fish on Top.

2 Tomatoes, peeled, and cut into small wedges ⎫ arranged
½ cup finely chopped celery ⎪ on the greens
1 hard-boiled egg, chopped ⎬ and shellfish,
1 small onion, thinly sliced, separated into rings ⎪ and chilled until ready
1 Tablespoon chopped chives ⎭ to serve

Caviar Dressing

½ cup sour cream ⎫ Mix together well.
½ cup mayonnaise ⎪ Pour on Bouilla-
1 Tablespoon prepared horseradish ⎬ baisse Salad at
2 tablespoons best black caviar ⎭ table, and toss proudly.

〰〰〰〰〰〰〰〰〰

* Mostly thanks to Helen Corbitt

Spinach Mousse (Serves 8)

2 ten-ounce packages chopped frozen spinach, placed in saucepan

1 can Campbell's Consommé (beef, 10½ ounces) Pour half of this over the spinach, and cook only until spinach thaws. While spinach is cooking, soak

2 tablespoons (2 packages) unflavored gelatin right in the remaining half can of consommé. When spinach has cooked, stir the soaked gelatin into it. Mix thoroughly, so as to dissolve the gelatin. Then remove from stove. Allow to cool somewhat.

½ teaspoon salt
½ teaspoon celery salt
freshly ground pepper, to taste
1 small onion, peeled and quartered
} Add this to the slightly cooled spinach. Blend thoroughly in blender. This calls for 2 loads, unless you have an extra-large blender.

1 cup sour cream, stirred into blended spinach.

Pour into mold that has been slightly coated with corn oil. This makes about 6 cups of mousse. Any mold will do — ring, or melon, or whatever attractive mold you have that will hold 6 cups. Chill until firm.

2 hard-boiled eggs, reserved, and sliced or chopped as garnish for mousse.

Unmold on a blue platter, if you have one. Surround with lettuce, sliced (or little cherry) tomatoes, some carrot curls, and the eggs. Have a dish of mayonnaise on the side, for those who want it. You will have delightful taste and color accents; in fact, just about the whole spectrum, a soul-satisfying sight. Serving spinach cold, in this happy state, is a pleasant change.

Lady Birley's Horseradish Mousse
(kindness of Peggy Ryan)

2 tablespoons butter, melted in pan

⅓ cup flour, stirred vigorously into butter

2½ cups milk, stirred gradually into above until lump-free

2 packages (tablespoons) unflavored gelatin soaked in
     ¼ cup cold water and stirred into above hot sauce
     until thoroughly dissolved

3 eggs, separated, whites beaten until stiff and set
     aside. Mix the yolks with the cream (below)
     and stir into hot sauce (above) and heat
     just to boiling point, not a second more.

3 tablespoons heavy cream

4 hard-boiled eggs, finely chopped
salt and freshly ground pepper, to taste
cayenne pepper, a pinch
4 heaping tablespoons horseradish   } stirred into
1 teaspoon vinegar   above mixture
1 teaspoon sugar

     Lastly, fold egg whites into all. Pour into 2-quart mold which has been oiled. Chill until set. Unmold and decorate with watercress and/or cucumber slices and/or garden lettuce. Excellent served with a roast beef dinner.

     Equally appropriate served with crackers

at a cocktail party. That is the way I first enjoyed it at Peggy Ryan's house. Everyone was enchanted with the dish, and Peggy not only shared the recipe with me, but a true story in connection with it.

Peggy wrote, "Perhaps I've told you the amusing story of Lady Birley's first serving of her famed Horseradish Mousse. A few years ago she planned a large dinner party for her Anglo-Irish friends at her country estate in Ireland, and engaged a caterer who was bringing all the china, crystal, and silver in his van. A group of the I.R.A. boys, angered at her English ties, held up the van and kept the caterer at gunpoint until the party was over. Undaunted, Lady Birley borrowed plates from her neighbors and, lacking a large platter, served the roast beef and Horseradish Mousse in a birdbath from her garden."

〰️〰️〰️〰️〰️〰️〰️〰️

very very good.
made for gus' nameday '88.
served on lettuce leaves — for 17 people!
can grapefruit sections

Marge's Western Salad (Serves 8 to 10)

1 cup mandarin oranges	mix, chill, serve, either as a salad,
1 cup pineapple chunks	with or without lettuce, or as a dessert.
1 cup shredded coconut	This salad has saturated the North, South
1 cup marshmallow bits	and East as well, but continues to stir
1 cup sour cream	enthusiasm. Especially good with ham.

delicious

1 chopped apple
(do not peel)

〰️〰️〰️〰️〰️〰️〰️〰️

Avocados with Hot Sauce (Serves 6 to 8)
(As served by Mary and Cecil Dawson)

2 tablespoons butter
2 tablespoons ketchup
2 tablespoons vinegar
2 Tablespoons Worcestershire Sauce
2 Tablespoons sugar
Salt and pepper, to taste
dash of Tabasco

} Mix all Together in double boiler and heat until ready To serve.

½ avocado to each person, stone removed, skin left on.

Place each half on a bed of watercress, if obtainable. Otherwise garnish with any suitable green. Pass The Sauce, piping hot, To be spooned into avocado.

Never To be forgotten was The dinner party at which Mary served This, and Cecil broiled five-inch-thick steaks. Well, maybe they were only four inches. The avocados filled the bill for vegetable and salad. What else was served? I've forgotten, nor does it matter. The Avocados with Hot Sauce stole the show.

George Sawyer's Avocado Salad (Serves 6)

2 avocados, peeled and cut in pieces
2 tomatoes, peeled and cut in pieces
2 bunches scallions, cut small and using plenty of green stem
Juice of 1 lemon
½ pint sour cream (1 cup) salt and pepper, to taste
6 slices bacon, cut up small with scissors, and baked
　　in oven until crisp, and drained on paper towel.
　　Mix everything together except the bacon.
Use that as a topping. Serve with lettuce or not, as
you prefer. So good it is close to immoral.

　　Scallions are not always available, so a
coarsely grated onion may be used instead. In
this case, use some chopped celery also, both for
flavor and crunch. Yes, George, I believe celery
improves this, even with the scallions.
　　Better to mix this dish at last minute, or the
whole lot gets too runny. Another way that has
proved satisfactory is to mix it all ahead (reserving
a little of the cream) and place it in a colander
over a bowl to drain, and keep in the refrigerator
for as long as you care to. Empty onto a round
platter or shallow bowl. Garnish with the reserved
cream and top with the bacon.

Horseradish-Beet Salad (Serves 4 to 6)

<u>1 medium can sliced beets</u>, drained, and cut into
slender julienne strips

½ cup sour cream
¼ cup prepared horseradish
Sugar
Salt   } to taste   } mixed
Cayenne pepper

<u>chives</u>, fresh or dried

    Fold the beets carefully into cream-horse-
radish mixture. Put into an attractive bowl.
Garnish with chopped chives. Chill thoroughly
until serving time.

    This is a marvelous accompaniment to
a New England Boiled Dinner which demands both
horseradish and beets. Instead of bothering to heat beets
separately to serve on the meat platter (if cooked with
everything else in the pot, beets make the whole dinner
bright red) and having a separate dish of horseradish,
you take care of the whole necessary taste combination
with this unique and delicious side dish.   Don't overlook
its possibilities with other meals also.

Borsch Salad

Using the recipe for Cold Borsch on page 57 soak 2 Tablespoons (2 packages) plain gelatin in ¼ cup cold water.

Bring consommé to a boil and dissolve the gelatin therein.

Blend the can of beets and onion in a blender and add to consommé.

Then add lemon and salt.

Chill in a ring mold. Turn out when firm. Garnish with lettuce. Put sour cream (or yogurt) in center of jelly.

This jellied borsch, so easily prepared, will establish your reputation as a gourmet cook whether you are or not. I nearly always double the recipe, for guests are inclined to resort to corners, hopefully unseen, where they wolf this concoction with hostess-flattering abandon. People think it is cranberry jelly! Interesting to watch their faces light up as the first bite indicates otherwise.

Three-Bean Salad (Serves 12 or more)

1 medium-sized can French style cut green beans ⎫
1   "   "   "   "   "   "   "   yellow beans ⎬ drained
1   "   "   "   kidney beans   ⎭ and mixed

2 small onions, thinly sliced and mixed into above

¾ cup vinegar   ⎫ Bring to a boil, no more,
¼ cup corn oil   ⎬ and pour over above.
¾ cup brown sugar ⎭

Salt and pepper, to taste

Refrigerate in glass jar. It will keep several weeks. Divine!

Once upon a time Camilla Baker brought this to a gathering after a funeral. Everyone was noticeably cheered. This was when the recipe was new and had still to take the whole country by storm. I've even seen the recipe framed in gift shops. This must say something about its universal appeal.

Frances Fretz's Cucumbers in Sour Cream (Serves 4)

1 good-sized cucumber, peeled, thinly sliced

1 cup sour cream
2 tablespoons vinegar
4 tablespoons sugar
sprinkling of cayenne pepper DILL
salt, to taste
pepper, freshly ground, to taste

} beaten together with egg beater. Fold in the sliced cucumber.

Serve in sauce dishes and garnish with paprika

A runny and ravishing treat. Have it at least once during cucumber season, and think of the good old days when no one had ever heard the word cholesterol.

Frances Fretz was a great beauty, and one who inspired some of Charles Dana Gibson's drawings of the famous Gibson Girls. I knew her as a mature, and still beautiful, woman. The joys of her well-set table were legendary in Easton, Pennsylvania. There I was privileged to partake, and this is the dish I liked best. The recipe was given me by her daughter, Wilhelmina Fretz Starr.

Italian Salad

Tomatoes
Mozzarella cheese } the colors of the
basil   flag of Italy.

     When garden vegetables are available, place lovely red slices of tomato alternately with thin slices of Mozzarella cheese until a platter is filled. Chop a generous handful of fresh basil and sprinkle over all. Chill until ready to serve. Lastly, just before serving, anoint sparingly with Basic French Dressing (page 139) This may be served in winter with dried basil, but I prefer to save it for one of summer's delights. Basil and tomato are soul mates, which fact the Italians particularly appreciate.

Tomato and Onion Salad

     Fill a glass bowl with alternate layers of sliced tomatoes and sweet red (or white) onion rings. Sprinkle with nothing but vinegar, sugar, salt, pepper. As good as it is simple.

Chicken Salad

     The best one I ever ate was simply white meat of chicken, seedless green grapes (you may substitute mandarin orange sections) and capers, bound together with mayonnaise.

Susan McMillan's Layered Salad (Serves 10 to 12)

<u>1 head iceberg lettuce</u>*, quartered, washed, drained, patted dry and cut up quite fine with a French knife.

<u>Several stalks of celery</u>, washed, scraped of strings, and cut into small pieces — making about 2 cups.

<u>2 green peppers</u>, washed, cored, cut in strips, chopped

<u>1 sweet onion</u>, finely chopped, or in very thin rings, according to preference

<u>1 box frozen peas</u> (10 ounces), ever so slightly cooked in a little salted water, drained; <u>no butter</u>!

Broccoli

Zucini Squash

Place the above in layers in your best large glass bowl, in order given, saving ½ the lettuce as top layer. (Start and end with lettuce.)

<u>1 cup sour cream</u>
<u>1 cup mayonnaise</u> } mixed together and spread <u>over</u> salad, <u>not stirred in</u>!

<u>2 Tablespoons Sugar</u>, sprinkled over above.

<u>¼ pound Cheddar cheese</u>, grated, and sprinkled over all.

Cover bowl with plastic. Refrigerate for 24 hours, or 8 hours at the least.

This is a party favorite, for it is totally ready a whole day ahead. It emerges cold and crisp to a degree. Being almost salt free (salt would make the greens weep), it is especially good with ham. But I use it with any and every meat. Excellent with boiled live lobster, and a blessed switch from cole slaw.

---

* Though I'm inclined to downgrade iceberg lettuce, it has its place, and this is an ultra-special recipe.

Otis Bricketts' Cabbage Salad (Serves 35 to 40)

10 pounds cabbage, shredded ⎫
1 bunch carrots, shredded ⎬ Place in large wooden
1 bunch celery, cut fine ⎬ salad bowl.
2 medium onions, chopped fine ⎭

1 cup salad oil, poured over above and tossed thoroughly so as to coat the greens

1 pint sweet mixed pickles, chopped fine, juice retained and poured over above greens ⎫
½ cup sugar ⎬
2 tablespoons celery seed ⎬ added to
2 tablespoons salt (or more, to taste) ⎬ above
1 tablespoon mustard seed ⎬ and mixed
⅛ cup vinegar (That's all!) ⎭ in well

1 pint salad dressing (not mayonnaise) Otis likes Pleezing,
but there are many good brands.

    Mix the salad dressing in fast, and thoroughly. Chill salad until ready to serve.

    Mr. Otis Brickett is famous for this salad in the Northeast Kingdom of Vermont, and generously gave me his recipe, which should be on record for posterity. There has hardly been a church supper, a benefit at the Knights of Pythias Hall, or at the Masonic Temple, or at the Elks', or at chicken barbecues on Danville Green, or a Dowsers' Convention, in the past 40 years, that Otis has not made this salad in quantity (This is his smallest recipe) and reigned as king of the salad bowl. He has always graciously produced it for the Danville Four Church Supper and Barn Dance in my barn, where we feed 400 people at a time, each summer. Because that supper invariably has the same menu, and is typical of the food of this region, I am noting it down — again for posterity. Hearty fare, but square dancing on a crisp August evening seems to call for just that. Everything is home made by willing committees from the Baptist, Catholic, Congregational, and Methodist churches.

Barn Buffet for 400 People

Roast Ham - page 99
Mustard

Baked Beans page 166
Tomato Relish page 299
Raisin Brown Bread page 219

Stuffed Eggs - page 123
Hot Rolls - page 207
Butter (from local creamery)

Potato Salad
Otis Brickett's Cabbage Salad page 158

Fruit Cup
Bessie's Ginger Cookies page 245

Coffee
(great fragrant urns of it)

Milk
(all the kids can drink)

Gnocchi Alla Romagna (Serves 8)
(Mariafranca Morselli's recipe, given to me by Bets Albright)

1 quart milk, brought to a boil
1¼ cups farina, added slowly to boiling milk while stirring constantly until very thick and lump-free. Remove from fire.

2 teaspoons salt
¾ stick sweet butter (a little less than ¼ pound)
2 eggs, beaten
¼ cup grated Parmesan cheese

stirred vigorously into above and then spread on well-buttered large shallow pan. You want a surface of about 11 X 15 inches. Lacking right-sized pan, use 2 smaller ones. Allow to chill for several hours.

When meal time approaches, spread the cooled farina with the remainder of that ¼ pound stick of sweet butter. I heat the butter slightly and spread surface with a pastry brush. Now cut the farina into nice-sized squares for serving (with a spatula) after cooking is completed. Sprinkle generously with grated Parmesan cheese. Slide pan or pans into preheated 350° oven and bake about 20 minutes, being watchful. At the very last, place beneath broiler for a few minutes (watching it every second!) until brown and bubbly. Simply divine!

Bring on, to applause, at an outdoor steak party, along with a bowl of green salad.

Confetti Rice (Serves 6)

1 cup uncooked rice, regular, not instant
    (Long-grained Carolina is best.)
2 cups chicken broth, your own, canned, or made
    with bouillon cubes
1 onion, chopped fine
½ green pepper, chopped fine
½ sweet red pepper (or canned pimento) cut fine
1 small can mushrooms, drained and chopped (optional)
salt might be needed if broth not sufficiently salty.

    Throw This all together in your favorite casserole dish, which has been buttered. You may combine it in the morning for the evening meal. Cover. Bake, covered, in preheated 350° oven for one hour. Stir, once, half way through the baking. A party favorite. Effortless. Fat-free for the diet-conscious. Its dryness well contrasted by having a creamed vegetable. Or a happy companion to creamed chicken.

Bess Piqula's Rice Ring (Serves 8)

1 medium onion
2 stalks celery
½ green pepper
} Chop fine and brown slightly in small amount of vegetable oil.

1 cup uncooked rice (not instant) added to above and cooked a little longer.

1 package Lipton's Chicken and Noodle Soup Mix
4 cups water
} Added to above. Cover and let simmer for 20 minutes, or until rice is cooked.

½ can cream of mushroom soup
½ can water
} mixed and added to above after it has cooked.

Butter a 10-inch ring mold and pack rice mixture into it. Keep warm by placing ring mold in pan of hot water. This ring mold may be made way ahead and heated just before the meal. Good with creamed turkey and peas. Colorful with center of ring filled with hot carrots and green beans.

Bess was one of the better cooks and home-makers of St. Johnsbury, Vermont. She said this rice ring always rang the bell.

Rice Soufflé (Serves 4 and does not fall.)

1 tablespoon butter, melted in pan
1 Tablespoon flour, mixed into butter
1 cup milk, stirred slowly into above roux and cooked until smooth
2 eggs, separated
2 cups cooked rice
¼ pound Cheddar cheese, grated
onion salt, to taste (or a little grated onion and plain salt)
pepper, freshly ground

Cool the white sauce made of first 3 ingredients. Then beat in the egg yolks vigorously with a spoon. Fold in the rice, cheese, and seasonings. Lastly fold in, gently, the egg whites which were beaten until stiff. Pour into buttered soufflé dish. Bake about 40 minutes in preheated 350° oven until puffy and nicely tanned. Wonderful. Especially so, made with left-over wild rice. (See page 165)

Rice Salad

As made by Maria Franca Morselli of Milan, Italy, who not only manages to be an outstanding botanist, but mother, homemaker, and cook. This salad served on a hot summer day at the Morselli Vermont farm, made a memorable meal, light and nourishing. It was served in a large glass bowl, with an extra bowl of garden lettuce for those who wanted to place the rice salad thereon.

cold, fluffy boiled rice (about ½ cup cooked rice per person)
Tomatoes, cucumbers, green peppers, celery — all chopped fairly fine, in amounts to embellish the rice, but not to overwhelm it. Likewise some cubes of Swiss cheese

Add to the above, canned or fresh crabmeat or lobster or shrimp or ham, cut into bite-sized pieces. Again, don't overwhelm. Remember this is a rice salad and the things added to it are supposed to emerge as delightful tidbits. Toss all together with dashes of best olive oil, lemon juice or vinegar, salt, freshly ground pepper, and chopped basil. Hopefully the basil is fresh from your garden, when a fairly lavish hand is called for. If dried basil is used, be circumspect.

Clear, hot soup was served first. With the salad (which happened to contain crabmeat and shrimp) we had crusty Italian bread and white wine.

Perfect Wild Rice

1. Plan about ⅓ cup uncooked rice per person.

2. Wash rice thoroughly in strainer under running water. It is liable to be quite dirty, for this is no factory product, but gathered wild, from canoes — a nice sort of dirt!

3. Put rice in the container in which you plan to cook it, and pour boiling water over it. Cover and allow to stand all night.

4. In the morning pour off any excess water that has not been absorbed. Again cover rice with water, but this time cold water. Add salt, to taste, and bring to a boil slowly. Simmer for a good hour, until kernels are really soft and sort of exploded. Check now and then so that rice does not scorch or run out of water.

5. Drain in a colander and rinse well with cold water. Now your rice is ready to heat when you are ready to eat.

6. Place rice in double boiler and heat it with a generous dollop of butter, and correct salt, if necessary.

Wild rice is excellent served just as directed above. If you must gild the lily, add chopped fresh mushrooms and onions which have been delicately browned in butter, or toasted slivered almonds, or raisins, or currants.

Having cooked wild rice to go with game, for a lifetime, I can guarantee that this way of preparing it produces the most palatable results. (See page 163 for Rice Soufflé.)

Boston Baked Beans (Serves 12)

<u>1 quart (4 cups) pea beans</u> ~ Pick over beans, discarding any that are imperfect. Rinse well in colander. Place beans in a bowl, cover with plenty of cold water, and allow to soak overnight. (They will swell markedly.) Drain, cover with water, bring to a boil and let simmer until skins of beans split when taken up on a spoon and blown upon. Drain the beans and pour into a bean pot.

(This <u>slow</u> simmering takes 1 to 1½ hours.)

<u>2 teaspoons salt</u>
<u>1 teaspoon dry mustard</u> (makes beans more digestible.)
<u>½ teaspoon ginger</u> (optional)
            This is a northern New England touch.
<u>¼ cup molasses</u>
<u>¼ cup brown sugar</u>
<u>¼ to ½ cup maple syrup</u> (Depending upon
            how sweet you like your beans.)

Stir together with some boiling water and pour over beans.

<u>1 onion</u>, peeled, and pushed into center of bean pot.
<u>½ pound fat salt pork</u> ~ Cut away from rind and into small cubes. Top the beans with this. Add enough more hot water so beans are submerged. Cover the bean pot and bake for <u>8 hours</u> in <u>250° oven</u>. Add hot water now and then to keep beans covered with liquid. The last hour of cooking, remove cover so that salt pork cubes brown and the water cooks down. You may want to turn oven to <u>300°</u> for better browning. Beans should be moderately runny but not swimming around the plate. Serve directly from the pot.

(See next page)

More Bean Talk

It seems that the farther north one goes, the bigger the beans get. Boston baked beans are made from small pea beans, as indicated. In Vermont "soldier beans" are often used. In Nova Scotia the dried beans are called "brown-eyed Bettys." Some people use dried lima beans. They are all good.

Warning: Beans that are over-sweetened get tough, not tender, as they cook.

A friend who lived in northern Maine, close to French Canada and its customs, said that during bird season a whole partridge, skinned of its feathers, is often found nestling in the beans, imparting its goodness, as well as drinking in the bean juices, and falling apart with tenderness at serving time.

At Vermont church suppers I have sometimes remarked on the deliciousness of the beans, only to have the kitchen crew admit that the great covered roasting pans of succulent beans came out of a can, doctored up with a touch of ginger, mustard, maple syrup, and/or brown sugar, and/or molasses. So there is a shortcut.

This is always the menu for a Saturday night baked bean supper at our house: Baked Beans (page 166)
Brown Bread (page 219)   Fish Cakes (page 114)
Tomato and Apple Relish (page 299)
Finger Greens (carrot-celery-cucumber)
Snow Pudding with Custard Sauce (page 257)

If there is a better meal I don't know what it is. Also, one feels approving Puritan ancestors hovering. Beans were baked on Saturdays in colonial times to allow sustenance on Sundays, without the sin of cooking on the Sabbath.

An old saying: "You don't know beans unless you come from Boston."

About Potatoes

The diet zealots seem to have turned 'potato' into a bad word, and a food that is taboo. What a shame. There is no gift of nature as benevolent as a potato, and there are no more calories in a potato than in an apple. Yet a dieter will piously down an apple. Apples are great, but so are potatoes, and one needs this root vegetable for myriad reasons of sound nutrition. Consider the spunk of the Irish, and the fact that these tubers were their main food supply for generations; and without them they were forced to emigrate.

Potatoes are an excellent source of complex carbohydrates. There's an interlocking dependence between carbohydrates and the capability of the tissues to transform protein into blood sugar. Proteins alone won't do it. Extreme restriction of carbohydrates (a present fad) causes the brain to starve for glucose, which brings on mental depression and inability to concentrate. The whole body lacks energy.

Not only in the present have the noble potatoes had a checkered career. When the Spaniards introduced them to Europe in the early 16th century, having found the Incas of Peru eating them enthusiastically, the tubers were hardly larger than peanuts. The Indians made a habit of eating the larger ones in a crop and saving the smaller ones for seed. Thus were they nearly bred out of sight. They were cultivated first

in Europe as a curiosity, and were reputed to be poisonous (as were tomatoes). The Germans seem to have been
the first (and the French last) to have risked eating them,
and, being great horticulturalists, breeding a larger and
larger strain. Certain religious groups frowned on potatoes
because they were not mentioned in the Bible, others because
the "eating of these roots doth excite Venus and increaseth
lust." As with the banning of books in Boston, this was
all that was needed to establish their popularity. They soon
became prominent in the daily diet of countless millions,
so that the world potato crop is second only to the wheat
crop. The improved nutrition, largely due to the increased
use of the potato, is alleged to have brought on the population
explosion.

Buy the best. The Burbank Russets of Idaho
have no peers. There are countless varieties, and, after
Idaho, the Northeast section of North America seems
to grow the best. Grow your own, if possible, for
solid satisfaction. The recipes that follow may encourage you to give this much-maligned but much-
loved vegetable the place it deserves on your table.

How To Bake a Potato

This may seem too elementary to discuss, but read on. There are several tricks to the act if you want a truly superb article. Having top grade potatoes, scrub the skins well and place the potatoes on oven rack in 450° preheated oven. Bake for <u>one hour</u>. Any time after the first half hour of baking, pierce each potato several times, enthusiastically, with a large sharp meat fork to let out the steam. This makes them more mealy. Remove from oven when hour is up and serve at once, having made a criss cross slash in each one of them, pushing both ends toward each other so the steaming potato pops up from the slash. Place a generous slice of butter on each one. I find the flavor of a baked potato so ravishing that I only shake a bit of salt thereon, and save the butter to eat with the crisp skins.

A potato wrapped in foil, before baking, is a modern heresy, making everything soggy and unappetizing. The only excuse for foil is when baking potatoes outdoors, over charcoal or in rosin. (Some people have a special iron pot about half full of rosin, hung from a tripod. A fire is built beneath the kettle. When rosin is bubbling-hot, foil-wrapped potatoes are dropped in for an hour. The rosin remains in the pot indefinitely, ready for the next cookout.)

Twice-Baked Potatoes
(Favorite company fare. No last-minute attention required.)

Bake potatoes (1 per person) as already directed. Cut in half lengthwise and scoop out all the potato into a beater bowl. Add butter, salt, pepper, to taste, and a generous amount of milk. Beat until fluffy and lump-free. (This can also be done with regular potato masher and ingredients stirred in by hand.) Put the mashed potato into the potato skins, discarding a few of the skins so that those used have an abundant, heaped-up appearance. Put a dab of butter or a slice of Cheddar cheese on each potato, along with a dash of paprika. Arrange in a shallow stove-to-table baking dish. Put aside and keep all day if you wish. About 20 minutes before meal time, pop into a hot oven and bake until thoroughly heated and slightly browned on top.

This way of serving potatoes is not only a cinch for the hostess but guaranteed to delight one's guests.

Baked French Fries

Cut up a potato per person in the same manner as for French Fries. Place in a large, shallow, generously buttered pan. (I use a cookie sheet with sides.) Bake in a hot (about 375°) oven for about an hour, turning potatoes with spatula a couple of times during baking. Salt and serve.

Aunt Helen, who enjoyed ill health, taught me this trick, and I have always been grateful. As she lived to be 90, I've thought that perhaps these potatoes may have helped to keep her going. Not rich and fatty, as are fried potatoes, and, to me, they taste as good.

A Vermont neighbor, who approaches 90, told me that in his boyhood it was considered hospitable to give each departing guest a hot baked potato to hold in mittened hands during the cold sleigh-ride home. How nice! I'll bet they fried them for breakfast.

Mashed Potatoes

Does anyone need directions for these? It would seem not, yet I recall one bride who said she was unable to serve them because she couldn't mash and add butter and milk and salt and pepper fast enough to get them to the table hot. It was a revelation to her that, once mashed, they could be returned to the stove and reheated while stirring constantly so as not to scorch.

An even better method (unless you're just having a good family time of it, and some willing member thereof, with a strong arm, assists in preparation) is to make mashed potatoes in the morning, plop them in lovely peaks into a buttered soufflé dish, and allow to cool until company arrives. Then heat quickly in hot oven and serve at once. If the peaks are a bit browned, so much the better. Mashed potatoes this way seem to taste better than when reheated in double boiler. The latter type are all too available in most restaurants.

Mashed potatoes are less starchy and more fluffy if mashed by hand rather than with an electric beater. And the more they are beaten by hand, the whiter they become. If I'm just doing a few potatoes, the hand masher does the trick. But with any quantity of potatoes I find it easier to put them through a ricer, then add butter, milk, salt and pepper, and beat with a spoon.

St. Patrick's Day Special
(Irish Champ, on page 175, is another.)

Chop <u>lots</u> of <u>parsley</u>, and I mean <u>lots</u>, and stir into mashed potatoes until they are bright green. Lovely to look at, delightful to eat. No salad course necessary, and no need to wait for St. Patrick's day either. Try this trick with <u>chives</u> also.

═══════════

Millie Lyon's Mashed Potatoes

Using <u>1 medium potato</u> and <u>1 medium white turnip</u> per person, peel, and boil them together in salted water until tender. Drain. (Save water for gravy.) Mash thoroughly and season, to taste, with <u>butter</u>, <u>salt</u>, <u>pepper</u>. Possibly a bit of milk will be needed, but turnips are watery and may supply sufficient moisture. This is a Pennsylvania Dutch practice, and devastatingly good with a crispy roast of pork — and apple sauce, of course. Kids (and adults) who think they don't like turnips can thus be conned into eating them.

═══════════

Riced Potatoes

I nearly always serve these with a roast of lamb (page 103) because gravy is usually a part of that meal, and good dry potatoes are a fine foil and sop for the runny gravy.

Peel 1 large potato per person, and boil in salted water until fork tender. Mash through a potato ricer onto well buttered stove-to-table dish. Let it mound up, as in a gentle snowstorm, never bearing down on it with the ricer. When your fluffy pile is completed, which will look for all the world like rice, sprinkle paprika thereon, nothing else, and put aside until meal time. Before serving, place in preheated 450° oven until piping hot and becomingly browned. (10 to 15 minutes)

Rita's Irish Champ (Serves 6)

6 potatoes, peeled, and boiled until tender
1 cup milk
1 bunch scallions, chopped fairly fine about
    half way up the stems. (Lacking scallions,
      chop 1 onion)
butter, a generous piece

Simmer together for 10 or 15 minutes, while potatoes cook.

Drain potatoes (saving water for gravy, soup, or bread), and mash thoroughly. Then stir in the hot milk mixture, using plenty of elbow grease. Add salt and pepper, to taste. Small wonder the Irish love potatoes.

Scalloped Potatoes (Serves 4 to 6)

1½ cups milk
1 medium onion, peeled and quartered
1 Tablespoon flour
Salt and pepper, To taste

} blended together in blender

+ par boiled

4 medium potatoes, peeled and cubed, and placed in buttered stove-to-table baking dish. Then pour above blended ingredients over potatoes at once. (Cut-up potatoes darken rapidly unless covered with fluid.)

2 tablespoons butter, dotted over all

⅛ pound Cheddar cheese, grated, and sprinkled over all as Topping

This dish may be held at this stage for some Time. I don't know why, but diced scalloped potatoes seem to taste better than the ubiquitous sliced.

As meal Time approaches, bake, *Less* uncovered, in 350° preheated oven for 1 hour and 15 minutes or 1½ hours. Just be sure potatoes are tender.

gard

Roasted Potatoes and Onions
(To accompany roast lamb or roast beef.)

Peel a potato for each person to be served. Cut extra-large potatoes in two. Cover with cold water, salt judiciously, and boil for about ½ hour. Then arrange the partially cooked potatoes around the roasting meat at least one hour before meat is cooked and preferably longer. Save the potato water!* Roasted potatoes always need this pre-cooking in water or they turn out hard as rocks. At the same time that potatoes are added to the meat roasting pan, pour one bottle or can of small white onions, juice and all, around the roast. Baste meat a couple of times with this good pan juice. Turn the vegetables once so they brown on both sides. Ideally the meat should roast long enough for most of pan liquid to evaporate. If you use a stove-to-table roasting pan (such as Corning Ware) you may remove roast from oven and serve as is and skip the gravy. Instead of gravy serve a creamed vegetable. But save that savory pan when the meal is over! Don't be guilty of washing away all that goodness until you have captured it by adding a couple of cups of cold water to the pan, let it simmer on stove, scraped up all the crusty business with a spoon, poured it into a refrigerator dish and stored it for future gravy or soup. You need no packaged meat seasonings if you save this elixir.

* Maybe you _do_ want gravy. Use potato water to make it. (Put potatoes and onions in buttered baking dish and reheat when ready to eat.) Or save potato water for making bread, substituting it for milk or water called for in recipe and making allowance for its saltness. Or use potato water in making gravy for a Shepherd's Pie next day. Just don't throw all that good nourishment down the drain.

Sweet Potatoes and Yams (Plan 1 potato per person) *

Baked: * Scrub skins well. Bake at 375° about 1 hour. Pierce with fork *Peels right off neatly.* during baking. Serve as is, with butter and salt.

Twice Baked: After baking, cut in half the long way, scoop out the potato, mash and mix with milk, butter, salt, and a touch of sherry, to taste. Pile into potato skins. Just before serving time reheat them in a hot oven.

Boiled: Boil in salted water with their well-washed skins on. This takes from 20 minutes to ½ hour.

Casserole: If speed is important use the canned potatoes. Otherwise boil, as above, peel, and put through ricer to remove all strings and lumps. To a can of yams or sweet potatoes, or 6 home-boiled, add ½ cup milk, 2 tablespoons butter, salt and pepper to taste, and ½ cup drained crushed pineapple. *add brown sugar* Mix well. Place in buttered casserole, top with a few marsh-mallows and bake in 350° oven until marshmallows are slightly browned (about ½ hour). This is what Esther Klarén serves with her baked ham slices (page 101).

Casserole Variations: Substitute orange juice and a dash of rum for milk. Omit pineapple and marshmallows. Fill either a casserole or orange-rind shells with the mixture. Top with mandarin orange sections and brown sugar. Bake at 350° until slightly glazed. (About ½ hour.) ½ cup chopped pecans or almonds may be added to either of above recipes.

Speedy Potatoes: Slice boiled potatoes into buttered baking dish. Embellish with thin slices of apple, or pineapple, or mandarin oranges, or pecans, or almonds, or any combination thereof. Add salt, brown sugar, dots of butter. 350° oven about ½ hour.

French Asparagus (Serves 4 to 6)

1/4 pound butter
1/4 cup bread crumbs
} heated together in dish in oven until crumbs are brown. Stir occasionally. (A small Corning-ware saucepan that goes from stove to table is ideal for this.)

2 hard-boiled eggs, chopped
1 tablespoon chopped parsley
salt and pepper, to taste
juice of 1/2 lemon (optional)
} added to above browned crumbs and spooned over hot asparagus.

Awfully good and has none of the uncertainties of Hollandaise Sauce.

Concerning asparagus: always keep it in water in the refrigerator, like a bouquet of flowers — upright and well immersed so it won't dehydrate. In preparing asparagus, be wasteful and cut off lots of the tough lower stem. (Save for Asparagus Soup if you want to.) Then, with a vegetable scraper, peel off the tough outer skin of the stems you will serve, stopping short of the tender tops, of course. This makes for a real delicacy. Asparagus may be cooked ahead of time, almost to doneness, allowed to cool, underanced, in its own water and reheated rapidly as guests are ready to go to table. Never keep it warm for any length of time or it will lose color and get mushy.

Aunt Hell's* String Beans

If you are fortunate enough to have really young, fresh green beans (Kentucky Wonders take the prize!), or wax beans, here is the way to fix them for maximum, mouth-watering goodness. Wash the beans <u>first</u>, otherwise good juices are sluiced away. Snip off both ends and line up beans on a chopping board. Take a French knife and cut the beans across in the tiniest of pieces — no bigger than this : □ With a proper knife it only takes a couple of minutes to produce an imposing heap. Place beans in cooking pan with <u>very little</u> water, a sprinkle of <u>salt</u>, a dab of <u>butter</u>. Cover, and cook fairly rapidly, taking care all water doesn't disappear. They are done in about <u>5 minutes</u> (crunchy, not mushy). Don't pour off any remaining water! Steam it off, with cover removed, if you think too much is left. Don't doctor beans with <u>anything</u>. Fancy embellishments are for the purpose of trying to make canned and frozen beans taste as good as these.

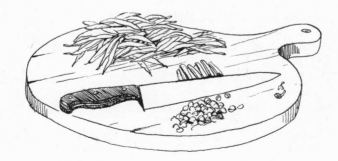

---

* This aunt, by marriage only, no blood relative, was a fine cook and I learned much from her. But the name, by which she was secretly called, indicates certain negative aspects of her nature.

Tasty +
Easy!
Easter 1989
+
Thanksgiving
'89

Carrots Lyonnaise (Serves 6)

3 tablespoons butter, heated in stove-to-table dish (if you have one).
3 medium onions, cut in thin rings, browned slightly in the butter. Cover, and allow to simmer 10 minutes in their own juices.

½ cup water
1 chicken bouillon cube
6 carrots, scraped and cut into julienne strips

} Add to onions, cover, and simmer 10 minutes, or less.

→ I cut chinese style

1 tablespoon flour
1 teaspoon sugar
pepper
½ cup water

} Blend thoroughly and add to above, stirring well. Cook about 3 minutes more. Test for salt. Serve at once, or cool and reheat later.

Baked Carrots
(Allow about 2 medium-sized carrots per person.)
Grate carrots on medium-fine grater onto a piece of waxed paper. Slide into a buttered stove-to-table baking dish. Sprinkle with salt and sugar. Dot with butter. Cover, and bake in preheated 350° oven for about ¾ of an hour.

Plain Boiled Carrots

Place cut-up carrots, very little water, salt, a dab of butter, and a sprinkling of sugar, into cooking utensil. (I use stove-to-table Corning Ware.) Cover, simmer slowly until carrots are just tender but not mushy. Never drain! If they seem too watery, boil at high heat with cover off for a minute or so. Much flavor and nourishment is in the juice. And if there are any left-overs they taste so much better and do not dehydrate if stored in the refrigerator in a little of their own liquid. A slotted spoon is ideal for serving boiled carrots.

Peas

Whether peas are frozen or fresh, cook exactly as in directions for carrots. Cooking with the butter and sugar imparts flavor. Sugar brings out the essence of some vegetables better than that suspected product, monosodium glutamate, which has never found its way into my kitchen. Lean on the side of undercooking — for color, flavor, nourishment.

Princeton Carrots (Serves 4)

4 large carrots, scraped, quartered lengthwise,
      quartered again, and then cut in half.

1 onion, cut into thin rings

1 tablespoon butter

} Simmer in small amount of salted water until crisp-tender.

grated rind of orange, a judicious amount

juice of the orange

1 tablespoon cornstarch

1 tablespoon sugar or honey

} Mix together. Bring to a boil, stirring constantly, until thick and clear.

There should be some liquid left when you have stopped cooking the carrots and onion. Drain it off, and stir the vegetable liquid into the orange-cornstarch mixture. Pour this sauce over the carrots. This may be done in the morning. Your vegetable is ready for last-minute reheating and serving. Use a double boiler for reheating, if possible, then there is no danger of scorching. Harvard Beets have been around for a long while. Why not Princeton Carrots?

There is the lazy way to do many things. If hurried, I often boil carrots (with or without onion), and stir in some orange marmalade, just before serving. Almost as good as above recipe.

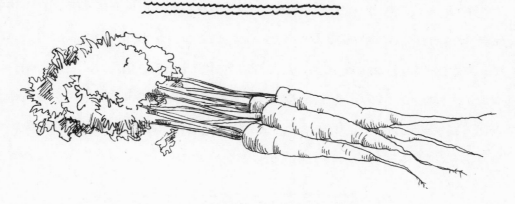

Double Boiler Celery — à la Betty Spencer

<u>celery</u>, washed, scraped of any tough strings, cut fine, quantity depending on number of people. Put in the top of double boiler.

<u>celery seed</u>
<u>onion salt</u> } added to above according to taste.
<u>butter</u> } Cook over boiling water until tender-crisp but not mushy.

<u>cream</u>, added shortly before serving and cooked just long enough for cream to heat.

Serve in sauce dishes. Excellent with game. Oh so easy and good!

~~~~~~~~~~~~~~~~

The fat, crunchy stalks of celery, near as the corner store, available the year round, have only been with us since 1874 when they were produced by Dutch farmers in Kalamazoo, Michigan. A far cry from the wild celery that sustained man through the ages — and just as beneficial. Loaded with vitamins and minerals, celery has ever been considered a cure-all medicine and an aphrodisiac, as well as good food.

~~~~~~~~~~~~~~~~

<u>John Cope's Dried Corn</u> is a product that should be in everyone's kitchen supply closet at all times. Just write John F. Cope Company, Inc., Manheim, Pa. 17545 and ask for the "Extra Fancy — Special Grade." Unless the corn is ripe in your garden, this is the next best way to have it. No Thanksgiving or Christmas is complete without it in food-knowledgeable Pennsylvania Dutch country. My two favorite ways of serving it follow. "So wonderful good," as they say in that part of the country.

<u>Cope's Baked Corn</u>* (Serves 6)

1 cup dried corn
3 cups milk
1 teaspoon salt
pepper, freshly ground, to taste
2 tablespoons sugar
2 eggs
2 tablespoons butter

Toss all into blender and blend well. Then pour into buttered baking dish and dot with the butter. Bake, uncovered, in pre-heated <u>350°</u> oven for 1 hour. Serve at once or turn off oven and hold if you must.

<u>Cope's Stewed Corn</u> (Serves 4)

<u>1 cup dried corn</u>, placed in pan in which it is to cook.
<u>2 cups boiling water</u>, poured over corn and allowed to soak at least 1 hour
<u>2 teaspoons sugar</u>   Add this to above after the soaking.
<u>Salt, to taste</u>   Place on stove and simmer, covered,
<u>butter, to taste</u>   ½ hour or more. Do not drain.
<u>½ cup milk or cream</u>, added to above after it has cooked. Cook 5 minutes longer.

*really a corn custard

Ordinary *Corn

3 eggs, beaten
½ cup melted butter
½ cup (yes, ½ cup) maple syrup
1 medium-sized can cream style corn **
salt and pepper, to taste

Mix all this together and pour into buttered baking dish. Bake in preheated 325° oven for nearly an hour.

"Sinfully good" says Virginia Jones, who gave me this recipe. I agree.

A Summer Medley (Serves 6 to 8)
(The Quineys' favorite)

2 tablespoons bacon fat, heated in large skillet
2 cups corn, cut from cob (fresh, uncooked)
2 cups fresh tomatoes, peeled, diced
2 cups sliced zucchini
1 teaspoon salt
1 teaspoon sugar
½ teaspoon ground cumin
⅛ teaspoon freshly ground pepper

Add to hot fat in order given.
Cover and cook 10 minutes — no more!

Enslaving.

* From Wiggins Tavern in Northampton, called an "Ordinary" in olden times.
** 16 ounces

Fiddleheads

Gathering fiddleheads is a joyous spring rite in Vermont, and one is given an unmistakable cue as to when to go out and pick them. After six months of white silence, there is a definite moment when, as though a baton were lifted, the frogs and peepers start fiddling. So, to music, one sets forth to harvest the still furled fronds of the ostrich fern, though others are edible (page 137). Man has been eating this enchanting green delicacy throughout the ages. The Abnaki Indians of New Brunswick cultivated fiddleheads, recognizing their curative powers, especially where scurvy was concerned.

Fiddleheads are available, in city markets, both canned and frozen; and in select markets of the North, for a short season, may be purchased fresh.

Directions for cooking:

Pick crosiers when very young (only 2 or 3 inches high). Wash, drain, and should there be any woolly, brownish skin, remove it. Cook in plenty of boiling salted water until crunchy-tender, no more. Drain.

1) Serve with butter, salt, pepper, and lemon juice (optional), or vinegar (optional). 2) Serve with traditional Hollandaise Sauce (page 312). 3) Serve with Mock Hollandaise (page 313). This dish is such a rare treat that it is traditionally served as a separate course.

Creamed Onions (Serves 8)

(Without which no Thanksgiving or Christmas dinner is complete.)

__small boiled onions__   Plan about 3 onions per person. I break down and use the bottled or canned variety and simmer them for a while in their own juice, as they have not been sufficiently cooked. If you are a purist, peel and boil your own. Save all juices for gravy or soup.

__2 cups rich milk__, the more cream in it the merrier
__4 Tablespoons flour__
__1 teaspoon dried thyme__, or more if you use fresh. This is the secret ingredient.

} Blend together in blender. Place in double boiler and stir over boiling water until thick and smooth.

__butter__, a generous piece stirred into the hot, thickened sauce. Then add __salt__ and freshly ground __pepper__, to taste. Add the boiled and drained onions. Heat and serve at once, or hours later. (A little __onion salt__ adds depth of flavor, but be careful.)

Or, place the completed creamed onions in a buttered casserole, or any open baking dish, and top with the dried commercial poultry stuffing. Bake at __350°__ until bubbly hot and browned on top. Never use this topping if you are serving a stuffed bird, for that would constitute the forbidden repetition of a theme. It is delicious fare with all meats, and especially non-stuffed poultry.

"This is every cook's opinion —
No savory dish without an onion,
But lest your kissing should be spoiled
Your onions must be fully boiled."

(Jonathan Swift)

Baked Apple and Onion

apples
onions
brown sugar
salt
butter
crumbs (bread or cracker)

Butter a casserole dish, size depending on number to be served. Put in a layer of apples, peeled and sliced, Then a layer of onions which have been separated into rings. Sprinkle fairly generously with brown sugar and sparingly with salt. Repeat the layers until dish is heaping. Top with crumbs and generous dabs of butter. Cover. Bake slowly, a little over 300°, for about 3 hours. The longer baked the better it is. Uncover for last half hour so crumbs will brown and juices evaporate somewhat.

The long, slow baking makes it disappear alarmingly. Hence the heaped-up dish to compensate for shrinkage. An unbeatable accompaniment for almost any meat dish. Onions cooked this long are completely digestible. The hot fruit-vegetable combination is unique and mouthwatering.

Baked Parsnips (Serves 4)

1 pound of parsnips (one package), scraped, cut first into quarters, then into eighths, then the long, thin strips cut in half. This gives an opportunity to remove any overly woody centers, though usually the centers become tender when cooked. Place these delicate strips in a well-buttered casserole that has a good cover. Sprinkle the parsnips with . . . .

salt, pepper, a touch of water, a generous sprinkling of brown sugar (or maple syrup, in which case eliminate the water), and dot with butter.

Cover, and bake in 350° oven for 1 hour. Once during the cooking stir them around in the baking dish so they are well coated with the sweet juices. Should there be any left-overs (which is doubtful), brown in a little butter in a frying pan the next day.

People either love or hate parsnips. To me they are one of Mother Nature's great gifts.

Baked Squash

Using frozen winter squash, or cooking and mashing your own, add butter, salt, plenty of pepper and brown sugar, to taste. Put in a buttered baking dish, and top with pecan halves. The dish is ready for later baking. Bake in 350° oven until piping hot, which depends on amount of squash. About ½ hour for an average-sized dish.

Plain Boiled Spinach

Nothing better, especially fresh spinach from the garden. Wash it diligently. Gritty spinach is an abomination. Remember that spinach is mostly water, and also enough water remains on leaves from washing, that none need be added when cooking. Bring to a boil, slowly, in a covered pan, and start turning it over and testing with a spoon almost as soon as it boils. The minute a spoon cuts through it easily it is done. Overcooking darkens and ruins it. Strain over a bowl,* chopping with spoon as you strain. (You may hold the spinach at this stage if necessary.) When ready to serve, return to stove. Heat quickly with salt and a generous bit of butter. Garnish with hard-boiled egg slices. Have a vinegar cruet on the table for diners to anoint spinach as suits their taste.

Do likewise with beet greens or Swiss chard.

*Spinach water may be incorporated in gravy, if you are having it, or saved for spinach soup another day.

Tom Sawyer's Succotash (Serves 8 generously)

1 dozen ears freshly picked corn, husked
2 pounds fresh shell beans (the kind with pink and
   white striped pods and beans), shelled
1 piece salt pork about 2 inches square, scored down to rind

Just cover the beans with water, add the piece of salt pork and cook, covered, until beans are tender. If they are good fresh beans it should take no longer than about 15 minutes.

While beans are cooking, scrape the raw corn kernels from the cobs, getting out all the lovely juice. Add corn to beans and water and simmer only 2 or 3 minutes. Add a dab of butter and taste test for saltiness. It may need a bit more salt, but be careful. Remove pork and serve at once in its delightful runny condition. Do not drain!

Hope for left-overs. Tom considers it even better when heated up the next day. It freezes well. This is a taste that generations of New Englanders would almost lay down their lives for. Tom, my brother-in-law, says that one of his biggest thrills is to see his grandchildren go for this succotash as avidly as he always has.

We are indebted to the American Indian for this recipe. He ingeniously planted beans and corn in the same hill so that the climbing beans were supported by the sturdy corn stalks. When beans and corn were ripe, and so lovingly entwined, it seemed natural to cook them together. They called the dish succotash, and so it remains to this day.

Scalloped Tomatoes (Serves 4)

1 can tomatoes (approximately 1 pound "regular size")
1 onion, cut into small pieces
2 slices bread, cubed
2 Tablespoons sugar
salt and pepper, to taste
butter

Mix all ingredients in proper-sized, buttered baking dish. Dot generously with butter. Bake, uncovered, long and slowly and until bread browns a bit — at least 1½ hours in 325° oven.

There is no meat, fish, cheese, or egg dish that is not enhanced by adding Scalloped Tomatoes to the menu. Everybody loves them and all the ingredients are as near as your pantry shelf, or should be. A favorite standby for the "What-shall-I-have-for-a-vegetable?" mood.

194

Heavenly Vegetable Casserole (Serves 12)
(Kindness of Charlotte Wells)

used 2 → 1 package frozen French style green beans (usual size)
1   "   "   baby lima beans   "   "
1   "   "   very best small peas   "   "
3 green peppers, seeded, and cut into narrow strips

} Place in just enough boiling salted water to keep from burning. Cook only until thawed and separate with fork. Drain & cool.

also grated one carrot.

1½ cups heavy cream, whipped   *cottage cheese*
1½ cups mayonnaise
grated Parmesan or Cheddar cheese (about ¾ cup)
freshly ground pepper
Touch of salt

} mixed

Butter a casserole of appropriate size. Place the barely cooked vegetables therein. Cover with the cream-mayonnaise-cheese sauce. Ready to bake at once or to hold in refrigerator if you care to be party-ready ahead of time. Bake, uncovered, in preheated 325° oven for about 50 minutes, or until brownish and puffy on top.

This is a rich and marvelous mixture. Avoid serving any other creamy food with it. (I like to serve it with roast tenderloin of beef and fruit for dessert.) There is only one drawback; if you want to keep table conversation on a high level and not have it degenerate into recipe swapping — don't serve this. People will be bent only on trying to ferret out the secret of its haunting goodness.

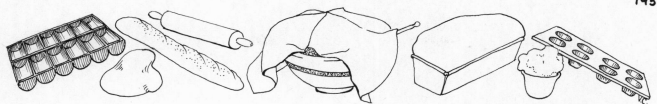

Bread

<u>Anadama Bread</u> (page 202) rising in the warming oven of the old Glenwood wood-burning stove at Bentley Farm.

———————————

Unfair Competition

"I can take the fluffy blonde with tinkly voice and dress size ten,
Nor fear brunettes whose glances fond bring out the Romeo in men.
I can cope with femmes fatales whose lines are lush and locks are red,
But shield me, please, from wholesome gals who serve my husband home-made bread."
                                                        — Betty Billip

———————————

"History... can tell us the names of the kings' bastards, but it cannot tell us the origin of wheat. Such is human folly."
                                                        — Jean Henri Fabre

———————————

About Bread

If you want praise out of all proportion to the effort involved, if you want to feel like the total, elemental woman (or man) who has joined the human race in depth, if you really want to make your family both happy and healthy — make bread. It has been made since the beginning of time, even by the ignorant, yet the most highly educated often pale at the thought of tackling what appears to be a difficult and mysterious rite. Absolute nonsense. It's easy, fun, rewarding.

It has been recorded that the patrician women of Rome, in the days of the Empire, no matter how many slaves they had, insisted on kneading their own bread, believing that it firmed and developed their breasts — a far more useful practice than the sterile exercises some women follow today for the same purpose. (Good for tummy muscles, too.)   Any psychiatrist would have to agree that the very act of kneading bread releases tensions and frustrations. And no matter how dark the day or the mood, by the time one has removed crusty loaves from the oven, and filled the house with a fragrance* no perfumer could capture, the spirit begins to heal.

Be sure to use <u>unbleached</u> flour in all recipes (unless specifically indicated otherwise). I use King Arthur, but am sure there are other good brands. The enriched white bleached flour, prevalent on all grocery shelves, has had some 16 elements removed from it, and 4 synthetic elements put in.   Avoid it like the plague. Because most store-bought bread is made with bleached flour, is loaded with preservatives, and

---

*I wonder if the fragrance has anything to do with the alcohol the bread emits as it cooks? The Reverend Mr. Graham (of Graham flour fame) wrote that there were distillery ovens in England, which captured the alcohol as the bread baked. What a joyous invention!

tastes like Kleenex, it is becoming a necessity to make one's own bread, both for flavor and for sound nutrition.

Use <u>raw sugar</u>, instead of refined, wherever practicable. I use <u>sea salt</u> in all recipes— and at table.

There is no necessity for fancy equipment in breadmaking. All you need is a large pottery <u>bowl</u>, a wooden <u>spoon</u>, and a <u>place to knead</u>. (If you never use sourdough, the bowl does not have to be pottery or the spoon wooden, but in case you do, these two things are a necessity. Because I make a lot of sourdough bread, this is standard equipment for me for every kind of bread.) A bread board, or even a Formica counter, will do for kneading. (An old man in this area remembers coming into our kitchen in his childhood, and seeing the grandmother of the family who then lived here, down on her knees on the floor, kneading bread on a well-scrubbed area. Talk about Yankee ingenuity!) Neither do you need one of those bread mixers with a crank on top. I can have the bread all made, with simple bowl and spoon, in the time it takes to assemble, disassemble, and wash that claptrap contrivance that appears with lustrous claims in the catalogues. Don't be misled, as I once was. Of course a butcher block is both ornamental and useful for kneading. So are heavy maple counters everywhere in one's kitchen. Aim toward that in your dreams for the perfect culinary workshop. In the meantime, it's better to turn out good bread than to have one of those picture-book kitchens where nothing takes place but the heating of TV dinners.

<u>Bread pans</u> are needed if you want to make loaf bread (which contains shortening), but just a <u>cookie sheet</u> will do for the French-style hearth loaves (which do not contain shortening and are harder and crustier). <u>Racks</u> are needed for cooling bread, and a rack from the oven will do in a pinch.

Try always to bake on <u>middle shelf of oven</u>. If you use 2 shelves, switch the bread half way through the baking. Otherwise one batch will be too brown on top, the other too brown on the bottom.

Bread freezes beautifully, ever ready for a quick treat. It is wise to undercook bread that is to be frozen, just a little. Then it can be quickly reheated and taste as fresh as on the day it was baked. There is no gift more welcome than a loaf of homemade bread, so cast your bread upon the waters of friendship, literally.

Now for the impossible—How To Knead Bread :

It is something that needs to be demonstrated in person, but here's for a try on paper, and a hope that the 1 - double 2 - 3 - rhythm of bread kneading turns you on.

First of all, forget exact amounts of flour, for flours differ. Just stir flour into the mixture as long as you can comfortably. Don't make the dough so stiff that you exhaust yourself stirring. It is easier to knead sufficient flour in later, than to stir it in earlier, and I think the yeast works better with plenty of moisture. The initial stirring is important, so stick at it patiently, for you are putting the gluten in the flour to work. Not a very lovely analogy, but it is similar to putting a piece of gum in one's mouth. At first it all breaks apart. Only with persistent chewing does it come together. Likewise with dough and the action of gluten, which proper stirring and kneading encourages. Another hint— loaf breads and rolls (containing shortening), are best with the least amount of flour you can manage to incorporate and still not have dough stick to kneading board, whereas hearth breads (without shortening) need plenty of flour to give them stability.

When you empty the rather runny dough onto the kneading area, be sure to have a good thick circle of flour to turn it onto. Then, with your hands, push up a fence of flour all around the dough. Then forget it for 10 minutes or so. Bread is better behaved if it has little naps along the way. When ready to knead, sprinkle dough all over with flour, push it in from the sides with the flour fence, and generally and gently tease it into shape until you can safely slide your two hands under the mass and fold ½ of it over the other. The forward fold is step ✕1. Now, with the heel of your hand, bear down twice, forcing the fold together. This is kneading, and it is that double step ✕2. Now turn the dough half way around, and this is step ✕3. Fold, press twice, turn. Fold, press twice, turn (always in same direction). As you do this, keep sprinkling flour over, under, around. Experience will teach you never to let it stick. It will also teach you to end up with a board about clear of flour, so there is little cleaning up to do. This kneading process takes about 10 minutes. When the dough seems springy and cooperative to your touch, when it is reluctant to pick up more flour, when you are reluctant to cease the happy rhythm, then is the time to quit.

When dough is properly kneaded, cut with a sharp knife (a serrated knife works best) into desired number of pieces for loaf or hearth bread. Knead each piece slightly on a bit of flour, and coax into desired shape. Just before placing into buttered pans, or onto buttered cookie sheet, cover your palms with soft butter and pat butter all over the dough, if recipe so indicates. Arrange dough, folded side down, for rising and baking. At this point make 3 or 4 diagonal slashes, with the knife, across the hearth bread. (Don't do this to loaves in bread pans.) Or better still, with hearth bread, slash the initials of the one you love in the dough. This reduces the recipient to putty in your hands, or maybe I should say dough. There is no better way to a person's heart.

The ideal temperature for raising bread is about 80°. Too much heat kills the yeast, too little makes the bread slow to rise. You will find a place in your house that is just right — near a heating unit, or a warm, sunny window, or in an oven that has been on for a minute, and then turned off. Dough does not like draughts.

Should you have to stop the breadmaking process for some reason, don't panic. Just place the dough in the refrigerator, and the yeast will respond to your cold treatment by delaying its action. When you are free to continue, bring dough back to room temperature, and proceed from where you left off. Let the dough adjust itself to your schedule, not the other way around. Dough is very cooperative, once you've learned its nature, and stopped being afraid of it.

Always cool bread on racks so it doesn't "sweat." This goes for biscuits, muffins, all baked goods. One can easily slide hearth bread onto racks immediately after removing from oven. But when loaf bread (in pans) is first taken out of oven, it is best to lay pans on sides for a few minutes. When somewhat cooled, remove bread from pans and cool completely on racks.

You'll fast develop into an old pro in this happy game. Once having bitten into real bread, created with your own hands, you'll agree with the old lady (a home baker of renown) I met in front of the shelves of bread at the corner store. She looked at the loaves dubiously and remarked, "I'd rather breathe my air than eat it."

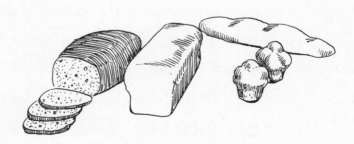

Frank Ryan's Anadama Bread
(2 large or 4 small loaves)

¼ pound butter ⎫
1 teaspoon salt ⎭ Place in your largest bowl.

2 cups water, brought to a boil in sauce pan.

½ cup yellow corn meal, poured slowly, while stirring vigorously, into the boiling water. Remove from heat at once and
   pour the mush over the butter and salt. Let cool to lukewarm.

1 package dry yeast, stirred into .....

½ cup lukewarm water, and allowed to work while cornmeal cools.

¾ cup molasses, stirred into lukewarm mush. Then stir in
   yeast also.

4 cups flour, stirred thoroughly into above. Give it all you
   have. Then you and the dough rest for about 10 minutes.
   Put about 2 cups flour on kneading board and spread
   into generous circle. Turn dough out onto flour and knead
   for about 10 minutes, incorporating sufficient flour to keep
   dough from sticking. Return dough to the large bowl (which
   has been washed and buttered) and let rise, covered, in warm
   place (2½ to 3 hours). It should double in bulk. Knock
   down dough with hands. Turn onto board, knead into shape
   for only a second. Cut into 2 or 4 equal-sized pieces.
   Shape lovingly and press into buttered bread pans.
   Let rise until doubled (about 1 hour). Place in preheated
   400° oven for 5 minutes, then, without peeking, turn heat
   to 350° and bake for 35 to 40 minutes for small loaves,
   a little longer for large loaves.   It is a matter of

judgment. I prefer the loaves made in smaller pans —
7½ x 3½ x 2½. One rarely sees the larger old-fashioned
loaves these days, but use whatever pans you have or like.
The story of the word "anadama" is pretty well known, for I
see it printed on the wrapping of what passes for bread in the supermarkets. But just for the record, here it is, briefly:

There was once a hardworking New England fisherman
who had a lazy, and, I suspect, gadabout wife. The fisherman
returned home one evening to find his wife not there, and the
only food prepared for him, as usual, was some cornmeal
mush. So he yelled, "Anna, damn her — I'll show her",
or words to that effect. He added flour and yeast and
molasses to the mush, and came up with such mouth-watering loaves of bread that he shared some with neighbors, who
begged for the recipe. It was dubbed Anadama Bread,
and has so remained to this day.

Frank Ryan's recipe for Anadama Bread is the best
I know of, and only faintly related to its poor cousin of the
grocery store. Frank's family of fine boys have thrived
on the homemade product.

The word lady derives from "loaf kneader",
"maker of bread".

Danish Beer Bread (4 round hearth loaves)

<u>1 twelve-ounce bottle of beer</u>
<u>2/3 cup molasses</u> } mixed in large bowl
<u>2 cups hot water</u>

<u>1 package dried yeast</u>, sprinkled into above, at once, and allowed to "work" for about 10 minutes while you go about your work.

<u>1 heaping quart measure rye flour</u> } stirred very vigorously into
<u>2½ teaspoons salt</u> } above. Cover, spoon and all, with a dish towel, and forget it for about a half hour.

<u>1 heaping quart measure unbleached white flour</u>, stirred into spongy dough above, a little at a time, and thoroughly. Don't try to stir in all the flour (unless you have a mighty right arm), only the amount the dough takes easily. (Empty the rest of the flour on kneading board, to be incorporated later, by kneading, which is easier than beating.) Cover again, this time with a warm, wet towel. Allow to rise in warm place until doubled in bulk — around 2 hours.

Now, the dough, having doubled its size, should be coaxed out of the bowl with the spoon (which I always leave in the dough), onto floured board. You will need more flour than was left in the quart measure. This is a pretty sticky mass, but by flouring generously all over, and handling deftly, you will be able to start kneading without any of dough sticking to board or hands. Knead it lovingly, adding more flour when necessary. When you have worked out all your frustrations on the dough, it feels springy, and doesn't want to take up any more flour — stop. Cut into 4 equal sections with a sharp knife. Shape into 4 lovely rounded balls. Place on a well <u>buttered</u> cookie sheet. <u>Butter</u> the mounds of dough, generously, all over. Let rise until nice and plump, but not spilling over the sides. (An hour or more.) Bake in preheated <u>400°</u> oven for <u>10 minutes</u>, and at <u>350°</u> for <u>about 25 minutes</u> more. Remove from oven and from pan, and cool bread on racks. Freeze any of the loaves not needed at once, in plastic bags. A real treasure is yours to take out of the freezer when the occasion demands.

This bread is fat free, so why not indulge in eating it with plenty of sweet butter? Fine with a boiled dinner of either ham (page 100) or corned beef. This fine-grained bread makes perfect sandwiches. Or serve thin slices of it, buttered, and cut in strips, for a cocktail snack. People seem to forget the cocktails and lean heavily on the staff of life only. If you have guests who are inclined to reach for the bottle too often, try this merciful cure. This bread served with Liver Pâté (page 18) will make the blind see and the lame walk.

〰〰〰〰〰〰〰〰〰

Consider the philosophical implications inherent in maple syrup production: It takes forty gallons of sap to make one gallon of syrup.

〰〰〰〰〰〰〰〰〰

Mother Sawyer's Oatmeal Bread
(2 large or 4 small loaves)

1 cup quick cooking oatmeal, placed in large bowl
2 cups boiling water, poured over oatmeal
½ cup molasses
1 Tablespoon salt
2 tablespoons corn oil
1 package dry yeast, soaked in
½ cup of lukewarm water, while oatmeal cools

} Stir this into oatmeal when it is lukewarm.

5 cups of flour, or less, stirred thoroughly into above mixture. Stay on short side of 5 cups if hard to beat in. Cover, spoon and all, with towel, and let rise in warm place until doubled. Then stir down and spoon into 2 large or 4 small bread pans which have been generously anointed with corn oil (not butter, for once). Let rise in pans until doubled. Bake in preheated 400° oven turned down to 350° when bread is put in, for about 40 minutes for small loaves, longer for large. Cool as directed on page 201. An excellent recipe for the beginner in the mystery and magic of bread-making.

Mother Sawyer was my sister's mother-in-law. Everyone called her Mother, for she had that sort of outreach to young people. I'll never forget the joy of visiting in her gracious home in Fitchburg, Massachusetts, and the countless small kindnesses that made one feel a welcome guest, not the least of which was this bread, toasted for breakfast — fragrant, chewy, dripping with butter.

Gladys Elviken's Potato Rolls (about 4 dozen)

1 package dried yeast, sprinkled onto
½ cup lukewarm water, in a large bowl; } Combine, and let
1 cup potato, that has been boiled and mashed. } stand in warm place
1 cup warm potato water (not hot!) } until spongy — about
⅔ cup sugar } ½ hour.

1 cup melted butter
4 eggs, well beaten
2 teaspoons salt
6 cups flour, about — enough to make a soft dough

} Stir into above sponge, in order given. Mix thoroughly, cover, let rise until doubled in bulk. (2 or 3 hours)

After dough has doubled, turn onto floured board and knead lightly and slightly. The less flour you can manage to use, the lighter the rolls will be. Roll, with rolling pin, to about an inch in thickness, and cut into circles with 2½ inch cutter.* Place on buttered cookie sheets, far enough apart to allow for expansion. Let rise until double in size — an hour or more. Bake in preheated 425° oven for 10 to 12 minutes, until pale golden brown. Serve hot.   Keep extras in deep freeze for last-minute reheating. Used as rolls for hamburgers —— wow!

There is no need to have any other recipe for rolls, for once these have been introduced, no one ever wants any other variety. Strong men have been known to weep for joy when first biting into one of these.

* An empty soup can will do in a pinch.

Bourne Biscuits
(makes an innumerable quantity of small rolls)

1 package yeast
½ cup lukewarm water } Pour water into large beater bowl. Sprinkle yeast on water. Let stand 5 minutes.

2 eggs, beaten
½ cup sugar
1 teaspoon salt
5 tablespoons corn oil
1 cup warm water } Mix together, add to above, and beat for 2 minutes with electric beater.

5 cups flour — Add half of the flour to above mixture, and beat for 3 minutes. Stir in the remaining flour by hand, with a spoon. If you can't incorporate all the flour into the dough, don't worry. Flours differ.

Cover bowl tightly, and refrigerate until ready to make biscuits. Dough will keep for a week. When ready for baking process, butter a cookie sheet, scoop out dough, a teaspoon at a time, roll into small balls with buttered hands, and pat down onto cookie sheet. Rolls should be small and dainty. Let rise for 3 hours. Bake in preheated 400° oven about 10 minutes. Keep remaining dough for another time. Or make the whole batch and freeze some.

I made the statement that, with the recipe for Gladys Elviken's Potato Rolls (page 207) you needed no other. I've changed my mind. This one is easier, and almost as good, and a perfect recipe for the uninitiated in dealing with yeast breads. A fool could make it, and when Helen Bourne first served these many years ago (and she is no fool!) her guests were enchanted.

~~~~~~~~~~~~~~~~~~~~~~~~~~

As a pleasant switch from garlic bread (which many people find indigestible), do the following:

Mix soft butter with chopped dried marjoram, basil, rosemary, thyme, tarragon, and chives, and spread on diagonally sliced French bread. (Heat in foil or not, depending on whether you desire it soft or crisp.) If you are an herb buff, as I am, use chopped fresh herbs, of course, using more of the fresh than you would the dried. My garden in summer, and windowsill in winter, yield all of these herbs. They are a cinch to grow and a daily blessing.

~~~~~~~~~~~~~~~~~~~~~~~~~~

Christmas Coffee Cake
(As made by Bets Albright)

½ cup boiling water, ¾ cup milk, placed in large, warm mixing bowl.
2 packages dry yeast, sprinkled over above warm liquid. Stir to dissolve yeast.
1¼ teaspoons salt, ½ cup sugar, 2 cups flour, stirred into above and
then beaten with a spoon, using plenty of elbow grease.
3 eggs, beaten, ⅔ cup melted butter (or corn oil), 4 cups flour (about),
thoroughly stirred into above mixture. Turn this dough out
onto a board spread with ½ cup flour. Knead 5 to 7 minutes.
Place kneaded dough into buttered bowl and cover. Let rise in a warm place until
doubled in bulk (about 1½ hours). Turn onto a lightly floured board. Cut into
3 equal parts, kneading each a little. Rolling out one section at a time (with a
rolling pin) into a long, thin rectangle, give each the following treatment:
Brush with melted butter, sprinkle with cinnamon and brown sugar and
raisins (seeded or seedless) and chopped pecans. Roll up the long way,
snugly, and form into a circle, uniting the ends. Coax onto buttered cookie
sheet. Take scissors and boldly snip all around each circle (from
outside toward center) cutting almost ⅔ through the dough, each snip
about 1 inch from the next. Let your 3 lovely circles rise until doubled
(½ hour or more). Bake in preheated 375° oven ½ hour (about). Watch it!
When baked and still warm, spread with confectioners' sugar
icing: milk, confectioners' sugar, and a dash of vanilla or almond or lemon extract,
mixed into spreadable consistency. Press red candied cherries surrounded by green
candied cherries, the latter cut to suggest leaves, into the icing. Cool on racks. Wrap in
plastic. Place each wrapped up circle on foil-covered cardboard, or on trays, or boards,
and wrap again in plastic. You may freeze them. Bets has brightened many a Christmas
for her friends, with gifts of these delightful edible wreaths.

About Sourdough

Unless you are lucky enough to have gotten hold of an old "starter" for the making of sourdough bread (mine began in 1885 in Portland, Oregon, and I have its pedigree as carefully written down as any family tree) there is available a sudden rash of starters. However, I would suggest making your own, just as your grandmother or great grandmother did.* It is all very simple, despite the fact that there are those who will consider you a cross between a witch and a genie if your refrigerator houses that bubbling mystery — a homemade sourdough starter.

1 package dry yeast, sprinkled onto
2 cups lukewarm water, preferably a bottled spring water, so as not to introduce the odd chemicals in modern reservoir water.
2 cups unbleached flour, stirred into above.

Step # 1 (uncovered)
This step is only taken once (a little like being present at The Creation).

This mixture must be stirred together in a scrupulously clean pottery or glass or enamel container. No metal, no plastic. Stir with a wooden spoon, and, for convenience, leave the spoon in it, for the mixture must stand, uncovered, in a warm room for 2 days, and be stirred once in a while.

After 48 hours, divide your slightly bubbly, sour-smelling starter into 2 non-metal, non-plastic containers. Into each stir

1 cup flour
1 cup milk
¼ cup sugar (scant) I use raw sugar.

Step # 2 (covered)
This step taken every time you feed starter forevermore.

* Well, not exactly the same way. Not having commercial yeast, she captured the wild yeast that is present in the air.

You now have 2 bowls of starters that could be called Abraham and Sara, progenitors of endless offspring. Unless you want to be proprietor of a bakery, I suggest you give one bowl away to a neighbor. It's convenient to have some of your progeny living near you, for in case you let your sourdough die, a relative is there to come back to the ancestral home. My sourdough offspring are all over Northern Vermont, a comforting situation.

After the feeding of the two bowls, as directed above, they must be covered and <u>refrigerated for at least 48 hours</u> before being ready for use in breadmaking. (A quart preserving jar may be used to hold sourdough starter, always leaving room for expansion, or a bowl with a plate on it. I prefer the latter, for it is easier to feed.)

So, <u>4 days</u> have gone by since you started on this mysterious journey. You are now ready to make sourdough bread. (See following pages.)

But first a few more directions about the care and feeding of sourdough starter. Every time you use the starter it must be fed according to Step #2 (previous page) with the <u>1 cup flour – 1 cup milk – ¼ cup sugar</u> combination, for you must never get down to less than 1 cup of starter. Then it must age for 2 days in the refrigerator before it has "worked" enough to use again. The starter may remain in the refrigerator for 2 or 3 weeks without refeeding, but no longer, or you'll have a funeral on your hands. If you don't use it, keep it alive by dividing and feeding. Either throw out half of it and feed what is left, or feed each half and give some away. Should you want to develop a lot of it (as I did for sale at a hospital benefit) it's as easy as raising rabbits. Just divide and feed every 2 days, and soon your refrigerator, and everyone else's within miles, will overflow with the lively stuff. Remember — <u>clean</u> containers that are not of metal or plastic.

Sourdough French Bread (2 big or 4 small loaves)

1½ cups warm water, placed in large glass or pottery bowl.

1 package dry yeast, sprinkled over above warm (not hot) water.

1 cup sourdough starter, mixed into above and allowed to rest at least 10 minutes, or more, depending on your whim.

2 cups flour
2 teaspoons salt
2 teaspoons sugar
} stirred vigorously into above with a wooden spoon for several minutes. Now add more flour, stirring in an amount that your strength and the batter allows. You want more of a sponge than a stiff dough. Flours differ, so absolute measurements are difficult to give.

Cover this dough, mixing spoon and all, with a towel, and let rise in a warm place until doubled in bulk. (2 hours or more)

1 cup flour
½ teaspoon soda
} Mix together and stir into above when it has risen. This is the most important step in sourdough bread making, so don't forget it!

Now turn the dough out onto wellfloured (be generous) kneading board. Forget it for 10 minutes or so. Then knead for about 10 minutes until you have a nice, springy, stiff dough. Cut into 2 or 4 equal parts with sharp knife. Shape into rounds or long loaves. Place on buttered cookie sheet, and thoroughly butter loaves with hands. Make about 3 diagonal slashes in loaves with knife. Let rise until doubled. (1 hour or more). Bake in preheated 400° oven for 40 or 45 minutes. This is BREAD!

Sesame Sourdough Bread

To the Sourdough French Bread recipe (on the previous page) add

1 cup Toasted sesame seeds

½ cup wheat germ

} Add these at the time the flour-salt-sugar is called for. In place of sugar, substitute ·····

2 Tablespoons honey

Then proceed as in previous recipe. This makes the most nourishing and delicious bread imaginable. As breakfast toast it is superb, and with it to fortify you, your blood sugar won't be down to zero by 11 A.M., and your energy likewise.

It is best to buy sesame seeds in bulk, at a health food store. If purchased from the herb shelf of a regular grocery store, in little bottles, the expense would be great. It is worth taking the trouble to toast the seeds. Spread in a pie plate, roast in 325° oven about ½ hour, stirring once or twice during baking. The flavor is greatly enhanced.

The sesame bread one buys has but a sprinkling of seeds on the surface, which have a way of falling off before they can be eaten. To incorporate them in the bread is a 4,000 year old trick. In an ancient Egyptian tomb there is depicted a baker doing just that. The ancient Greeks were sustained in battle by sesame seeds, and the blacks who were brought to the Western hemisphere, brought the seeds along, unable to imagine life without them. The Turks, in modern wars, have been credited with superior stamina due to sesame.

Sourdough Pancakes   (Serves 4)

<u>1 cup sourdough starter</u>
<u>1 cup flour</u>
<u>⅓ cup milk</u>
<u>⅓ cup warm water</u>

} Mix together, cover, and allow to stand at room temperature <u>overnight</u>. (Remember to take 2 eggs out of refrigerator.) (Also remember to feed starter!)

<u>2 eggs</u> (room temperature) well beaten
<u>2 tablespoons corn oil</u>
<u>2 tablespoons sugar</u>
<u>1 teaspoon salt</u>
<u>½ teaspoon soda</u>

} Mix this together in the morning and stir into above. If too thick, add more milk. Let whole mixture rest a bit, and then pour, to desired size, on well-heated griddle. Best pancakes you ever ate. Serve with plenty of butter and maple syrup, of course.

This is as good a time as any to expound on a heresy that infiltrates the country here and there, and that even my heroine, Fannie Farmer, condones. That is the <u>heating</u> of maple syrup. First, it turns the lovely syrup to water; second, it reduces the pancakes to a mound of mush. Please, <u>please</u>, don't ever be found guilty of joining this subversive group. Have your maple syrup at <u>room temperature</u>, your plates and pancakes piping hot —— then you'll be happy, and so will I.

More About Sourdough

It has been said that one reason real French bread is so good is because some of the "starters" of France have been kept alive for generations.   Start the process yourself and your grandchildren will be rich inheritors.

You may be surprised that I recommend buttering the French bread before the last rising, a most untraditional treatment. It's just that I like it better that way. It is still crusty, but not so much so that more crust flies onto floor and table than into one's mouth. However, skip the butter if you prefer, and let your rising bread suffer from dry skin. Neither do I follow the bricks-in-the-oven-and-spraying routine. Why make life so difficult? The fight isn't worth the candle.

Why yeast (commercial) <u>in addition to</u> sourdough starter? This is due to the time factor. It would take about 36 hours to make bread with just the starter. The excellent flavor and quality of the bread is still made unique by using the sourdough. It makes a much whiter product also. Then, in pioneer times, it was discovered that baking soda or "saleratus," as it was then called, made a lighter, better-tasting product, and offset the acidity of the starter. Commercial yeast and baking powder didn't come along until after the Civil War, and the latter was viewed with deep suspicion for it was reputed to be an anaphrodisiac. Where men were men, they wanted energizing sourdough breads, and none of your new-fangled nonsense.   Sourdough has been credited with putting proper bacteria back into the digestive tract when illness or modern medicine may have destroyed them.

Columbus discovered America, but who bothers to mention that through him the Americas discovered sourdough? Thanks to Columbus and the sourdough aboard his ship, the Western hemisphere inhabitants were introduced to leavened bread. It had long been enjoyed in Europe and The Middle East, having been discovered by the Egyptians around 4,000 BC.

In early New England the leaven was often called "emptyings," because the frugal housewife scraped her breadboard clean of all excess flour and bits of dough, and put them back into the starter pot. In Wisconsin it was called "spook yeast," and as the hardy pioneers pushed farther West, the name "sourdough" took over.* The most important thing a prospector carried with him to the California or Alaska gold rush, was his sourdough pot. On cold nights he is reputed to have slept with it to keep it warm. There were no supermarkets, and the loss of one's sourdough consigned the bereft individual to hardtack, until a generous friend came along and shared his leaven. Those who went to the Klondike, always carrying sourdough from home, became known by that name. In this day and age, when homemade sourdough bread is nearly as extinct as the whooping crane, the word means, to many, only a Klondike prospector, and is not associated with bread at all.

A renewed surge of interest in a real staff of life on which to lean, is indicated by the fact that the Department of Agriculture recently committed fifty thousand dollars of the taxpayers' money to find out whether San Francisco sourdough bread can be made anywhere else and still be as tasty. Wasted "dough"? Not if it alerts more housewives to the joys inherent in good bread, and the discovery that a living, breathing pot of sourdough in one's home makes for good company. Then farewell to the rows of aerated paste that pass for bread in the supermarkets.

---

* Sometimes called "wilderness yeast" also.

Very good

Baking Powder Biscuits

(Makes about 14 biscuits in a matter of minutes.)

<u>2 cups flour</u>
<u>3 teaspoons baking powder</u>   } Mix together in a bowl.
<u>1 teaspoon salt</u>
<u>1 teaspoon sugar</u>

Used Crisco

<u>3/4 cup milk</u>, scant
<u>1/3 cup corn oil</u>   } Combine and pour over above dry ingredients. Stir
<u>1 beaten egg</u> (optional)   together lightly. Don't overdo it. Drop by the spoonful onto a <u>buttered</u> cookie sheet. Bake in 450° oven <u>12 to 15 minutes.</u>

The variations of this basic recipe go on and on. My favorite is <u>parsley biscuits</u>: Toss <u>at least 1/2 cup well-chopped parsley</u> into this recipe, more if you care to. It is difficult to overdo it.   Likewise with <u>chives</u>. Or make <u>sage biscuits</u> to go with pork, chicken — provided you have fresh sage, and be careful, a scant <u>1/4 cup chopped sage</u> is sufficient. Make <u>rosemary biscuits</u> to go with lamb or chicken. Be even more careful. A <u>heaping tablespoon of fresh rosemary</u> is ample. One winter day I snipped off a bit of every herb on my window sill in the kitchen: <u>rosemary</u>, <u>sage</u>, <u>basil</u>, <u>tarragon</u>, <u>parsley</u>, <u>chives</u>, <u>savory</u>, <u>thyme</u>, <u>dill</u>, <u>marjoram</u> — just snips. I chopped them all together with a French knife and tossed the fragrant green confetti into the biscuit dough. The resultant <u>herb biscuits</u> were the fancy fillip needed to complement a plain beef stew.

Though I usually make drop biscuits, there are times when I roll out the dough on a floured board, and cut it into decorative shapes or letters, and bake them on a cookie sheet. "Happy Birthday" written in biscuit letters on a game pie (page 82) for example, is more acceptable in our family than a sweet birthday cake. In fact, I always use the above recipe in place of pastry for any meat pie, cooking the pie and biscuit dough separately, before combining, so that the topping is not soggy on the bottom.

HAPPY BIRTHDAY VICTORIA

Boston Brown Bread

1 cup rye flour
1 cup corn meal (yellow)
1 cup graham flour
1 teaspoon salt
1 ½ teaspoons baking soda
1 cup seeded raisins (the large, sticky ones)

} Mix together thoroughly in large bowl.

¾ cup molasses
2 cups buttermilk

} Mix together and stir into above mixture.

Pour into well-buttered old-fashioned brown bread mold, or melon mold. Mold should be about ⅔ filled. Cover. Steam for 3 hours. (Simply place in kettle of boiling water, the water reaching about ⅔ of the way up on the container.) The steaming kettle must be covered, the water therein boiling gently. After brown bread has steamed 3 hours, remove from steaming kettle, uncover, and bake in 350° oven for about 10 minutes, or until top of bread is dry. Unmold, slice, serve steaming hot. To reheat, use a double boiler. Left-over brown bread makes good toast. If mold is not large enough to hold all of recipe, use a second mold. Even coffee tins will do. No words are needed in praise of this Saturday night staple of proper Bostonians.

My Grandmother's Brown Bread Mold (still going strong after 100 years)

Refrigerator Bran Muffins (makes dozens and dozens)
(By Eva Lindley)

(Always ready for a crowd or a few, at the drop of a hat.)

2 cups all-bran cereal (Kellogg, Nabisco, or combination of both)

1 whole box seedless raisins, added to above bran

2 cups boiling water, poured over combined bran and raisins, and put aside to cool

1 cup white sugar, placed in very large mixing bowl

1 cup corn oil

2 cups molasses

4 eggs, well beaten

1 quart buttermilk

3 more cups all-bran cereal (dry)

} stirred into white sugar in order given

5 cups flour

5 teaspoons soda

1 teaspoon salt

} stirred together and added to above combination

Lastly, mix into above, the cooled raisin-bran mixture. Store this batter in covered quart jars in refrigerator. It keeps perfectly for as long as 2 months. Spoon into buttered muffin pans (filling each section about 2/3 full), and bake in preheated 400° oven for exactly 20 minutes. Allow to cool slightly in pans, on a rack. The muffins come out of pans more easily if given a short rest period. Ever so good served hot, cold, reheated, and frozen and reheated.

A bottle of Refrigerator Bran Muffins makes an excellent hostess gift when you go visiting, especially if recipe is attached.

Johnny Cake (serves 6 to 8)

1 cup yellow corn meal
½ cup flour
⅓ cup sugar
2 teaspoons baking powder
¾ teaspoon salt

} Mix in a bowl large enough to hold all ingredients.

1 egg, beaten
½ cup milk
2 tablespoons corn oil

} Mix together and stir into above very quickly and carelessly, no more.

Pour batter into buttered 8-inch square pan. Bake in preheated 450° oven for about 20 minutes. Cut into 9 large or 16 small squares. Serve hot.

Quicker to make, for a group at breakfast, than toast, and a welcome change.

No one seems to be sure of how the word "Johnny Cake" evolved. Some say it is a corruption of "journey cake" that early travelers in this country carried to sustain them. Others say it derives from French Canadian "jaune (yellow) cake." Whatever the background, it has endured because it's good.

Popovers (makes 6)
(A never-fail magic recipe)

2 eggs, broken into a bowl.

1 cup milk ⎤ stirred into eggs, with a spoon, until just blended.
1 cup flour ⎬ Don't worry about lumps. Pour into 6 copiously
½ teaspoon salt ⎦ buttered custard cups. Set cups in muffin pan for secure handling. Cups should be ¾ full of batter. Put into a cold oven and then turn on heat to 450°. Bake exactly ½ hour, with no peeking! Remove from oven, puncture necks of popovers in several places, with a sharp knife. Return to oven for 10 minutes with the heat off. Remove from cups and serve at once, or cool on rack for later serving. Reheat on cookie sheet in 350° preheated oven for 5 minutes.

Pancake Ideas — To any pancake batter, add blueberries, or chopped apple, or (best of all) some raw fresh corn scraped off the cob. If you make blueberry pancakes, instead of serving with plain maple syrup, blend some fresh blueberries into the syrup in the blender. You will be surrounded by the broadest and bluest breakfast smiles.

Apple Muffins — To any muffin recipe, add a good cup of chopped apples. Sprinkle top of muffins with cinnamon and sugar, before baking.

Blueberry Cake (page 235) makes a fine breakfast hot bread.

Cake ~ Cookies

About Cake and Cookies, 225 through 228

Daffy Sponge Cake (page 229) in the Daffodil Bed at Bentley Farm
A Dali-esque conception, but spring in Vermont, after six months
of snow, is mind-blowing, and almost anything can happen.

When I was in grammar school, I was thrilled by Wordsworth's
"The Daffodils," and learned it by heart, to recite at a school function. My
father was persuaded to put down the Boston Evening Transcript
long enough to listen to me practice. Those were the days when elocution
was much in vogue. I gave it all I had, gesticulating dramatically, and
waited breathlessly for his comment which was, "What nut wrote that?"

About Cake ~ Cookies

If you think baked goods mixes are "just as good", then why the line-up of enthusiastic buyers at our country bake sales? The rule for these sales is "no mixes" (a priori admission of their flaccidity), and people fall all over themselves to acquire honest-to-goodness home-baked foods. Their frantic grasping would bring tears to my eyes, except that my puzzlement is so complete it turns off the tears. Why any able-bodied, half-way intelligent person with such staples in the house as flour, sugar, salt, spices, baking powder, yeast, butter, eggs, and milk, can't combine same, and come up with his own home made treat, is beyond me. The miles of aisles of mixes (of doubtful age) in our supermarkets would seem to testify to a population of idiots. Like pollution, the mixes have become a distressing part of modern life. Ever read what is in the mixes — adulterant this, preservative that, dried the other? Not only is the air becoming dangerous to breathe, but foods to ingest.

I watch in horrified fascination as people fill up their grocery carts with costly mixes, costly T.V. dinners, costly processed foods of all kinds, that they are conned into buying; and then I see them pick up margarine instead of butter, to save money!

If threat to health and pocketbook is not enough, the psychological approach may encourage you to get creative in the kitchen. A certain Philadelphia psychiatrist who deals with mentally ill children, with marked success, says that the first question she asks the mother of a disturbed child is, "When did you last bake a batch of cookies for this child?" The answer is, almost invariably, "But I don't bake" (consternation and boredom with anything so inconsequential, written all over the mother's face). Session one ends by the psychiatrist saying, "Go home and bake some cookies, and say to your child, 'I'm baking these cookies that you will love, because I love you.'"

Another psychological angle: I read, some time ago, that there emerged from several costly "think tank" sessions, the shocking realization that mixes were giving women inferiority complexes. Their creativity was so cut down by the fact that they didn't even need to break an egg to produce a reasonable facsimile of a cake, that it was damaging the female ego. Ergo — no dried egg for her mix! Give directions for beating a real egg and the little woman won't end up on a psychiatrists couch.

Then there's the matter of storage space. If you stick to basic commodities you won't have to add an ell to the kitchen to store all those stale, half-used boxes of heaven-knows-what (with their fabulous, irresistable, Madison Avenue photography).

Now for a few practical hints concerning cake and cookie making:

1) Always preheat the oven to designated temperature. Test your oven control now and then, for accuracy, by using a separate oven thermometer. Correct temperature spells success.

2) The middle shelf in the oven is best, baking things uniformly, top and bottom. If you must use 2 shelves, switch the pans half way through the baking, to even up the browning process.

3) Always place pans on racks after removing baked goods from oven. This prevents "sweating", which happens if the pans are placed on a solid surface.

4) Do use butter to grease all baking pans where greasing is called for. It takes very little of it and pays off in flavor. (Recipes will indicate any exceptions.)

5) No need to bother with sifting flour these days, which makes for speedier preparation. Use <u>unbleached flour!</u> (I use the King Arthur brand.)

6) Don't bother to bake if you use fake vanilla*. Commercially baked goods reek of it. Why be an accessory to the crime?

7) When it comes to using nuts, as one often does in cakes and cookies, we are fortunate in having them all shelled in tins or plastic bags. Don't empty them onto chopping board. Pick them out of containers by hand, leaving residue in the bottom. The residue may contain little pieces of shell, which are distressing to bite into. Shells in cakes or cookies are in a class with pieces of core in apple pie, except that shells are more destructive and might break a tooth. Chop nuts with a French knife. It's a cinch, and so much quicker and more effective than a nut grinder. (see page 328)

8) Nearly all home-baked cakes and cookies freeze perfectly, ready for any emergency, and fresh and moist (or crisp) as when they were just baked. Cake and cookie mixes, on the contrary, come from the freezer drier than an Egyptian mummy.

* Imitation vanilla contains waste paper and wood pulp along with coal tar. I'm all for recycling, so long as I don't have to eat the end result.

The recipes that follow use just enough salad oil (in place of butter) to doff one's hat to Dr. Paul Dudley White, and enough butter so as not to be a zealot. The middle-of-the-road approach makes sense, for food fads change every decade. An interest in health foods, so called, is to be recommended up to a point, but when one goes so far as to make a child's birthday cake out of whole wheat flour, he has fallen off the tightrope we all must walk. Nutrition is still an inexact science.

"There should be fragrance, when a house's door
Is opened, welcoming the ones who come,
Whether it be sunlight on the floor
And plants along a window sill, or some
Warm odor from a kitchen: baking bread,
Or peanut-butter cookies laid to cool,
A steaming cocoa pot, or toast that's spread
With cinnamon and sugar. After school
Or play, a child — and after work, a man —
Finds home a little lovelier, scented so,
For always, opening a door, they know
Someone is there before them, and they can
Detect, besides the fragrances that greet
Them, warmth of real affection, doubly sweet."

Elaine V. Emans

Daffy Sponge Cake

(So-called because it is yellow as a daffodil, and people go daffy over it.)

5 egg whites, beaten until stiff and put aside (in smaller beater bowl)

5 egg yolks ⎫
1 cup sugar ⎬ Beat together in large electric beater
3 Tablespoons cold water ⎭ bowl, the longer the better, until pale and fluffy.

1½ Tablespoons cornstarch, placed in measuring cup
flour (preferably cake flour) spooned into above cup until cup is full.
1¼ teaspoons baking powder ⎫ put on top of above cup.
¼ teaspoon salt ⎬ Shake contents of cup slowly into egg yolk mixture, beating just enough to incorporate the dry ingredients, no more.

2 teaspoons lemon extract, stirred into batter with spoon. Then fold in gently, and not too thoroughly, the stiffly beaten egg whites. Pour batter into tube pan, <u>not greased</u>. Bake in preheated <u>325°</u> oven for <u>1 hour</u>. Invert pan the minute it is taken from oven. Let cake cool <u>thoroughly</u> before removing from pan by running knife around side, to free cake, and then around bottom. (This calls for a 2 part pan, as illustrated.) Leave plain, dust with confectioners' sugar, or frost.

230

Three things to keep in mind in making sponge cake:

1) Beating eggs makes cake light. Over beating of batter makes cake tough.

2) Eggs at room temperature make the best cake, though they separate more easily when chilled. So separate your eggs the minute you take them from refrigerator. Go about your business for an hour or so — then on with the cake making.

3) Direction for beating whites first is purposeful, for egg white on the beater will not harm the yolks. Whereas, if yolks are beaten first, you must wash and dry the beater carefully before touching the whites. The least bit of yolk or water or any foreign substance interferes with beaten egg whites assuming their proper fluffiness. (See page 119 for the further understanding of egg whites.)

Variations of Daffy Sponge Cake

1) **Jelly Roll** (Serves 12) (Be sure to have waxed paper on hand.)

Line the bottom of a cookie sheet that has sides, with brown paper. No greasing of anything. Pour in one recipe of Daffy Sponge Cake batter. Bake about 20 minutes in preheated 325° oven. Remove from oven, place on rack, allow to cool completely — for an hour, or a day if it suits your fancy. Cut around 4 edges of pan with a knife. Invert pan onto waxed paper that has been well coated with confectioners' sugar. Tear off brown paper. Spread generously with your favorite jelly. (I like raspberry best.) Any jam is good also. Now, coax the cake gently into a roll with the aid of the waxed paper. Don't panic if first fold cracks a little. Just keep rolling and coaxing with the waxed paper. When rolled, wrap it firmly in the same waxed paper, so that it holds its shape and acquires the sugar as a coating. Another outside wrapping of foil is helpful. Serve with whipped cream which has been slightly seasoned with sugar and vanilla. Keep jelly roll in refrigerator if to be served within a day or so. Or freeze for longer storage.

My cookie sheets with sides measure 12" x 17½". One pan holds this whole recipe and serves 12 people. An official jelly-roll pan is smaller and would only hold ½ this recipe. I treasure my pans above fine jewels, often doubling the sponge cake recipe, making 2 rolls, and having enough for a party of 24. Make an effort to acquire pans of the larger size, even if you have to go to a Tinsmith.

Small amounts of jelly left in numerous jelly glasses? Mix all together and use for jelly roll. Always beat jelly with a spoon to soften, and make more spreadable, before putting on jelly roll.

All jelly roll recipes I have ever found call for rolling the cake instantly, while hot. The process is nerve-wracking, the result soggy. I discovered this cold method quite by accident, and am addicted to it. This cold cake is so pliable it can be waved around like a flag, and not fall apart. I've waved it at various cooking demonstrations, so far without disaster!

2) <u>Cream Roll</u>

Spread cake with <u>whipped cream</u>,* seasoned as specified on page 231, roll, store in freezer. Slice, ice cold, and serve with hot <u>Butterscotch Sauce</u> (page 318) and toasted slivered <u>almonds</u>. (Um-m-m!) <u>Chocolate Sauce</u> (page 319) and <u>walnuts</u> or <u>pecans</u> is another variation. A Vermont touch is <u>maple syrup</u> and <u>butternuts</u>. Or a fruit garnish is excellent and makes for a lighter dessert: <u>strawberries</u>, <u>raspberries</u>, or slices of <u>banana</u>, or <u>mandarin oranges</u>. Use your imagination.

———————

3) <u>Chocolate Roll</u>

Add <u>4 tablespoons cocoa</u> to the measuring cup along with the cornstarch. Then fill cup with flour and proceed as directed. (You will have 4 tablespoons less of flour.) Be sure to substitute <u>vanilla</u> for lemon extract. Roll up with whipped cream. Freeze. Serve plain or with hot Chocolate Sauce (page 319) and pecans.

Here's what my friend, Bill Rough, did with this Chocolate Roll recipe. He substituted <u>3 tablespoons dark rum</u> for the water, and used a dash of <u>rum</u> in the whipped cream filling in place of vanilla. Inspired! No further embellishment needed.

———————

4) <u>Orange Sponge Cake</u>

Substitute <u>orange extract</u> for vanilla. Frost with <u>Orange Frosting</u> (page 322). This may be either a regular cake or

* <u>1 cup heavy cream</u>, whipped

a roll.   Or make as for a jelly roll, but do not roll. Spread
with orange frosting. Chocolate sponge cake spread with orange frosting
is a happy combination also. Cut into tiny squares. This will serve
30 or more people at a tea.

5) Lady Fingers
       Make your own with this same Daffy Sponge Cake
recipe. Line cookie sheet with brown paper. Make fingers of the
batter by dropping from teaspoon or using pastry bag. Or make
little circles and when cool put together sandwich-wise with the
frosting of your choice .   325°oven for about 12 minutes.

6) Apricot Dessert (Serves 12 or more)
       Make the sponge cake according to basic recipe and
bake and cool as for jelly roll. Cut sides free and turn cake out onto
confectioners'-sugared waxed paper . Do not roll. Remove paper,
and top with the following apricot glaze:
   1 box dried apricots (about 11 ounces) just covered with water, and allowed to simmer, uncovered , until tender and water reduced
   1½ cups sugar, added to apricots toward end of simmering
   1 tablespoon (package) plain gelatin, soaked in ¼ cup cold water
and stirred thoroughly into hot apricots. Blend in blender. Cool. Stir in
   1 cup heavy cream, whipped. When thickened to spreadable
consistency , spread on cake and garnish with
   Toasted slivered almonds   Chill. Serve in generous squares.
This is a marvelous dessert for a buffet supper of the balancing-on-
lap variety. For a cheaper and less rich topping, you may

substitute evaporated milk for cream. Whip <u>1 cup of very cold evaporated milk</u> until it begins to thicken. Add <u>2 tablespoons lemon juice</u> and whip until thick.

7) <u>English Trifle</u> (A great way to use up left-over sponge cake or lady fingers — and oh so good!)

     Line the bottom of your best glass bowl (a shallow one) with thin slices of <u>sponge cake</u>, or with <u>lady fingers</u> — the more stale the better. Spread each piece with any sort of <u>jelly or jam</u> that your cupboard yields, or spread lightly with canned, fresh, or frozen fruit such as <u>strawberries</u>, <u>raspberries</u>, <u>peaches</u>, <u>pears</u>, <u>apricots</u>, <u>oranges</u>. Sliced <u>bananas</u> are good. Now drizzle some <u>sherry</u> over all. Don't drown the thirsty cake, just give it enough for abstemious absorption. Next, pour on a generous layer of cold <u>Boiled Custard</u> (page 257). You may call the trifle complete at this point, or further embellish it with <u>whipped cream</u> and some <u>chopped nuts</u>, according to your taste and calorie consciousness. Chill all day in refrigerator.

8) <u>Tipsy Pudding</u>

     This is first cousin to above except that generous splashes of <u>rum</u> are used instead of sherry. <u>Rumtopf</u> (page 317) is ideal for this dish, and so are chopped <u>macadamia nuts</u>. Which reminds me that I served this to a United Nations delegation of 35 people in the fall of 1971. See pages 351 through 354.

<u>Daffy Sponge Cake</u>, for its versatility, flexibility, digestibleness, takes all prizes. And people of every age and stage love it.

Blueberry Cake (serves 8)

1 egg
⅔ cup sugar } Beat egg well. Add sugar gradually.

1½ cups flour
2 teaspoons baking powder } Mix together and add alternately
½ teaspoon salt } with liquids, below, to egg mixture, above.

⅓ cup milk
3 tablespoons corn oil } mix
1 teaspoon vanilla

1 cup blueberries, folded into batter at the last. Pour into 8 inch square buttered pan.

2 tablespoons sugar
½ teaspoon cinnamon } Mix and sprinkle on top of batter. (Blueberries and cinnamon are soul mates.)

Bake in preheated 400° oven about 40 minutes. Cool* in pan on rack. Serve with Lemon Sauce for a dessert that will put the whole family in a happy and cooperative mood.

Lemon Sauce (serve either warm or cold)

1 cup sugar, 2 tablespoons cornstarch, 2 cups water, mixed, and stirred over heat until thick and smooth. A double boiler is best. 4 tablespoons butter, 1 tablespoon grated lemon rind, 3 tablespoons lemon juice, ½ teaspoon salt, added to above when cooked and still hot.

Blueberry Cake is an excellent substitute for coffee cake, served hot or cold, with butter, for a morning coffee. I also use it instead of blueberry muffins for breakfast. Less trouble than muffin tins. The page of the notebook in which I keep this recipe is spotted, yellowed, almost worn out — a sure sign of merit.

*or serve hot from the oven.

Alice Montgomery's Orange Cake

1 orange
1 cup raisins
} Cut orange in pieces, peel and all, and remove seeds. Put orange through grinder, using smallest blade and catching the drip in a dish. Grind raisins. Set aside.

2 eggs, thoroughly beaten in large beater bowl

¾ cup sugar, slowly added to above

¾ cup buttermilk
½ cup corn oil
1 teaspoon orange extract
} added to above

2 cups all-purpose flour
1 teaspoon soda
½ teaspoon salt
} Thoroughly mixed together and then added gradually to above. Beat until well mixed, no more.

When cake is all combined stir in, by hand, the orange and raisins and juice, withholding about 2 tablespoons of the mixture for frosting. Pour cake batter into well buttered 9"x12" pan. Bake in preheated 375° oven for 45 minutes. Cool on rack in the pan. Frost. Cut in squares when ready to serve. I keep the cake in the pan until used up. It may be baked in a sponge cake pan if you prefer, or in layers, thus making an attractive round birthday cake. It is a moist, elegant product, and Mrs. Montgomery made it for all festive occasions in her family life.

Frosting

Into the bowl with the orange-raisin-juice mixture you have saved, put about 3 tablespoons of soft butter, the juice of ½ an orange, ½ teaspoon orange extract and about ¾ box of confectioners' sugar. Just keep adding sugar and stirring until you have a frosting of the right consistency to spread.

Spice Cake (24 pieces of cake)

1 cup seedless raisins ⎫ Bring to a boil, that's all, in pan large
1 cup water ⎬ enough to hold the whole recipe.
½ cup salad oil, stirred into above, then cooled

1 egg, beaten ⎫ combined and stirred into above
1 cup sugar ⎭ when it has cooled.

1¾ cups flour
¼ teaspoon salt
1 teaspoon baking soda
1 " cinnamon
1 " nutmeg
1 " allspice
½ " ground cloves
½ cup chopped nuts (I like pecans best)

⎫ Mix well and
⎬ stir into above.

Pour into well-buttered 9 x 12-inch pan.
Bake in preheated 375° oven for 25 minutes. Cool completely, in the pan, on a rack. Then frost with butter-cream frosting. (Soft butter, confectioners' sugar, vanilla, a bit of cream, well beaten together in any amount you care for.) Leave in pan until ready to serve. Cut into 24 squares.

This is a moist, spicy, absolutely delicious cake that can be made faster than you can read the directions on a box of cake mix. An old-fashioned treat, too often overlooked.

Peach Cake (Serves 8 or more)

¼ pound + 2 tablespoons soft butter } Put butter in large beater
1¼ cups sugar ---------------------- } bowl. Add sugar gradually
while beating constantly until light and fluffy.

3 eggs, beaten into above, one at a time

½ teaspoon almond extract, beaten into above

1¾ cups all-purpose flour } mixed together and then stirred by
1 teaspoon baking powder } hand into above mixture

Pour batter into ungreased sponge cake pan.

Arrange . . . . .

4 or 5 sliced fresh peaches or 1 package frozen peaches, thoroughly drained,
around on the top of the batter, pressing peach slices down
into batter, just a little, and sugaring fresh peaches slightly.
Bake in preheated 350° oven for 1 hour. Allow to
cool completely in the pan, on a rack, right side up.
Remove cold cake from pan. Invert onto your best
serving dish. Embellish the top with

whipped cream that has been slightly sweetened and has had a few
drops of vanilla added. Sprinkle . . . . .
Toasted, slivered almonds over the whipped cream.

Rich and delectable. Everyone needs a moment
of abandon, now and then.

Bible Fruit Cake

1) 1 cup Psalms 55:21 (use either or both)
2) 2 cups Jeremiah 6:20 (last part of verse)
3) 6 Job 39:14
4) 3 Tablespoons 1st Samuel 14:25
5) ½ cup Judges 4:19 (first sentence)
6) 4½ 1st Kings 4:22 (first part of verse)
7) 2 teaspoons Leviticus 2:13
8) 2 teaspoons Amos 4:5
9) 2nd Chronicles 9:9 (½ teaspoon each of cinnamon, clove, nutmeg)
10) 2 cups Numbers 17:8, chopped
11) 2 cups both things in 1st Samuel 30:12, chopped (4 cups total)

Mix in large beater bowl in order given, beating in eggs until light and fluffy. When you get to the nuts and fruit, mix by hand, following Solomon's advice for making a good boy (Proverbs 23:14), and you will have a good cake. Bake at 250° for 2½ hours in 4 small bread pans*, buttered, and bottom lined with buttered brown paper. Allow to cool in pans, on sides, on racks. Then run knife around edges, and turn out cakes. Good eaten at once, but even better aged by wrapping in cheese cloth soaked in sherry or any whiskey. Wrap in foil. Keep in cool place.

(Key to Bible Fruit Cake on next page.)

* 7⅜" x 3⅝" x 2¼" deep

Key to Bible Fruit Cake
(Don't let the children see this! Make them look it up.)

1) butter or oil (I use corn oil)
2) sugar
3) eggs
4) honey
5) water
6) flour
7) salt
8) baking powder
9) spices
10) almonds
11) figs and raisins

This makes a perfect Christmas gift. Fun for children to figure out and prepare during the Advent season. This sort of recipe was the rage at quilting and sewing bees in the early 1800's. So old it is new. Often called "Scripture Cake" in old recipe books. This is not just a game. It is also an excellent cake.

Perfect Brownies (16 squares)

½ cup soft butter (one ¼ pound stick)
1 cup sugar — — — — — — — — } creamed together

3 eggs, added one by one to above, and well beaten in by hand
1 teaspoon vanilla, added to above

1 cup chopped nuts (walnuts or pecans)
¾ cup flour
1 teaspoon baking powder — — — — } mixed and stirred into above

2 squares chocolate, melted, and stirred into above

Turn into buttered 8-inch square pan, and bake in preheated 350° oven for 25 minutes, no more. Cool in pan. Cut into 16 squares.

(An almost-as-good brownie may be made by substituting ⅓ cup corn oil and ½ teaspoon salt for the butter.

Nested Cookie Cutters

If you ever see cookie cutters like these, be sure to latch onto them.

New England Marguerites (24 gems)

<u>2 eggs</u>, lightly beaten
<u>1 cup dark brown sugar</u>, firmly packed
<u>½ cup flour</u>
<u>⅓ teaspoon salt</u>
<u>¼ teaspoon baking powder</u>
<u>1 teaspoon vanilla</u>
<u>1 cup chopped pecans</u>

} stirred into eggs and spooned into buttered gem pans — just a little in each section. (2 pans, 12 sections each)

<u>48 whole pecans</u> —- Press 2 on each gem.

Bake in preheated <u>325°</u> oven for <u>about 20 minutes</u>. Better undercooked than over. Then place pans on rack and allow to cool enough for easy handling. Coax from pans carefully with dull knife and cool further on racks. They fall a bit and are supposed to, turning them into chewy delights. Sort of a cross between pralines and pecan pie, but better than either. They freeze perfectly.

If you are lazy or hurried, you may substitute a buttered 9 x 12-inch baking pan, cook the batter all in one sheet and cut into cookie bars with sharp knife. I use (and prefer) my grandmother's iron gem pans which make an oblong gem or cookie, rounded on the bottom. Fortunately these are still being manufactured and they may also be found in antique shops. Unfortunately people seem to use them more for wall decorations these days than for the luscious baked goods they produce. Regular round muffin tins do just as well if you lack the oblong variety. In my youth Marguerites were pear shaped, but I have never been able to find such pans.

Should you be fortunate enough to have a supply of <u>butternuts</u> (a rare luxury!) they may be substituted for pecans.

No luncheon or tea was complete in Newton Centre, Massachusetts, where I grew up, without Marguerites. They were purchased from the Woman's Exchange, which, if memory serves me correctly, held forth in Bond's Store near the railroad station where all Newton Centre fathers entrained for their jobs in Boston. I never wasted any time getting home from school when Mother entertained, in hopes there would be some Marguerites left over for me. They taste as good to me today as they did then.

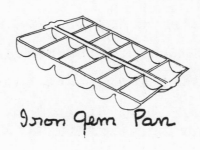

Iron Gem Pan

244

Glorified Oatmeal Cookies

(About 10 dozen small cookies. Make bigger ones if you want to.)

3/4 cup corn oil
1 cup brown sugar
½ cup granulated sugar
2 eggs
¼ cup water
1 teaspoon vanilla

} Toss into large beater bowl and beat together.

1 cup flour
1 teaspoon salt
½ teaspoon soda
1 teaspoon cinnamon
½ teaspoon cloves
½ teaspoon nutmeg

} Mix together and add gradually to above, until well beaten in.

3 cups uncooked oatmeal
½ cup pecans, chopped
½ cup almonds, chopped
1 cup raisins   choc chips
1 sixteen-ounce box or jar of mixed, candied fruit that comes all chopped

} Stir all this into above, by hand. Drop by teaspoonful onto buttered cookie sheets, firming and shaping with buttered fingers. Bake in preheated 350° oven for 10 to 15 minutes. Watch carefully. Cookies that are too brown are a disaster. Scoop off and cool on racks.

In every home where there are children, the cookie jar should be filled with these delicious and highly nutritious cookies. Excellent for mailing to young people away at school. They will prevent you from getting a letter, as did one mother I know, saying, "Thanks, Ma, for the crumbs." There wasn't a whole cookie in the lot, the cookies being the fragile kind, which these are not.

Peanut Butter Drop Cookies (about 8 dozen)

1 cup peanut butter, smooth or chunk style
½ cup butter (1 stick) soft, or ½ cup salad oil } Place in beater bowl
2 teaspoons vanilla   and beat together
½ cup sugar   thoroughly.
1 cup honey
2 eggs

2½ cups flour   } mixed and slowly beaten into
1 teaspoon baking soda } above emulsion

1 cup coarsely chopped dry roasted peanuts, stirred into above
by hand

Drop, by the teaspoon, onto buttered cookie sheets, pressing down a bit, to shape each one. Bake in preheated 375° oven about 10 minutes, watching ever so carefully. Better undercooked than scorched.   These are the peanutiest peanut cookies you'll ever encounter. Real energy boosters.

Bessie's Ginger Cookies

1 cup sugar
1 cup molasses   } Bring to a boil. Keep stirring until butter is
1 cup butter (2 sticks, ½ pound)   ) melted. Cool. When cool, stir in . . . .
1 egg, well beaten, and ½ teaspoon salt
1 teaspoon ginger, 1 teaspoon cinnamon, 1 teaspoon soda ~ Stir thoroughly into...
2 cups flour, and add all to above. Add as much more flour as is needed to make a soft dough. Chill in refrigerator an hour. Break off pieces of dough. Roll thin on floured board. Cut into cookies of desired shape. Slide onto buttered cookie sheet. Bake in 350° oven about 8 minutes. Cool slightly before lifting off pan.

Rice Krispie Squares (24 two-inch squares)

<u>Butter</u> a 12×9-inch pan, generously, and set aside.

<u>½ of a quarter-pound stick of butter</u> (¼ cup) melted in large saucepan.

<u>40 large marshmallows</u> (or 4 cups of miniature marshmallows) added to melted butter, and stirred constantly over low heat until marshmallows are melted.

<u>½ teaspoon vanilla</u>, added to above.

<u>5 cups Rice Krispies</u>, stirred into the marshmallow syrup, until well coated. Immediately transfer this warm mixture to the buttered pan. Press it firmly and evenly therein. Cool. Cut into squares with a sharp knife.

~~~~~~~~~~~~~~~~~~

There is nothing remarkable about this recipe except its goodness. A fine snack, loved by children and adults alike. Just the touch for a dessert cookie when something a little sweet and very crisp is called for.

When my nephew served in the army in Korea, great quantities of these confections went to the Far East. He said they were the top choice of his outfit — ahead of candy, conventional cookies, or cake.

~~~~~~~~~~~~~~~~~~

<u>Rum Cookies</u> (no cooking)

<u>1 whole box Vanilla Wafers</u> (12 ounces) reduced to crumbs with
mortar and pestle, or rolling pin.

<u>1 cup confectioners' sugar</u>
<u>1½ cups finely chopped nuts</u> (I use pecans, but walnuts or almonds will do.)
<u>1½ tablespoons cocoa</u>
<u>2 tablespoons light corn syrup</u>
<u>½ cup rum</u> (dark rum is best)

    Combine all ingredients and mix thoroughly. Roll into
small balls with buttered hands. Drop into a paper bag that contains
some confectioners' sugar. Shake gently, to coat the cookies.

    An excellent accompaniment to a fruit dessert. They
freeze well. Wrap individually in waxed paper and twist the ends —
like old-fashioned molasses kisses. Fine for a holiday gift box.

<u>Pecan Puffs</u> (makes about 30)

<u>½ cup soft butter</u> (1 stick)
<u>2 tablespoons sugar</u> } creamed together
<u>1 teaspoon vanilla</u>
<u>1 cup flour</u>
<u>1 cup finely chopped pecans</u> } added to above and well mixed. Pick up
dough by teaspoonful. Roll into balls. No
need to butter hands. Place on buttered
cookie sheet and bake in preheated <u>300°</u> oven for <u>1 hour</u>. When cool,
give them the paper-bag—confectioners'-sugar-treatment as above.
Devastatingly good! You may substitute 1 cup <u>sesame seeds</u>,
toasted (page 214) for the pecans. Highly nutritious for a child's
lunch box.

good

Shortbread (Scottish) (Makes 36 fingers)

As made by Jess Fairhurst, who grew up close to Loch Lomondside

Have a cookie sheet ready, lined with brown paper. (No butter)

½ pound (2 sticks) soft butter ⎫ Cream together zealously, no shirking. Do it
½ cup confectioners' sugar ⎬ by hand with a wooden spoon. No mechanical
(2½)   ⎭ beaters, please. (Use a wide, large mixing bowl.)

2¼ cups flour, added gradually to well-creamed fluff above. Stir and stir, lovingly, for this is a once-a-year Scottish rite. When all is well combined, put the mixing spoon aside, and, with your bare hands, go to work and knead this mixture, in the bowl, for at least 5 minutes. Squeeze, press, pat, pound, anything to blend the 3 ingredients thoroughly. The warmth of your hands works a certain magic. Lastly, gather into a ball, mopping up every last crumb in the mixing bowl. Plop the ball onto the waiting brown-papered cookie sheet. Press and pat with your buttery hands until you have a rectangle that measures about 7×9 inches, and is smooth and crack-free. Now take a fork and jab it in rows, up and down the rectangle. (See Figure 1). It resembles a cross between a Babylonian cuneiform tablet and a fat I.B.M. card. Next, take a sharp, slim knife and cut the tablet in 5 long strokes, up and down, then 5 strokes across, to make 36 fingers. (Figure 2). Bake in a pre-heated 300° oven for 1 hour (or until lightly brown on top). Remove from oven and place on rack. If any further cutting seems necessary to separate the pieces, score again, while hot. (If scored when cool, it will crumble.)

+ ½ tsp almond extract

Used 9 X 13 "pan"

←— 7" —→

↑ 9" ↓

9X13?

Figure 1

Figure 2

or 325° for about 40 min.

(next page)

Cool. Separate into fingers, and store in a tin with tight-fitting lid. Put waxed paper between the layers of shortbread. Keep in cool place.

———————

Jess prepares many tins of shortbread for her friends a good month before the holidays, ready for the festivities of Christmas and the New Year. Having been a recipient of this treat for over 40 years, I've never bothered to make it myself. But now, many letters and phone calls later, I've written it down for posterity, and even managed to make a reasonable facsimile of Jess's perfect production.

This seems a lot of discussion for a simple, three-ingredient recipe, but as its preparation and usage are as surrounded by tradition as the Stone of Scone, a brief description would not do it justice.

Marcia's Cookies (about 90 cookies)

2 cups dark brown sugar
1 cup soft butter (2 quarter-pound sticks)
2 eggs, and 1½ teaspoons vanilla —

Place in large beater bowl and beat until well combined and fluffy. Then beat in .... thoroughly.

2¼ cups flour (scant)
½ teaspoon soda
½ teaspoon salt
1 cup chopped nuts (almonds or pecans)
1 cup grated coconut
1 twelve-ounce package semi-sweet chocolate bits

Toss all this together in a bowl and mix thoroughly with a spoon. Then stir, by hand, into above mixture. Drop by teaspoon onto buttered cookie sheet. Bake in 350° oven for 8 to 10 minutes. Cool slightly before lifting from pan.

(Marcia is a young lady destined for fame in the culinary world.)

———————

Made Feb. '09. Did not add coconut. Nice cookie, but nothing special

Scottish Fancies

1 egg, well beaten
½ cup sugar
1 tablespoon corn oil, trimming, or melted butter
1 cup uncooked oatmeal, quick or regular
½ teaspoon salt
1 teaspoon vanilla

Mix all together well with a spoon, in order given. Put batter, a teaspoonful at a time, onto cookie sheet with sides, that has first been buttered and then generously anointed with corn oil. With a fork, dipped in cold water, press each cookie into a round, flat shape. Bake in preheated 325° oven for about 15 minutes. Watch it! These are ancient standbys, made in minutes, crisp, toothsome, and too often overlooked, probably because they have a tendency to stick to the pan like glue. The butter-oil routine seems to overcome this. If cookies run in together, as they are apt to, cut apart with a sharp, thin paring knife before lifting up cookies by sliding same knife carefully under each. This should be done while cookies are still warm. Cool them on rack.

Sesame Cookies (kindness of Nancy Hays)
(Makes about 60 paper-thin, addictive wafers.)

1 cup sesame seeds* that have been washed in a strainer under running water

⅓ cup water

} Mix together in a saucepan, and bring to a boil over moderate heat, stirring often. Cook about 5 minutes, or until water is nearly absorbed by seeds.

¼ pound stick of butter, stirred around in above mixture until melted. Remove from heat.

1 cup dark brown sugar
¾ cup flour
¼ teaspoon salt
1 egg, unbeaten
1 teaspoon vanilla

} Stir all this into the above seed mixture in the order given.

Drop cookie batter, a teaspoonful at a time, onto slightly buttered cookie sheets, well apart, so that they run together as little as possible. I get 20 cookies to a sheet. Bake in preheated 350° oven for 10 to 12 minutes. Cool slightly in pan before cutting apart, for they are bound to run together a little. They lift from pan with the greatest of ease. Any cookies not used right away I keep refrigerated, or frozen in plastic bags.

Sesame has sustained soldiers on the march, through the ages. You'll feel like jogging with a heavy pack after eating these.

*Buy by the pound from any health food store. Too costly in bottles from an herb rack.

100 Spice Cookies
(They won't last long!)

2 cups seedless raisins)
1 cup water ....) simmered together for 5 minutes, and cooled.

1 cup salad oil (I use corn oil))
2 cups dark brown sugar)
3 eggs)
2 teaspoons vanilla ...) Beat these ingredients together in large beater bowl. Then stir in the cooled raisin mixture, by hand.

4 cups flour
1 teaspoon baking powder
1 teaspoon baking soda
2 teaspoons salt
1½ teaspoons allspice
1½ teaspoons cinnamon
½ teaspoon nutmeg ...) Stir together well, and add to above, stirring by hand.

1 cup chopped nuts (I prefer pecans), stirred in last.
Chill dough in refrigerator for at least 20 minutes — a very important step. Drop from teaspoon on buttered cookie sheets. Bake in 350° preheated oven for about 15 minutes. Watch. A soft cookie which holds its shape nicely. They do not run together. They freeze well. Not crumbly, so they mail well. Have good keeping quality.

Dessert

Snow Pudding with Custard Sauce (page 257)
A refreshing dessert, cool as the icicles hanging outside the Bentley kitchen window.

"The setting sun, and music at the close,
As the last taste of sweets, is sweetest last..."
— William Shakespeare

About Desserts

There are many custard recipes in this section, a treat too often neglected in this country today. Custard is standard fare in all fine hotels throughout the world, and Americans grown queasy from travel and strange food, may be observed going for this delicacy as a baby for its bottle. But for some reason it is overlooked in the American home, replaced in most cases by the ubiquitous commercial ice cream. Whenever I serve custard to guests there are cries of nostalgic delight, and the question, "Why don't we ever have this at home any more?"

Because custard curdles if overcooked, some people are afraid to make it. Equipped with a double boiler, the determination to stir constantly for a few minutes, the alertness to remove the custard from the heat the second it begins thickening, the care to strain it, the use of a lavish hand with pure vanilla extract (no imitations!), any dolt can turn out an excellent custard sauce in short order.*

When it comes to baked custards, again, do not overcook. Most cook books tell us to test baked custards with a silver knife. What for? I don't like to break the perfection of the surface, and only slight experience informs one when custard is done. The silver knife is in a class with straw from a broom for cake testing, both hangovers from the era of the wood stove and its uncertainties. Because cook books recommended such techniques in eighteen-hundred-and-froze-to-death, they keep right on, out of habit. With a modern temperature-controlled oven there is little guess work. Holes throughout a baked custard indicate too hot an oven or too long cooking. Remove custards from oven when

*Custard sauce, soft custard, boiled custard are all different names for the same thing.

wavy — firm, not solid, keeping in mind that they continue to cook somewhat as they cool. I leave them standing in the pan of hot water in which they baked, until cooled and easy to handle. Err on the side of under rather than overcooking.

Butter the containers in which custards are baked. The dishes wash more easily, the custards may be turned out on a plate effortlessly, if you care to serve them that way, and the touch of butter adds flavor.

I often bake individual custards in punch cups. It's an attractive switch from the usual pottery variety.

When serving custard for dessert, avoid eggs in any other form at the outset of the meal.

Featherlight desserts, as well as heavier pies and shortcakes, are included in this section. The hearty desserts will be more appreciated if the first course is light. One of the better meals is a bowl of soup followed by a generous serving of strawberry shortcake. Who needs more?

In the pie section I have not indicated, as a rule, how many people one pie will serve. 6 or 8 people is usual, but many factors are involved: the diners' wishes, the richness of the pie, the necessity of stretching the servings for a crowd, or being extra generous with a few.

If meat and vegetable course is substantial, taper off at dessert time, serving small portions of one of the lighter desserts, or just fruit, or just Irish coffee (page 15). Guests will be grateful.

There is no substitute for real lemons. Be not conned into buying those plastic replicas that symbolize all that is loathsome in modern merchandising. They also cost more!

Old-Fashioned Boiled Custard (1 quart)
(Serves 6 to 8)

4 egg yolks
¾ cup sugar
1½ tablespoons flour
¼ teaspoon salt

Stir together briskly in top of double boiler.
But do not place over boiling water until
milk is added.

3 cups milk, scalded, and stirred into above. Cook over boiling water,
stirring constantly until custard thickens slightly. Remove from
heat at once, or it will curdle. STRAIN and cool slightly.

1 tablespoon(!) pure vanilla extract, stirred into custard. Chill,
covered, (so it won't form a skin), in refrigerator.

You now have a beautiful, basic, vanilla sauce ready for the creation
of countless desserts.

Alice Roosevelt Longworth is on record as having disliked
boiled custard in her youth at the White House because it had "horrid strings
of egg in it." Inexcusable! Had the White House chef strained the custard,
she would have suffered no such trauma.

Snow Pudding (serves 6)

1 envelope plain gelatin, sprinkled into a bowl, and covered with....
¼ cup cold water, and allowed to soak a few minutes.
1 cup boiling water, poured over gelatin and stirred until totally dissolved.
¼ cup lemon juice, ½ teaspoon lemon extract, ¼ teaspoon salt, stirred into
above along with 1 cup sugar. Chill mixture until syrupy, but
not jelled. Beat with egg beater until foamy. Fold in......
4 egg whites, stiffly beaten. Pour into mold that has been coated lightly
with corn oil, or pour into best glass bowl. Chill until set.
Unmold, or serve directly from glass bowl — with Boiled Custard (above)
for the lightest and most refreshing of desserts.

Floating Island (Serves 6)

Beat 4 eggwhites until stiff, and then gradually beat in 3 or 4 tablespoons sugar, a sprinkling of salt, and a few drops of vanilla. Plop great clouds of this airy nothing onto individual dishes of chilled Boiled Custard (page 257), or onto a large, shallow bowl of custard (for serving at table). Do not make this meringue too far ahead of serving, or it begins to sag. Last minute treatment is best.

———————

In the book Tracy and Hepburn by Garson Kanin, it speaks of the famous pair going out for dinner (something they rarely did), to a place called "Cochon d'Or" in Paris. There they enjoyed a perfect dinner, the dessert that delighted Spencer Tracy being — you've guessed it — Floating Island.

———————

Pompadour Pudding

This is almost the same thing as the above, but, as children, we considered it a step up the ladder from plain Floating Island. It simply has a little grated bitter chocolate folded into the meringue, along with more sugar.

———————

Boiled custard makes a fine sauce for any fruit dessert. It is especially good poured over sliced bananas, garnished with chopped peanuts. Pour custard over Jell-O desserts.

———————

Crème Brûlée (Serves 6)

<u>2 cups light cream</u>, scalded in double boiler

<u>4 egg yolks</u>, well beaten

<u>3 tablespoons sugar</u>, added gradually to above yolks, beating as you add. Then stir in the scalded cream.

<u>1½ teaspoons vanilla</u>
<u>¼ teaspoon salt</u>
} Stir this into above mixture. Then pour through a fine strainer into proper-sized baking dish. (I use soufflé dish.) Place in pan of hot water and bake in preheated <u>325°</u> oven for <u>about 45 minutes.</u> (See page 255 for a discussion of that delicate balance between done and overdone.)

<u>¼ cup brown sugar</u>, either light, dark, or brownulated, sprinkled evenly over surface of the hot baked custard. Turn the oven to <u>broil</u> and return custard to oven, close to broiler. With oven door open, keep a sharp eye on the brown sugar. Broil until sugar commences to bubble, and to liquify slightly. This only takes seconds, and careful watching, or your lovely dessert might be a smoking ruin.

Refrigerate well, before serving — a whole day or more is best. A rich and smooth custard that is a real pièce de résistance. Only dainty servings are called for.

Oh-So-Easy Blender Custard (about 6 cups)

2 cups milk
2 eggs
1/3 cup sugar
1/4 teaspoon salt
1 Teaspoon vanilla

Toss all into blender. Blend thoroughly. Pour into buttered custard cups, with no necessity to strain the blend. Place in shallow pan to which hot water has been added, to a depth of about 1 inch. Over each cup sprinkle nutmeg. Bake in preheated 325° oven for about 50 minutes.

Maple Custard (about 7 custards)

2 cups milk
4 eggs
1/2 cup maple syrup
1/4 teaspoon salt
1/2 teaspoon vanilla
1/4 teaspoon maple flavoring
nutmeg (optional)

Blend thoroughly and proceed as directed above. 45 minutes baking time should be sufficient, because there are more eggs than is usual.
Chilled custards may be garnished with a few chopped nuts. Butternuts are the last word, if available.

Maple syrup poured over plain baked custard is good, and a reasonable facsimile of, and less work than Caramel Custard.
(page 262)

Made Oct 2010. Delicious, but could use 1/3 c. sugar. So, I made Caramel Sauce on next page. good

Classic Baked Custard

Milk must be scalded. Use egg yolks only. The proportions are 1 cup scalded milk to 2 egg yolks to ¼ cup sugar to a sprinkling of salt to ¼ teaspoon vanilla. A grating of nutmeg over all. Multiply these proportions, depending on your need. Amounts given would only serve 2 or 3. The egg yolks are stirred together vigorously with the sugar, salt, vanilla, and then the scalded milk is stirred in. STRAIN, and pour into baking dish, then sprinkle with nutmeg. Use separate buttered custard cups, or put everything in one buttered baking dish. Proceed as with Blender Custard (page 260).

This custard has a slightly different quality than the blender variety, is more traditional, and probably better because it involves a little more work. There will be left-over egg whites, which may please you or not. They seem to worry me, sitting in the refrigerator bothering my conscience. They may be frozen for future use, or turned into meringues, or angel pie, or angel food cake. Most definitive cook books will give recipes for the aforementioned.

~~~~~~~~~

Custard Bread Pudding (old-time favorite)

Pour scalded milk over cubed bread and let soak. Add a beaten whole egg per cup of milk, some raisins, sugar, salt, vanilla, nutmeg — according to taste. Bake in pudding dish as for any custard. Serve warm with cream or Hard Sauce (page 320). Easy does it on the bread. A little goes a long way. Optional embellishments are a little grated lemon rind stirred into unbaked pudding, and some dots of butter on the top.

~~~~~~~~~

"Your dressing, dancing, gadding, where's the good in?
Sweet lady, tell me, can you make a pudding?"

~~~~~~~~~

Low Heat

Caramel Custard (8 or 9 custard cups)

3/4 cup sugar, placed in heavy iron pan over _low_ heat, and stirred now and then until caramelized. (It turns into a brown syrup.) This takes more time than attention.

3 cups milk, scalded. Into the scalded milk, slowly spoon the caramelized sugar, and stir and stir and stir until all sugar is dissolved.

3 eggs
1/4 teaspoon salt } Beat slightly, and into this pour the hot sugar-milk mixture.

1 teaspoon vanilla, added to above, and then strain the whole mixture through a fine strainer into a good pouring pitcher, and pour into 8 or 9 _buttered_ custard cups.

nutmeg, grated over each cup.

Place cups in shallow baking pan. Add about 1 inch of hot water to pan. Bake in preheated oven of 325° for 50 minutes or more. Chill. If you are ambitious, turn chilled custards into attractive sauce dishes (by running knife around edge of custard), and spoon Caramel Sauce over each. This is the classic way. Or serve the custards in their own cups, topped with Caramel Sauce.

Caramel Sauce

1 cup sugar, caramelized, as indicated above (in the same pan, which I trust you haven't gotten around to washing as yet).

1 cup boiling water, added slowly to caramelized sugar, and boiled for 6 minutes, stirring often. Chill. Add dash of _brandy_ (optional). Makes about 1 cup, just enough for 8 or 9 custards.

Be careful. Don't boil at first!

Applesauce Custard (Serves 4 to 6)

3 eggs, separated, putting whites in the smaller beater bowl, yolks in the larger. Beat the whites until they begin to stiffen, and, while still beating, very gradually add

6 tablespoons sugar, and beat until stiff, lastly adding.....

⅛ teaspoon salt

½ teaspoon vanilla   Set this meringue aside. Without changing the beater, or whacking off the last of the egg whites, beat the 3 egg yolks well, that are in larger bowl, and then add

3 cups applesauce, sweetened to taste. Beat until well mixed. Canned apple sauce will do. Or quarter, core, and peel fresh apples, add a little sugar, and very little water, stew until tender and water evaporated. Cool. The beating turns this into applesauce.

1 teaspoon grated lemon rind) Beat this into yolk - apple mixture.

½ teaspoon vanilla _____) Then plop just a little of the meringue into this, and fold in gently, by hand. Place in soufflé dish. Top with remaining meringue. Bake in preheated 300° oven for 20 minutes or more, until meringue looks tan and happy. Chill all day. A light and tempting dessert is all ready.

Rice Pudding

Make this when you have left-over <u>rice</u> in the refrigerator. Add cooked rice to <u>boiled custard</u> (page 257) until the mixture holds its shape. Add some chopped glazed <u>fruit</u>, or <u>raisins</u>, or crushed <u>pineapple</u>, a grating of <u>lemon rind</u>, perhaps a touch of <u>cinnamon</u> or <u>nutmeg</u>. To make it extra special, fold in or top with some <u>whipped cream</u>. Garnish with chopped <u>nuts</u>, if that strikes your fancy. The variations are many. Do a little tasting and testing, and use your imagination.

Pumpkin Custard (Serves 8)

<u>2 cups cooked pumpkin</u> (I use canned pumpkin)
<u>1 cup milk</u>
<u>1 cup cream</u>
<u>½ cup maple syrup</u>
<u>4 eggs</u>, well beaten
<u>1 Tablespoon brandy or rum</u>

} Mix together thoroughly.

<u>½ cup sugar</u>
<u>½ teaspoon salt</u>
<u>1½ teaspoons cinnamon</u>
<u>1½ teaspoons ginger</u>
<u>¼ teaspoon nutmeg</u>

} Mix and add to above. Pour into 1 large baking dish, buttered, or into separate buttered custard cups. Place in a pan containing about 1 inch of hot water. Bake in <u>325°</u> oven about <u>1 hour</u>. (See page 255.)

Serve cold, garnished with <u>whipped cream</u> and <u>pecans</u>.
(You may add chopped <u>crystallized ginger</u> to the cream for further embellishment, if it strikes your fancy.)

Holiday Steamed Pudding (Serves 6)

2/3 cup flour
1 teaspoon baking powder
3/4 teaspoon baking soda
3/4 teaspoon salt
1/2 teaspoon cinnamon
1/4 teaspoon nutmeg
1/4 teaspoon cloves
2/3 cup sugar
2/3 cup currants
2/3 cup raisins
2/3 cup grated raw carrots
2/3 cup grated raw potatoes
1/3 cup milk

Place all these ingredients in a bowl. Mix well and put into thoroughly buttered steam mold. I use a melon mold, but anything with a tight cover will do, so long as it is not more than 2/3 full of batter. Place in a large kettle containing boiling water which should come about 2/3 of the way up on the mold. Cover the kettle and let boil slowly for about 3 hours. (Longer cooking will do no harm if dessert time is delayed.) Unmold onto serving dish and serve hot — with Hard Sauce (page 320).

I always double this recipe for Thanksgiving and Christmas. It seems to have superseded Plum Pudding on the menu completely. Everyone likes it better, and certainly it is better for one. The suet in old-fashioned plum pudding is considered lethal these days. No need to wait for the holidays to serve. An excellent dessert at any time of year. Children love it.

A Melon Mold

Blueberry Grunt (Serves 4)

2 cups (1 pint) fresh blueberries, well washed and drained ⎫

⅓ cup sugar

1 cup water

¼ teaspoon cinnamon

⅛ teaspoon salt ⎬ Combine in saucepan, cover, and cook until blueberry skins burst, about 5 minutes.

2 tablespoons lemon juice, added to above after the 5 minutes.

1 cup flour

1½ teaspoons baking powder ⎫ Mix together and then add . . . . . .

½ teaspoon salt

about ½ cup milk (enough to make soft drop dough).

Drop the dough from a teaspoon onto boiling blueberries. Cover, and cook 12 minutes without peeking. That's it. Serve warm, with a sugar bowl handy for those with a sweet tooth, and with a pitcher of honest-to-goodness cream. Sweetened whipped cream with a touch of vanilla is also traditional. Take your choice.

———————

For many years I sought a recipe for Blueberry Grunt that could approach what my husband's grandmother used to make in Wallace, Nova Scotia. I did not have her recipe, and there were those childhood memories to compete with. After years of trial and error, Perce pronounced the above recipe perfect. No faint praise. A terrible name for a tasty dish. Sometimes called "Blueberry Flummery" or "Blueberry Slump."

Never-Fail Pie Crust

(Enough pastry for a 9-inch, one-crust pie)
Be sure to have waxed paper on hand!

2 cups all purpose flour*
1 teaspoon salt
½ cup corn oil
¼ cup cold milk

Stir ingredients together, lightly, in order given. Form into a ball. Flatten and shape into a circle on a piece of waxed paper. Cover with another piece of waxed paper and roll out, with a rolling pin, to desired size. Peel off the top piece of paper. Place pie plate, upside down, onto the pastry. Holding pastry and plate together, turn plate right side up. Gently peel waxed paper off pastry. If pastry tears, it is easily mended. Press pastry firmly onto plate with fingers and a fork. If you are going to bake shell with nothing in it, prick it all over with a fork so that pastry will not blister. Otherwise do not make holes in pastry, for the filling will hold it down. Make a nice, rippled, upstanding edge with your fingers, and then push edge inward a bit, so it is not stuck to rim of pie plate. This holds the filling in better, so it doesn't run over, and also keeps edge from browning too fast. A good pie should not be stuck to the pie plate anywhere after it is baked. Ideally, it should slide around in the plate. This makes for easy serving. This recipe is a little more than enough for one pie (see page 275), so you have plenty of pastry to play with to make a good high, thick collar.

Warning: Never chill this pastry before rolling. Chill it all you want after it is arranged in pie plate. In fact, I always place the pie plate in the refrigerator while preparing filling.

For baking pie shell alone: Bake in preheated 475° oven for about 10 minutes. Cool on rack for maximum crispness.

* I use King Arthur unbleached flour.

The pie crust recipe on previous page is just enough to place on top of the large deep-dish pies with which I celebrate the blueberry (page 269) and apple (page 269) seasons. I never make a two-crust pie (the bottom crust is always soggy), and this way one always has a crispy crust, either over or under; and one crust, to my way of thinking, is sufficient pastry for anyone.

There are purists who disdain pastry made with oil. I can't imagine why. This is one sure-fire pie crust which never fails, and, if present research is correct, corn oil is better for one than animal fats. Another advantage is that there is no floury board to clean up after rolling the pastry. And most important — This pastry is tender and delicious.

〜〜〜〜〜〜〜〜〜〜〜〜

For a pleasant variation, add <u>2 tablespoons of sesame seeds</u> to above pie crust recipe.

〜〜〜〜〜〜〜〜〜〜〜〜

Deep Dish Apple Pie

Make this whenever you can get your hands on good tart winter apples. Butter a baking dish of sufficient size for the number to be fed. Figure one or more apples per person. Quarter, core carefully, and peel apples, until you have filled the dish. (Apples cook down considerably.) For every 6 good-sized apples, use ⅔ cup sugar mixed with 1 tablespoon flour, ¼ teaspoon cinnamon, ⅛ teaspoon nutmeg, a dash of salt, a touch of vanilla, a touch of lemon extract (or grated lemon rind, or lemon juice, or both — just a little). Sprinkle this mixture over the apples. Dot with butter. Cover with pie crust (page 267), and with fork or knife mark a large A in the pastry. Slide into preheated 450° oven for 10 minutes, and then turn oven down to 350° and bake 50 or 60 minutes more, depending on size of pie. (I usually double or triple this recipe.) Serve slightly warm, or at room temperature, with sharp store cheese (called rat-trap cheese in New England). The pie drips with juice. The crust crunches. Oh happy day!

Deep Dish Blueberry Pie (for 4 to 6)

1 quart blueberries, picked over, washed, well drained and put in buttered baking dish. Mix together 1 cup sugar, 2 tablespoons flour, sprinkle of salt, touches of vanilla and lemon extract (or lemon juice), and ⅛ teaspoon cinnamon. Pour over the blueberries and stir around a little. Dot with butter. Put on a top crust (page 267), and mark it with B — happier diners you'll never see. Have a dish of vanilla ice cream on the table for piling atop the warmish or room temperature pie.

Apple Tart (Serves 6)

1 unbaked pie shell (page 267)
6 medium-sized pie apples — Used "Rome" - a little dry.
⅔ cup sugar
2 Tablespoons flour
¼ teaspoon cinnamon
⅛ teaspoon nutmeg - No
dash of vanilla
  "   " lemon extract
  "   " salt

+ brown
sugar?

(try next
time)

Needs cream or ice cream with it.

Stir all this together thoroughly. The vanilla and lemon will make small lumps, but never mind. Go easy on the vanilla. It is to enhance, not overpower, the apple flavor.

butter

Cut apples into quarters, pare and core carefully. An apple pie containing bits of core is a desecration. Cut each quarter into 2 or 3 pieces and arrange in swirl pattern in the pie shell. Carefully spoon sugar-spice mixture over the apples. Dot with butter. Bake in preheated 450° oven for 10 minutes. Turn oven down to 350° and bake 40 or 50 minutes longer. Cool on rack.

Serve with cheese, of course! My grandfather used to say, "Apple pie without cheese is like a kiss without a squeeze."

This is the way apple pie is often made in Pennsylvania Dutch country. Not nearly as heavy as a two-crust pie, and the bottom crust really gets crisp.

Eggnog Pie (with Rum, by Gum)

Prepare a baked pie shell (page 267) or a graham cracker pie shell (273).
1½ tablespoons (1½ packages) plain gelatin, soaked in . . . .
⅓ cup cold water
4 eggs, separated ⌣ Place yolks in blender, whites in beater bowl.

1 cup milk
¼ teaspoon salt } Put these ingredients into blender with the egg
⅔ cup sugar   yolks and blend. Pour into top of a double
boiler. Add the soaked gelatin. Cook over
boiling water, stirring constantly, until custard
just thickens, and gelatin is dissolved. Allow
this mixture to cool until gelatin begins to set,
no more! Then stir in . . . .

3 Tablespoons rum (I like dark rum best.) Now fold in, tenderly, the
4 egg whites, beaten until stiff.
1 cup heavy cream, beaten until fluffy ⌣ Fold only ½ of this
whipped cream into above, reserving the rest.
Heap this cloud-like mixture into pie shell. Chill until firm. Then
spread remaining whipped cream on top of pie. Sprinkle with . . .
nutmeg, generously. Chill thoroughly before serving. This is
sensationally good fare.

Funeral Pie (Raisin Pie)

So called in New Jersey, in the old days, because it appeared often at the imposing collations provided by neighbors at the time of a funeral, and the ingredients were at hand throughout the year. Don't let the name turn you off. Some of the best food in the world has been served after funerals, causing the mourners to cheer up and want to go on living.

– – – – – – – – – – – – – – – –

a baked pie shell (page 267)

1 cup raisins (seeded or seedless)
1 cup water
½ cup sugar
} brought to a boil

2 Tablespoons butter heated in pan large enough to hold all ingredients
3 tablespoons flour, well stirred into butter
} Pour hot raisin mixture into this slowly, stirring constantly. Cook until thick.

2 egg yolks, beaten
1 teaspoon grated lemon rind
3 tablespoons lemon juice
} Mixed and then stirred into above after it is removed from stove. Cool thoroughly and pour into baked pie shell.

Cover with meringue (page 274). Bake in preheated 325° oven for 10 to 15 minutes.

Graham Cracker Lemon Pie
(Dave's Favorite)

Crust

20 square graham crackers crushed to crumbs. (I use large mortar and pestle for this. Lacking this equipment, use a rolling pin.)

¼ cup butter (½ stick), melted

¼ cup Sugar

Mix well. Press into pie plate.

Filling

2 egg yolks, well beaten

1 can Condensed Milk (the thick, sweet kind.)

grated rind of one lemon

½ cup lemon juice

Mix well. Pour into graham cracker pie crust.

Does not make a lot, so I added peach slices.

Meringue

See directions under Mrs. Crane's pie — ← *Very good*
(page 274).
Top the pie with meringue. Bake in preheated 325° oven until meringue is lightly browned. (10 to 15 minutes). Chill and serve.

This pie is always made in our family for any special homecoming.

Mrs. Georgina Crane's Maple Syrup Pie

1 cup maple syrup
1 cup milk
2 tablespoons butter
} Heat slowly, stirring constantly, to prevent curdling. Keep below boiling point.

2 egg yolks
1 tablespoon water
} beaten together

2 tablespoons corn starch
⅛ teaspoon salt
1 teaspoon vanilla
pepper, just a dash (yes, pepper!)

} Mix together thoroughly. Add a little hot milk mixture to this, then return this to pan containing the remaining milk-syrup mixture. Cook, stirring constantly, until just thickened, no more. Pour this filling, while still hot (this is most unusual, but Mrs. Crane knows whereof she speaks) into a

baked pie shell (page 267) Before baking the pie shell, Mrs. Crane brushes it with milk. She says it makes a browner crust, more impervious to hot filling. Now cover the pie with

Meringue ← Very good

Beat the 3 remaining egg whites until stiff, gradually adding, while beating, 4 tablespoons sugar, ⅛ teaspoon cream of tartar, dash of salt. The more you beat in the sugar, the less the meringue will weep. Place pie in preheated 325° oven and bake until meringue takes on a pleasing tan. Cool on rack. A traditional and elegant Vermont favorite.

Mrs. Crane is famous for her cooking prowess in this area. Whenever her baked goods are brought to church supper or bake sale, they are the first to be snapped up. She has been

Turning out good food since girlhood, learning at the knee of her Scottish mother how to do things right, and with a flair.

Mrs. Crane used to teach school at the little one-room red schoolhouse on Badger's Brook in North Danville, boarding at the Paquin farm on weekdays, and walking to and from her home at Danville Green every weekend. It was five and one-half miles each way. She received the sum of six dollars per week for her labors. "And," she says, "I managed to save money out of each week's pay!"

The schoolhouse (still standing) where Mrs. Crane taught.

Left-over pie dough that you hate to throw away? Roll it out, and sprinkle with grated cheese, or cinnamon and sugar, and cut into fingers, and bake quickly. Or cut into squares, place a dab of jam thereon, fold over, pinch together, and you have some small tarts ready for baking. Children coming in from school are appreciative of such snacks.

Favorite Rhubarb Pie

2 cups rhubarb, cut into small pieces

2/3 cup sugar
2 tablespoons flour
2 egg yolks
2 teaspoons water
salt, just a shake

Mix this together vigorously. Then add the rhubarb and stir until well coated. Turn into unbaked pie shell (page 267). Put into preheated 400° oven for 20 minutes. Reduce heat to 350° and bake exactly 20 minutes more. Cool on a rack. Serve this pie with maple syrup! This is an old New Jersey tradition worth perpetuating. Don't be skeptical. Try it and LIVE.

Cherry Pie

Make the cherry pie in exactly the same way as the rhubarb pie above, using two cups of sour red cherries, canned or fresh. If you use canned cherries, be sure to use those packed in clear, unsweetened juice, and drain them. Never buy the kind that comes in a sea of paste, supposedly ready for the pie shell. Also, use a judicious few drops of almond extract in the egg mixture. This enhances the cherry flavor. Skip the anointing with maple syrup, which is suitable for rhubarb pie only. A bride's qualifications were questioned in song by the old refrain, "Can she bake a cherry pie, Willy-boy?" With this recipe — she can.

Emma Lou's Strawberry Pie
(The most!)

1 baked pie shell, cooled (page 267)

1 eight-ounce package cream cheese, softened
½ cup sugar
1 teaspoon grated lemon rind
2 tablespoons lemon juice
2 tablespoons milk
} Cream together thoroughly and spread on bottom of pie shell.

1 quart fresh strawberries, washed, hulled, dried, and placed, stem side down, on the cream cheese mixture.

2 ten-ounce packages frozen strawberries, thawed and mashed in saucepan.

½ cup sugar
3 tablespoons cornstarch
} Mix, and stir into above mashed berries. Bring to a boil, stirring constantly. Cook until thick and clear. Cool. Pour over fresh berries in pie shell.

1 cup heavy cream, whipped
1 tablespoon sugar
1 teaspoon vanilla
} Stir into whipped cream. Garnish top of pie with this. Refrigerate until serving time.

Admiral Perkins' Pie (Thanks to Renee Nash)
For the height of the strawberry season.

<u>1 baked pie shell</u> (page 267)
<u>fresh strawberries</u>, washed, hulled, <u>dried</u>, arranged carefully in pie shell in
    one snug layer.
<u>1 jar of red currant jelly</u> (about 10 ounces) — Beat it with a spoon until easy to
    spread. Lather the berries with it. Put pie to rest in refrigerator
    <u>all day</u>.
<u>½ pint heavy cream</u>, whipped (not seasoned), and spread on pie
    just at serving time.

Nothing could be simpler — or better.

Because our son was born on Christmas day, a birthday party always took place at the half year, June 25th. We had a wisteria vine that crawled all over the back of the house, and on this, one year, I had the bright idea of tying bunches of bananas. At a given signal, the kids were allowed to swarm all over the vine, pick the fruit, skin it, pick up a 10¢ store banana-split dish, and proceed to a long outdoor table on which were spread three kinds of ice cream, every sort of gooey sauce imaginable, nuts, whipped cream, cherries. Happier, messier children you never saw, stuffing themselves to their hearts' content. This became an annual custom, because nothing could be dreamed up to exceed the delight this orgy induced. Don't ever try it indoors, unless you are indifferent to rugs, walls, and furniture awash with sticky syrup.

Old Fashioned Strawberry Shortcake (Serves 8)

2 cups flour
3 teaspoons baking powder
½ teaspoon salt
1 heaping Tablespoon sugar
} Mix together well, in bowl of sufficient size to hold whole recipe.

⅓ cup corn oil
¾ cup milk, scant
} Combine oil and milk and pour over above dry ingredients. Mix only enough to moisten, just a few quick strokes. Too thorough mixing produces tough shortcake. (Miriam Lusk recommends a beaten egg added to wet ingredients, and Mary Morris says that a little grated nutmeg added to dry ingredients is a Nova Scotia trick, and makes the best shortcake ever. I'm inclined to agree with both suggestions, but give them as optional.) Now, turn the dough out onto a well-buttered cookie sheet, and, with buttered hands, coax the dough into the shape of your serving platter, or spoon out as separate biscuits, whichever you desire. Bake in preheated 450° oven for 10 to 12 minutes. When shortcake is cool enough to handle, split in half and butter generously. Shortcake should be a tiny bit warm when served, and only combined with berries at last minute. Shortcake may be made ahead and reheated before serving. Use 2 quarts strawberries, hulled, washed, mashed lightly, sugared to taste, and allowed to come to room temperature. This is important. Ice cold berries are not as flavorful. Reserve a few of the handsomest berries for garnish, leaving stems on.

Whip ½ pint heavy cream. Sweeten with 1 tablespoon sugar and ½ teaspoon vanilla. Refrigerate until ready to use.

Spread the mashed berries between and on top of shortcake layers. Now plop great mounds of whipped cream over all, and garnish cream with reserved whole berries. This is summer's dreamiest dessert! Serve only the lightest meal before the shortcake, so that appetites are still keen. (Just soup and shortcake makes a fine meal.)

I often cheat and use frozen berries, being sure they come to room temperature for the sun-ripened taste, and butter the platter on which the warm shortcake is placed, and use a blue platter for color interest, and combine at the last second, to achieve a crunchy rather than a soggy dessert.

Make Raspberry Shortcake and Peach Shortcake in exactly the same manner as above.

The Fire Chief in St. Johnsbury, Vermont, one Hubert Simons, is a friend of mine. His birthday falls right in the midst of the wild strawberry season. His most cherished childhood memory is of his mother making him a wild strawberry shortcake, complete with candles, every year. It takes a whole day to pick two quarts of wild berries. This birthday shortcake dripped as generously with strawberries as is recommended in the above recipe. Talk about your love feasts! Lucky Hubert.

Vanilla Ice Cream (2 quarts +)

1 recipe chilled Boiled Custard (page 257)
1 quart medium cream
2 Tablespoons vanilla (in addition to that in custard)
½ cup sugar – – – "   "   "   "   "
Mix and churn.

———————————

My father, who made glorious vanilla ice cream every Sunday for 60 years, when taste-testing before churning, always called for "more vanilla, more vanilla!" I believe the total of 3 tablespoons would match his liberal hand. As children, waiting to lick the dasher, we would suggest variations of this recipe by the addition of peaches or strawberries or chocolate. Papa, as we called him, looked both grieved and incredulous. "Put anything on the ice cream you want to, but we are not going to mar perfection by putting any foreign substances in it."

———————————

Save orange rinds from the morning juice. Fill them with orange sherbet. Keep frozen until ½ hour before serving time. They need to thaw somewhat.   Likewise with lemon or lime rinds. Fill with their matching sherbets. These need bases cut off a bit, and to be placed in small punch cups for serving. Easy, light, festive, colorful desserts.

———————————

Pour green crème de menthe into champagne glasses, so as to fill stems and a little more. Put a scoop of vanilla ice cream in each green puddle.

———————————

Milk Sherbet

juice of 3 lemons
1½ cups sugar } Mix together in ice cream freezer can.

I quart cold milk, poured slowly into lemon-sugar mixture, while stirring constantly. (It is necessary to add milk slowly or sherbet will have curdled appearance. This does not affect its quality, just the way it looks.) Churn in ice cream freezer, and serve.

We made gallons of this when the children were little, and ice was kept in sawdust under the barn, ready for sherbet-making on a hot summer day. The children furnished the muscle power in turning the crank, as well as the appetites to eat up every drop of this refreshing treat. If you want to keep a bunch of kids busy and happy all afternoon ——— try this.

Ever tried putting chopped crystallized ginger in whipped cream, for the topping of pumpkin or squash pie?

Apple Torte (Serves 4 to 6)

1 egg
3/4 cup sugar } beaten together

1/3 cup flour
1/4 teaspoon salt
1 1/2 teaspoons baking powder
1 teaspoon vanilla
1/2 cup chopped nuts
1 cup chopped apples } added to above in order given, stirring well with spoon.

Turn into buttered pie plate. Bake 30 minutes in preheated 325° oven. Cool on rack. Serve with a side dish of whipped cream or vanilla ice cream. Pecans or almonds or walnuts are equally good. Take your choice. If expense is no object, and the delicacy available, use macadamia nuts. Sensational. This is one of the easiest and best of recipes, whatever nut is used.

———

Trying to track down the difference between a "torte" and a "tart" is a bit like chasing moonbeams. Both words seem to come from the Latin "tortus" which means "making round." In modern usage and generally speaking, a tart is an open pastry shell holding various fillings, whereas a torte refers to a large family of round, flat, sweet, cake-like desserts containing eggs, nuts, fruit, and is usually fat free.

Blueberry Toast (Serves 4)

3 slices of bread, trimmed of crusts, cut in half, and 3 of the halves placed in a buttered baking dish.

1 egg, well beaten
¾ cup milk
½ teaspoon vanilla
Salt, a slight sprinkle
} Mix and pour over bread, and allow to soak for a good 10 minutes.

2 cups blueberries
⅓ cup sugar
2 tablespoons water
} Simmer 5 minutes. Then pour over soaked bread. Paint remaining 3 bread slices with a little butter and top the dish with these. Place in preheated 350° oven and bake until delicately browned. (Around ½ hour.) Dust with:

confectioners' sugar, generously
cinnamon, sparingly — Serve hot with a pitcher of cream.

Crows' Nests
(An old-Time Vermont favorite)

This dessert was made often by the grandmother of Mary Bisson and acquired its name because it is untidy looking, as is a crow's nest.

shortcake dough (page 279)
butter
brown sugar
pie apples
maple syrup

Pat or roll out one recipe for shortcake on a floured board. Spread with soft butter, brown sugar, and thinly sliced apples that have been peeled and carefully cored. (Amounts according to your taste.) Roll up as for jelly roll. Slice and place each slice on well-buttered cookie sheet. Bake in preheated 450° oven for exactly 12 minutes. Serve warm with maple syrup. A recipe to crow about.

Baked Bananas, Texas Style

Have one banana per person.
Slit the skin on inner curve of banana,
pry open a bit — enough to dot the fruit
with butter, brown sugar, and a dash of
cinnamon and dark rum. Make foil
cradles to hold bananas and prevent
them from tipping over. Bake for
exactly 20 minutes in preheated 400° oven.
Add another dash of rum, when cooked, if
you feel so inclined. Serve hot.

Danville, Vermont, happens to be the
headquarters of The American Dowsers' Society.
At our annual convention I met a Mr. Wood
from Texas, who not only talked dowsing,
but cooking. He said, "I've collected over
one thousand cookbooks." When I asked
if he had a favorite recipe, he immediately
came up with the simple dessert above.

Bing Cherry Jelly (Serves 6)

1 large can Bing cherries, drained, juice reserved. (These cherries are the dark, luscious, sweet variety.)

2 cups of juice from cherries (Increase by addition of water, if necessary.)

1 box Cherry Jell-O~ Dissolve Jell-O with the cherry juice, as directed on Jell-O box. Cool until syrupy. Then add cherries and

almond extract ~ Just a drop does the trick, enhancing cherry flavor, provided it is not overdone.

Place the mixture in a mold, glass bowl, or stemmed dessert glasses. Serve with whipped cream. A great Washington's Birthday special.

This jelly makes a good salad, served with cottage cheese.

～～～～～～～～

For one of the easiest and best desserts ever:

Mix seedless grapes (well washed and dried), with sour cream. Place in your best glass bowl and chill. Just before serving, sprinkle liberally with brown sugar. (If you put sugar on too far ahead, it gets runny and unattractive looking.)

～～～～～～～～

Date Jelly (Serves 6)

1 package pitted dates (8 ounces) } simmered a few
1 cup water   } minutes until dates
                                     are softened.

½ cup sugar, added to above and simmered
        for an additional 5 minutes.

1 envelope plain gelatin (1 tablespoon) } soaked together a
¼ cup cold water   } few minutes and then
                                          stirred into hot date
                                          mixture until well dissolved.

juice of 1 lemon, added last, to all of above.

Cool the mixture sufficiently to put in blender. (Never put too much of anything too hot into a blender. It sort of explodes.) When thoroughly pureed, pour into individual punch cups, stemmed glasses, or your best glass bowl, and chill until set.   Serve with whipped cream slightly seasoned with sugar and vanilla.

A dainty dessert to the eye, but sufficiently energizing to keep a camel driver going all day.

"Peel Me A Grape" (Serves 6)

2 cups freshly squeezed orange juice
1 tablespoon (1 package) plain gelatin
2 cups Tokay grapes that have been peeled, halved, seeded
Sugar, to taste
orange extract, a few drops

Soak the gelatin in ¼ cup of the orange juice for a few minutes. Bring remaining juice just to a boil, pour over the gelatin and stir until thoroughly dissolved, and stir in the grapes, sugar, and extract. Spoon into best stemmed dessert glasses. Chill. Serve with topping of cream cheese thoroughly mixed with honey, and of consistency to hold its shape. Fresher and fairer than springtime. A dessert for extra special guests, or to bear as an offering to a sick friend.

Grape and Orange Fruit Cup

Peel and seed grapes and prepare an equal amount of fresh orange sections (all pulp removed), combine, and sweeten to taste. That's all. A lot of goodness, a lot of work. (In the days of tail-gate parties at football games, shared with dear friends, this was often my contribution. We all tried to outdo each other with tempting delights.)

Mae West's famous line, "Beulah, peel me a grape," that drew so many laughs years ago, has placed the peeled grape in a class by itself. It is a delicious delicacy, well worth the trouble of preparation. Instead of knitting in front of T.V.—try peeling grapes. The skins peel off easily with the aid of a vegetable knife. And, once the grapes are split, the seeds are quickly removed with one flick of the thumbnail.

Steamed Rhubarb (Serves 8)

1 quart rhubarb that has been cut into small pieces. Place in double boiler. Cover, and allow to steam over boiling water for exactly ½ hour. No peeking.

¾ cup sugar
¼ teaspoon soda
½ cup water
} Mix together and pour over the cooked rhubarb. Do not stir! Clamp the lid back on quickly. Cook for 2 minutes more. That's all. Sauce is ready to serve, hot or cold. Excellent as dessert, or accompaniment to meat.

Once tried, you will never make rhubarb sauce any other way. (Rhubarb leaves are poisonous, so keep them away from small toddlers who are at the bent-on-suicide-eat-anything stage. Children will eat things that animals know enough to shun. Strange that the stalks of this plant should be so healthful and harmless, when the leaves are not. One of those paradoxes of nature.)

Danish Dessert

Stir 1 tablespoon cornstarch into 1 thawed 10-ounce package of frozen strawberries. Bring to a boil, stirring constantly until thick and clear. Combine this with Steamed Rhubarb (above). Chill. Serve with cream. As delightful as it is Danish.

Feather-Light Orange Cake (Serves 12)
(Must be made a day ahead)

2 packages Orange Jell-O, emptied into large bowl
1 cup boiling water, poured over Jell-O and stirred until thoroughly dissolved
grated rind of 1 orange ⎫
2 cups orange juice ⎬ Add to above and chill until syrupy, but
1 cup sugar ⎭ not jelled.

1 cup   + 1 cup plain yogurt
2 cups cream, whipped, and folded into Jell-O mixture when it is syrupy.
1 ½ a large, stale angel food cake (or 1 small cake, if obtainable)

    Tear the cake into tiny pieces and fold into above mixture.
    Put into slightly oiled ring mold, sponge cake tube pan, or
    melon mold. Refrigerate 24 hours. When ready to unmold,
    place container in hot water for a second. Garnish with.....
Mandarin orange sections that have been well drained.

    For speed and efficiency, this dessert may be made and
    remain in a pretty glass bowl. No unmolding necessary,
    though it loses its cake-like appearance. Also, I cannot
    tell a lie, I use store-bought angel cake. Be sure angel
    cake is at least a day old.

9-9-93   Made for sister Helen's arrival.
       9 X 11 pan - cut in squares — I did
                   not like.

Raw eggs!

Amundsen's Dessert

(Enough for 20 normal people, or 10 pigs. It turns most people into the latter.)

<u>1 package lady fingers</u>, plain, <u>not</u> filled, containing 18 double fingers.
Or substitute little fingers of stale sponge cake.
Line a 9"x13" shallow pan with the fingers.

<u>½ pound (2 sticks) soft butter</u>
<u>1 pound confectioners' sugar</u> (1 whole box) } Cream together in electric beater bowl.

<u>4 eggs</u>, separated, adding egg yolks, one at a time, to creamed butter and sugar, above, and beating in thoroughly.
Beat egg whites until stiff, and reserve.

<u>2 teaspoons vanilla</u>, beaten into butter-sugar mixture. Now fold in the stiffly beaten egg whites, and spread the mixture evenly on the lady fingers.

<u>1 can crushed pineapple</u>*, medium size, well drained, spread over the above. Top with......

<u>½ pint heavy cream</u>, whipped. Cover snugly with foil. Refrigerate at least 24 hours. Cut into small squares. A triumph. Rich, yes, but only dainty servings needed. Excellent for a large group because all work is completed a day ahead.

I call this Amundsen's Dessert because Gladys Elviken (who gave me the recipe) recalls that her mother served this to their friend, Roald Amundsen, the great Norwegian explorer, on his last visit to their home in Madison, Wisconsin, just before his fatal trip in 1928.

* about 20 ounces

Carol's Marcia's Lemon Bisque (Serves 8)

3 egg yolks ⎫ Beat well together in a saucepan.
5 tablespoons lemon juice ⎬ Place on heat and stir constantly while
½ cup sugar ⎭ bringing just to a boil, no more. Cool.

3 egg whites, beaten until stiff ⎫ Fold together carefully. Then fold
1 cup cream " " " ⎬ into above cooled sauce. Pour
into a 9 inch pie plate.

½ box vanilla wafers (about 40 wafers) crushed fine, and
sprinkled over top of above fluff.

Freeze for 3 or 4 hours. Remove from freezer ½ hour before serving. A delightfully refreshing dessert!

This may also be prepared in an 8 × 8 inch pan, and cut in squares, but I like it best served as a pie. It may also be prepared days in advance of serving, but wrap it well after it has frozen.

〰〰〰〰〰〰〰〰〰〰〰〰〰

Going on a picnic? Take along some oranges, some sugar lumps, and a paring knife. When dessert time arrives, cut a little round hole in the top of each orange and plunge the knife around carefully within the fruit to release juices but not break the skin. Press a sugar cube into each opening, and pass the oranges around. Children love to squeeze the sweetened juice into their mouths, and not just the children. Neither does it have to be a picnic.

〰〰〰〰〰〰〰〰〰〰〰〰〰

Chocolate Mousse (Serves 6)

½ cup semi-sweet chocolate chips, melted over boiling water
3 egg yolks, beaten until light in color, and then stirred into the melted
chocolate immediately after removing chocolate from heat
1 teaspoon vanilla, stirred into above
3 egg whites, beaten until stiff and folded into above

Spoon this mixture into pots de creme, demi-tasse or cocoa cups, or sherbet, or even cocktail glasses. Chill several hours. Serve with a dollop of whipped cream.

This is exactly like a status recipe from a famous French cookbook (first published in 1806, and which went into 32 editions), except that there were no chocolate chips (or morsels) in those days. They just used chocolate and sugar. This is a dreamy and sophisticated dessert that takes but a few minutes to prepare. The ingredients may appear not sweet enough. They are. How does it solidify without cooking? I don't know, but it does.

A Chinese saying:
"Into no department of life should indifference be allowed to creep; into none less than the domain of cookery."

Preserves ~ Sauces

About Preserves and Sauces, 297, 298

<u>A Corner of Gladys Elviken's Pantry in Danville</u>, <u>Vermont</u>
— on a fall day — a place of pure magic in any season.

    "I put up some plums today, and some tomatoes too, off our own place. I wonder if they will keep? Mother put up lots of things for us this summer, jelly and jam and lots of things. They look so pretty, I think, on a table in rows with the sun shining through them."

    From a letter to her aunt and uncle, by Edna St. Vincent Millay

<u>About Preserves ~ Sauces</u>

Along with a heaping woodbox that was once the symbol of preparedness and bounty, has gone the preserve closet with its rainbow of colors and its promise of good eating throughout a long winter. Well, almost gone. There are a few who still adhere to the thrifty practice of preserving some of summer's bounty, and the new generation seems to have a nostalgia for the old ways. Then, too, there are the modern techniques with a deep freeze.

A number of my favorite preserves follow. But I am prone to make the relish type of thing on the spot, and have it eaten up in its fresh state, rather than heaping the larder with long-lasting foods. (See pages 148 through 156, as well as certain meat accompaniments in this section of the book.)

There are few jelly recipes, for they appear on every container of pectin, and, followed to the letter, give perfect results. Wild jellies are especially rewarding to make, and mostly unobtainable commercially. I always try to make chokecherry jelly because the country roadsides are heavy with that fruit, and it goes so well with game. Wild grapes, raspberries, blackberries, plums, rose hips, are also plentiful in this area and make unique jellies for gift-giving. They also inspire non-controversial conversation at one's own table (except that the jellies <u>are</u> different shades of RED).

If you are interested in herb jellies, see my book <u>Let Herbs Do It</u> (Houghton Mifflin Company) for directions. It also gives instructions for herb-teas, herb-recipes, and lore not contained in this book.

Washing preserving jars and jelly glasses in a mechanical dishwasher will, as a rule, make them sufficiently sterile. The old-fashioned and tedious boiling method can usually be dispensed with.

Use enamel or stainless steel vessels when cooking preserves of any sort.

Every cook who aspires to making jelly should invest in a ten-cent-store enamelware double boiler for melting paraffin. Keep an expendable spoon in it for all time. If you use your best double boiler and a good spoon, and try to wash them, you will understand this advice. Melting in a double boiler is a very necessary safety precaution, too. Hot paraffin (heated directly on fire) can be dangerous. Store this inexpensive and handy equipment with your extra paraffin, jelly bags, canning jars, etc.

Authorities disagree as to who invented the double boiler. Bible tradition (not Scripture) says Miriam, the sister of Moses, thought it up. Another claim is that Italy gave the double boiler to the world through one Maria de Cleofa. The "bagno maria" went to France with Catherine de'Medici and her retinue of chefs. It became the "bain marie" of French cuisine, and one of the keys to the greatness of French cooking. Here it is called a plain old double boiler. Anyway, it has been around for a long, long while, and a supply of double boilers is imperative for any kitchen that produces good meals.

Tomato and Apple Relish (Makes about 6 pints)

2 quarts ripe tomatoes, peeled and chopped
2 cups tart apples, peeled and diced
1 cup celery, chopped
1 cup onion, chopped
2 green peppers, chopped
2 sweet red peppers, chopped
1½ cups vinegar
1 stick cinnamon
1 tablespoon salt
2 tablespoons mustard seed
½ tablespoon whole cloves
2¾ cups sugar

Combine all ingredients in a large kettle. Simmer slowly, uncovered, until mixture is thick and clear. This takes about an hour. Fish out the cinnamon stick. Seal in clean, hot, pint jars — the relish — not the cinnamon! The fragrance that permeates your kitchen at this point, is nearly mind-blowing.

This relish is a must for your preserve closet. I always use it with a baked bean dinner, and it turns a hamburger into a gourmet meal.

Pocono Pickles (10 quart jars)

Slice young cucumbers very thin (skins left on), until you have

6 quarts of cut-up cucumbers

6 onions, sliced thin and separated into rings

1 cup salt

Combine and let stand 3 hours. Then drain off all juices and put cucumbers and onions in large kettle.

6 cups vinegar

6 cups sugar

½ cup mustard seed

1 tablespoon celery seed

Mix this together and pour over cucumbers. Bring just to a boil, no more! Pack in clean, airtight quart jars.

To be preserved in quantity and eaten in quantity; not a garnish, but a crunchy sort of salad-vegetable that will enhance any meal, especially a fresh trout dinner (page 108). Serve a full sauce dish per person.

A Pocono native said, "We mountain folk are brought up on these. I'm surprised they aren't eaten in other places." So am I.

Blender Orange Marmalade (about 12 jelly glasses)

Scrub* 1 lemon and enough oranges to make
2 quarts of coarsely cut-up fruit, from which all seeds have
been removed. Use very best grade oranges — of
Seville type, if possible.
2 quarts of water, added to fruit and blended in blender ever so
briefly. You do not want a mush, you want small pieces
of rind throughout. Unless you have a huge blender, this
must be done in several separate loads. Pour into an
enamel kettle. Cover. Let stand overnight, or 24 hours. Then
bring to a boil, slowly, and simmer, covered, for 2½ hours.
Then stir in......
8 cups sugar ~ Boil, uncovered, this time. Stir often, being
careful not to scorch as mixture thickens. When the
marmalade jellies slightly (as it cools on the stirring
spoon), it is done. This takes about 2½ hours.
Pour into sterile jars and cover with paraffin.

    This product is an enormous improvement over
"boughten" marmalade. Great for gifts, provided family
forays on your stock are not too frequent. So much
easier to make by the blender method than the old-
fashioned cutting by hand, with precious juices
escaping everywhere.

~~~~~~~~~~~~~~~~~~~~~~~~~~~~~~~

* Citrus fruits are often coated with rather lethal chemicals, to prevent spoilage.

Grammy Root's Rhubarb Jam
(about 10 glasses)

5 cups rhubarb, cut small ⎫ Stir together and let boil
5 cups sugar ⎬ for 20 minutes. Bring to
boil slowly, to draw juices.

2 packages Strawberry Jell-O, stirred into cooked
rhubarb until completely dissolved.

1 cup crushed canned pineapple (1 small can), added fast,
and thoroughly stirred in.

Put in sterile glasses or jars and top with
hot paraffin. Store in cool place. Keeps indefinitely.
Delicious on toast, in sandwiches, as topping for ice cream,
or filling for cake. The easiest jam you'll ever make.

I hope you have a patch of (or can buy) real
strawberry rhubarb, the stalks a beautiful pinkish red, and
so superior to common green rhubarb.

~~~~~~~~~~~~~~~~~~~~~~~~~~~~

Frozen Tomatoes
If you have an over-supply of red, garden-fresh
tomatoes, simply scald them just enough for easy peeling, slip off
the skins, and pack the whole tomatoes carefully into quart jars. Cover the
jars and place in deep freeze. Lovely, when thawed, for winter use.

~~~~~~~~~~~~~~~~~~~~~~~~~~~~

Strawberry Jam

1 one-pound box of frozen, cut up, sweetened strawberries
1 cup Sugar

Put the above together in a saucepan, having let the strawberries thaw somewhat. Bring to a boil, and when thoroughly mixed, thawed, and bubbling, allow to simmer for 5 to 7 minutes, no more. Remove from heat, pour into a jar. When cool, place cover on jar, and keep refrigerated until used up, which won't take long. Oh so good with breakfast toast or muffins, or drizzled over ice cream.

This makes a rather runny, totally elegant, bright red jam. I make only one batch at a time, so it is always fresh and colorful, which can't be said of some long-stored jams. No paraffin to bother with. Of all the commercially frozen fruits and vegetables, I think that strawberries lend themselves best to freezing. Unless you have a strawberry patch of your own, and can pick the fruit at the peak of ripeness, frozen berries seem to be the next best thing.

It's fun to make the house redolent of a wild strawberry patch in a summer hayfield — on a February day, for instance. That's what it will be if you boil up this jam. And what a cinch.

Moose Missy Jelly

Moose Missy is the name sometimes used for mountain ash in this area. I was surprised to learn that jelly can be made from the spectacular orange berries this tree produces. Louisa Paulsen, a neighbor, gave me this recipe, which came to her by way of Austria. It is one recipe in this book I have not tested, and, as it is winter as I write this, will not have an opportunity to do so before publication. But it is worth anyone's try, so here goes:

2 pounds mountain ash berries — Soak the berries overnight in water to which ¼ cup vinegar has been added. Pour off this water in the morning. Then add sufficient fresh water to cover berries. Bring to boil. Boil 3 minutes. Pour off this water also.

2 pounds tart apples — Wash, cut in quarters, leaving skins on, cores in.

1 quart water — Add water and apples to berries. Boil until fruits are tender. Transfer to a jelly bag to drip for several hours or overnight. Then squeeze out all juices possible.

2 pounds sugar — Add to berry juice and stir together in a large kettle. Boil until jell stage* is reached.

1 vanilla bean or 1 teaspoon pure vanilla extract — If bean is used, put it into the kettle for duration of cooking, fishing it out at the last. If vanilla extract is used, add it toward end of cooking process. Skim froth off jelly. Pour into jelly glasses. Cover with paraffin.

* "Until jell stage is reached" is fraught with pitfalls. (Read Meg's experiences in "Little Women.") When the hot liquid "sheets" as it is poured from a spoon is one test. Another is to drop a little of the hot brew onto a cold plate. If it jells, it is done. This is the time-honored way of making jelly, the apples supplying the pectin. Real buffs refuse to make jelly any other way. It should work, and if it does, you will feel like the smartest cook on earth, your ego soaring to unaccustomed heights. Good luck.

Mummie Hansen's Cranberry Sauce (Serves 8)
(A Nova Scotian Recipe)

1 quart cranberries, well washed
1 pint sugar (2 cups)
1 cup water

Place in saucepan. Bring to a boil. Cover. Simmer 13 minutes without stirring.

New England Cranberry Jelly (Serves 8)

1 quart of cranberries (washed)
2 cups boiling water

Boil for 20 minutes, uncovered. Rub through a strainer. (Or cool and blend in blender.)
Then cook for 3 minutes and add . . . .

2 cups sugar
dash of salt

Cook for 2 more minutes and pour in a mold that has been slightly coated with corn oil. Chill. Unmold.

No holiday feast is complete at our house without cranberry sauce at one end of the table and cranberry jelly at the other, to satisfy two violently opposed preferences. Perhaps we should settle for the following delightful relish and be done with it.

Cranberry Relish (Serves 8)

1 pint cranberries (washed)
1 orange (scrubbed), cut into a few pieces and seeds discarded

Put through food grinder, using medium blade.

1 cup sugar, thoroughly stirred into above. Goodness increases by being made a day ahead of use.

Betty Lilly's Baked Pineapple (Serves 8)
(To be served with meat course)

<u>5 slices of bread, cubed, and soaked in</u>
<u>1 (number 2) can* crushed pineapple</u> (sweetened or unsweetened according to your taste)

<u>½ cup (1 stick) soft butter</u> ⎫ creamed together in
<u>¾ cup sugar</u> ⎭ beater bowl

<u>3 eggs</u> ⎫ added to butter and sugar and
<u>dash of salt</u> ⎭ beaten until light. Then
stir in, by hand, the bread-
pineapple mixture.

Place this mixture (which will look curdled),
in buttered soufflé dish. Hold for later baking, or
bake at once in preheated <u>325° oven for 50 minutes.</u>

It becomes slightly browned on top, a bit puffy,
and is a triumph of goodness. Excellent with
ham, especially a boiled ham dinner (page 100).
(Relax, the curdled look disappears in baking.)

〰〰〰〰〰〰〰〰〰〰

* (2½ cups, or about 20 ounces)

Ginger Fruit (Serves 8)
(To serve with meat)

1 can pear halves (1 pound 14 ounce size), syrup and all
1 can apricot halves "   "   "   ", drained
4 tablespoons chopped crystallized ginger
4 thin slices of lemon, cut in quarters

     Arrange fruit and pear juice attractively in baking dish. Sprinkle ginger over all. Tuck in lemon slices. Bake in preheated 325° oven, uncovered for ½ hour or more. Serve hot or cold. A fine accompaniment to any meat, and especially good with ham or chicken.

Quick Vegetable Relish (Serves 6)

1 cucumber, peeled
1 green pepper, seeded
celery, several stalks, scraped of strings   } cut up fine
1 large can tomatoes, drained

Season with salt, pepper, paprika, sugar, and vinegar — to taste.

     This seems ever so garden-fresh in mid-winter. Especially good with roast beef. Fills the bill for salad and/or vegetable. Serve in glass bowl.

Old Vermont Beet Relish
(As served by Yvonne Bedard)

4 cups finely chopped cabbage (medium blade of food grinder)
Either white or red cabbage may be used.
4 cups finely chopped beets (medium blade of food grinder)
Use either canned or home-boiled beets.
½ of a 5-ounce bottle of prepared horseradish
1 teaspoon salt
1½ cups cider vinegar
1 cup sugar
freshly ground pepper, to taste

Mix all of above ingredients together and store in covered glass jar in refrigerator. It will keep indefinitely. This is a superb dish. Yvonne says it is especially good with roast beef. True! Thank you, Yvonne. (She found the recipe in The Green Mountaineer Cook Book.)

"A fine sauce will make
even an elephant palatable."
grimod de la Reynière

Herb Butter

1 pound soft butter, beaten in small beater bowl until fluffy.
4 chicken bouillon cubes, crumbled
      or 4 teaspoons chicken broth powder
      or 4 packages chicken broth mix
¼ teaspoon dried savory leaves
"   "   "   basil   "
"   "   "   tarragon   "
"   "   "   marjoram   "
    2 teaspoons onion salt
    2 teaspoons garlic salt
    ½ teaspoon freshly ground pepper

½ cup lemon juice

Mix together thoroughly and beat into the butter until well blended. While still beating, add the lemon juice very slowly. Turn into an 8-inch square pan, spreading evenly. Freeze an hour or so, until firm enough to cut into small squares. Then place pan in a plastic bag and keep in freezer, ready for enlivening vegetables and meat. A few of the herb butter squares, softened, and spread on thin slices of bread, and baked until golden, make an excellent cocktail snack, or accompaniment to soup.

If you are lucky enough to have fresh herbs, chop them fine and use 1 tablespoon of each.

This butter melted over a plain old canned vegetable transforms it, likewise a hamburger. I am never without it in the freezer. When you need the 8-inch square pan, just transfer butter squares to a plastic bag. They do not stick together, once thoroughly frozen.

Fool around with other herb combinations when your garden burgeons.

Basic White Sauce
(the easiest and most digestible way)

1 cup milk
2 tablespoons flour
salt and pepper, to taste
— Place in a blender, in order given. Blend. Pour into top part of a double boiler. Place directly on burner and stir constantly until thickened.

1 or 2 tablespoons butter — Add to sauce as you heat and stir. When sauce is cooked, place over hot water, to hold.

The basics are above, the variations numerous. Light cream may be substituted for milk if you desire richness. A beaten egg yolk may be stirred in at the last minute before serving, for further enrichment.

For anyone on a low fat diet, substitute a chicken bouillon cube for the butter and salt.

For low salt diets, substitute herbs for salt. Use only a pinch of dried herbs, be more generous if herbs are fresh.
dill for fish, eggs, potatoes
rosemary or tarragon for chicken
basil with cheese or tomatoes
Thyme with Tuna fish, onions, almost any creamed vegetable
sage with Turkey
celery seed or savory may be used to make any food more savoury.

Egg Sauce

<u>2 cups milk</u>, measured in metal quart measure

<u>2 medium onions</u> ⎫
<u>½ bay leaf</u> ⎬ added to above and brought
<u>1 whole clove</u> ⎭ just to a boil, no more

<u>4 Tablespoons butter</u>, melted in large enough pan to hold all ingredients

<u>4 Tablespoons flour</u>, mixed into above butter, to make a roux. Pour hot milk mixture slowly into roux, stirring over heat until smooth and thick.

<u>salt</u> ⎫
<u>pepper</u> ⎬ To Taste, added to above. Then strain the sauce, discarding onion, bay leaf, clove.

<u>2 hard-boiled eggs</u>, chopped, and added to sauce

    This is the sauce that must always be served with poached salmon on the Fourth of July — plus garden peas and new boiled potatoes. Lacking fresh-killed salmon, have Steamed Salmon Loaf (page 111).

    This sauce makes a fine breakfast dish, served on toast and garnished with bacon.

Hollandaise Sauce (Serves 4)

<u>3 egg yolks</u> - - - - - - - - - - - } Put in top of double
<u>1/4 pound butter</u>, cut in pieces } boiler. Stir continuously over boiling water, until butter melts, no more.

<u>juice of 1/2 lemon</u>, added to above the minute the butter has melted. Stir until hot and <u>slightly</u> <u>thickened</u> and, again, NO MORE.
That's it.

Serve at once, or store in glass jar in refrigerator, and reheat by placing jar in hot water, and stirring sauce constantly until warm enough to serve.

This sauce turns any vegetable into a food for kings. Especially good on broccoli or asparagus. Transforms fish also.

≈≈≈≈≈≈≈≈≈≈≈≈≈≈

"She that is ignorant in cookery, may love and obey, but she cannot cherish and keep her husband."

17th century proverb

≈≈≈≈≈≈≈≈≈≈≈≈≈≈

Mock Hollandaise Sauce

<u>2 chicken bouillon cubes</u>, dissolved in
<u>2 cups boiling water</u>

<u>4 tablespoons butter</u>, melted in top of small double boiler over
<u>4 tablespoons flour</u>, stirred into butter until smooth. Now
boiling water
pour the bouillon slowly into the roux, stirring
constantly until thickened and lump-free.
Allow to simmer along for <u>about 10 minutes</u>.
<u>2 egg yolks</u> ‑ ‑ ‑ ‑ ‑ ‑ ‑ ‑ } beaten together in small bowl.
<u>2 tablespoons lemon juice</u> } Add to it slowly, while stirring
constantly, about ½ of the above
sauce. Then pour it all back
into double boiler, stir, and remove from heat
and from boiling water at once. Stir in
<u>another 2 tablespoons butter</u>

Your Hollandaise is ready to serve at once, or to
refrigerate and reheat over boiling water at last
minute. <u>Just</u> bring up to piping hot, but no more. Eggs
can curdle.   Excellent on asparagus or fiddleheads
in the spring of the year, or anything else that is
enhanced by Hollandaise Sauce.
        There are so many attractive double boilers
these days. Do have them in all sizes, so that you may refrigerate, heat, serve — all in the same pot. It saves
unnecessary labor.

Mushroom and Onion Sauce (Serves 4)

1 large Bermuda onion (or several regular onions) cut fairly
    small and browned very slowly in butter. Scrape and stir often.

8 or 10 large fresh mushrooms (or equivalent in small ones) well
    washed and sliced, stems and all. Add these to onions after
    onions have cooked about ½ hour. Keep on cooking for about
    another ½ hour, adding more butter. When all the water the
    mushrooms have exuded is evaporated, and all is nice and
    brown, crumble......

2 chicken bouillon cubes over the mushrooms and onions, and pour in

1 can cream of mushroom soup — Stir and scrape to get up all
    the good brown residue in the pan, and to spread the bouillon
    cubes throughout. Transfer to a double boiler, ready to heat
    and serve at meal time.

Pour this sauce over a roasted tenderloin of beef for a
royal treat (page 97). Budget bound? Then pour it over
pan-broiled hamburgers (page 83). For a thinner sauce, served
separately, add milk or cream until the consistency pleases you.

Bourbon Glaze for Ham

After the ham is well baked, cut off the skin, leaving as much fat on the ham as is possible. Score the fat in criss-cross fashion, with a sharp knife : ⧄ Play Tick-tack-toe by pushing a <u>clove</u> into each section.

<u>2 cups brown sugar</u>
<u>1 tablespoon dry mustard</u>
<u>¼ cup (about) bourbon whiskey</u>
} Mix this together well. Then, <u>with your hands</u>, press and pat it all over the scored, studded ham. It is hard to make it stick, but the cloves help. You may now put the ham into a <u>400°</u> oven for <u>close to ½ hour</u>, to glaze. Watch it. Some glaze runs into pan and is lost, but this is one of those wasteful processes that produce such deliciousness that the cost is not counted.

I go one step further in embellishment. After the sugar mixture is patted all over the ham, I take

<u>1 regular-sized can of sliced pineapple</u>*, drain, cut the slices in half, and arrange these fans with circle side <u>down</u>, wherever possible, so as to catch and hold more of the glaze, and nail them in place with a toothpick stuck through a <u>maraschino cherry</u> : ⌣ I cover the ham in this manner, and then place in <u>400°</u> oven.

Put this colorful, browned, fragrant baked ham on your best platter, surround with parsley, and serve whenever you feel like it. It will stay hot for a long while. The pineapple is removed at carving time, to be served with each helping of ham.   Or let the whole thing chill for a day. You can then bring forth the best-looking roast that ever graced a cold buffet.

―――――――

* (about 16 ounces)

Sauce for Venison

Melt ¼ pound of butter and 1 glass of red currant jelly together over a low flame. When well blended, add about ⅓ cup sherry. Serve hot. Good with wild duck, too.

———————

In the days when Asher Odenwelder presided over a really magnificent cuisine in his home on South Fourth Street in Easton, Pennsylvania, he served the best cut of venison, sliced paper-thin, seared, for seconds only, on a hot griddle, and then transferred to a platter containing the above bubbling hot sauce. Ambrosial fare.

———————

Always serve parsnips with venison. Asher did.
(See page 190)

———————

Raisin Sauce (for ham or tongue)

⅓ cup brown sugar, firmly packed
1 Tablespoon flour
½ tablespoon dry mustard
dash of salt and pepper

} Mix together in a saucepan.

1¾ cups water
¼ cup vinegar

} Stir into above dry ingredients, thoroughly. Bring to boil, stirring constantly. Then add:

½ cup seedless raisins
1 tablespoon butter

} Allow all this to simmer for 10 minutes, giving the sauce an occasional stir.

Serve hot.

———————

Rumtopf

You will need a large crock that holds about a gallon and has a firm cover. (I have one of those decorative jars that says "Rumtopf" right on it. It looks important sitting on the kitchen armoire, and is conveniently at hand.)

As summer approaches, keep on the alert for the following fresh fruits: <u>strawberries</u> (hulled), <u>cherries</u> (stoned), <u>gooseberries</u>, <u>red currants</u>, <u>red raspberries</u>, <u>plums</u> (peeled and sliced), <u>apricots</u> (peeled and sliced), <u>peaches</u> (peeled and sliced), <u>pears</u> (peeled and sliced), <u>fresh pineapple</u> (cut small). When you have fresh fruit, put a layer in the jar with an <u>equal weight of sugar</u>. Then pour on sufficient <u>dark rum</u> to submerge the fruit. That's all there is to it. Keep going, layer after layer, until the fruitful season wanes. Don't ever dip into your hoard until it has aged at least <u>6 weeks</u>. Probably your first layer of fruit will consist of strawberries. They will float in the rum for a day or so, but, with total inebriation, sink.

<u>Do not use the following fruits</u>: <u>apples</u>, <u>black currants</u>, <u>blackberries</u>, <u>bilberries</u>. Better to skip <u>blueberries</u> also.

When I first made Rumtopf I was bitterly disappointed to find that the colorful array of fruits soon turned to an uninteresting tan. However, the taste proved so superb that color was forgotten. <u>Don't forget to stir contents of crock well, before using</u>. Also, you may substitute <u>honey</u> for sugar, if you wish.

Rumtopf is my favorite to enliven Tipsy Pudding (page 234). Excellent poured over ice cream. Should you happen to be entertaining royalty, strain out the fruit and pour remaining elixir over cracked ice for a summer drink. In winter, turn the juices into a hot toddy.

Old-Fashioned Butterscotch Sauce

1¼ cups dark brown sugar ⎫ Mix in sauce pan.
⅔ cup light corn syrup   ⎬ Bring to a boil and
4 Tablespoons butter   ⎭ simmer until a soft
ball is formed when dropped in cup of cold water.

¾ cup light cream   ⎫ stirred into above when
1 teaspoon vanilla ⎬ it is cooked

Serve warm or cold over vanilla ice cream. I often serve this with a Daffy Sponge Cake Whipped Cream Roll (page 232). Toasted almonds, used as garnish, make either of these desserts almost immorally good.

The sauce keeps well in covered jar in refrigerator. Just set jar in pan of hot water to reheat. (It is really more devastating served warm.)

Chocolate Sauce (about 2 cups)

2 squares (2 ounces) unsweetened chocolate, cooked until melted, in top of double boiler.

1 can (14 ounces) sweetened condensed milk) stir into the
1/4 teaspoon salt   } melted chocolate.
2 teaspoons vanilla

boiling water, slowly stirred into above until the sauce is of consistency you desire. Using an egg beater makes for a more perfect blending. Serve warm, as is, or refrigerate for future use. 1/4 cup water is about the right amount if you serve immediately, 1/2 cup water, if you are going to refrigerate. The sauce thickens appreciably when cold.

No one needs to be told to serve chocolate sauce over vanilla ice cream. Try it sometime over orange sherbet for a refreshing change. (You know how good a chocolate-covered orange cream candy is. This is a similar taste sensation.)

Hard Sauce (for 6 or 8)

¼ pound soft butter (1 stick)
2 cups confectioners' sugar
2 tablespoons milk
1 teaspoon vanilla
nutmeg

Cream butter thoroughly while adding sugar gradually. Keep beating as you add milk and vanilla. This may all be done by hand or in electric beater bowl. When you have a nice, fluffy, well mixed product, heap it onto your prettiest plate. Sprinkle generously with nutmeg and refrigerate until ready to serve.

Children have been known to eat almost anything so long as there is Hard Sauce on it. In a less sophisticated age than this, it was often called "fairy butter."

~~~~~~~~~~

Whipped Evaporated Milk (A fine substitute for whipped cream)

1 small can (1 cup) evaporated milk ~ Pour into small beater bowl. Chill in deep freeze about 15 minutes. Beat with electric beater until it begins to thicken. Then add · · · · · · ·

2 tablespoons lemon juice ~ Beat until very thick and stiff. Sugar, to taste, and 1 teaspoon vanilla, stirred into above. Refrigerate until ready to use. It keeps nicely for several hours.

~~~~~~~~~~

Cream Cheese Topping

For a dessert topping that is especially good on fruit,
and less rich than whipped cream or hard sauce:
Mix a room-temperature package of cream cheese
with sufficient honey to produce a nice consistency.
Top with a pinch of cinnamon or nutmeg.

This is particularly pleasant on a fruit cup of
watermelon and blueberries. (Blueberries call for the pinch
of cinnamon.)

Melba Sauce

2 cups frozen raspberries, thawed (the sweetened kind)
2 teaspoons sugar
2 teaspoons cornstarch } Mix, and cook over low heat, stirring,
until clear and slightly thickened. Strain
out the lovely red juice, and keep in jar in refrigerator.*

Half a fresh or canned pear, with a scoop of vanilla ice cream,
Topped with this sauce, makes the delightful dessert known as Pear Melba.
Do the same thing with a peach half and you have Peach Melba.
(Lacking ice cream, I have substituted the Cream Cheese Topping above.)

Dame Nellie Melba, the famous Australian
soprano, took the world by storm at the turn of the century.
She must have been a lover of good food, for chefs were prone
To name their culinary inventions after her.

* Keep the juice, not the pulp!

Confectioners' Sugar Frostings

<u>Orange Frosting</u>:   Thoroughly blend a <u>tablespoon of soft butter</u> with some <u>confectioners sugar</u>, the grated <u>rind of an orange</u>, a touch of <u>orange extract</u> and real <u>orange juice</u>. Keep in mind that a little liquid goes a long way with this sort of sugar. For a large cake I use a whole box of sugar, but add it alternately with little splashes of orange juice, so as not to get the frosting too runny. Keep beating and adding sugar and juice until you have a smooth spreadable frosting. The more you beat the nicer it will be.

<u>Lemon Frosting</u>:   Same as above, using a <u>lemon</u>.

<u>Chocolate Frosting</u>: Melt <u>a square or 2 of unsweetened chocolate</u> in a double boiler, along with <u>1 tablespoon butter</u>. Remove from heat and beat in <u>confectioners' sugar</u> with a little <u>milk</u> or <u>cream</u> and a dash of <u>vanilla</u>.   You may substitute <u>rum</u> for vanilla, <u>cream cheese</u> for butter.

<u>Mocha Frosting</u>:   Mix ½ tablespoon of instant <u>coffee</u> with <u>2 tablespoons</u> of <u>cocoa</u> and stir in enough <u>hot water</u> to dissolve. Add a <u>tablespoon</u> of <u>butter</u>. Stir in the <u>sugar</u> alternately with touches of <u>cream</u>.

Flavors, colors (you may use vegetable coloring), are nearly endless in this type of frosting.

I knew a little girl, named Elise, who made a birthday cake for her father. She tinted it blue for Yale, with a deep <u>blue</u> frosting! Not recommended, but memorable.

Household Hints

Bentley Farm ~ Danville, Vermont ~ 1840

Every kitchen needs one central work area.
This is mine, and the things I like about it
are listed on the next page.

———————————————

"To make routine a stimulus / Remember it can cease...."

Emily Dickinson

General Hints

1) There's a view of a small garden to feed my soul,* and a sustaining breeze when window is open.

2) On the right are <u>narrow</u> shelves holding all herbs and spices in alphabetical order for easy grabbing. Ditto for the lengthening lists of paper, plastic, aluminum rolls of things that make housekeeping simpler every year, but are hard to store conveniently. They rest on <u>tipped-up</u> shelves, out of their containers, the easier to know when re-supply is necessary. Scissors are at hand for these, the metal, saw-toothed edges of the boxes they came in discarded, because I'm forever cutting my fingers on them, and like this system better anyway. There's a <u>timer</u> with a loud bell, on one of the shelves, without which I'd burn everything.

3) Refrigerator (not showing) is just to right of herb shelves, so no need to move to get at its contents.

4) Good overhead light.

5) On the left, those three bumps are the mixing bowls most often used, hanging on the side of a cupboard which holds all the things necessary for baking, sandwich making, and cooking in general.

6) The drawer on right holds all sharp knives, firmly on a magnetic rack. Drawer on left holds measuring spoons, mixing spoons, scraper, butter spreader, etc.

7) The counter is made of chopping-block maple for kneading bread, rolling pastry, chopping anything.

8) Beneath the drawers is waste basket, and stool to sit on — a real throne with all necessities within reach.

---

*"If thou of fortune be bereft / And in thy store there be but left
Two loaves, sell one and with the dole / Buy hyacinths to feed thy soul."
James Terry White

If all this sounds smug, it is. I had the rare opportunity after 35 years of housekeeping, to start from scratch on the kitchen of my dreams. If I can pass on suggestions to help others in their planning, this is my purpose. When we are young we aren't sure what we want in kitchen and house conveniences. Experience helps us to know.

Dozens of household hints follow, but here are two favorites:

1) Always have a dish of <u>room-temperature butter</u> in your most accessible cupboard, ever ready for a quick sandwich, and a hundred other uses in cooking.

2) As you scan and use various cookbooks, write down <u>name</u> and <u>page</u> of favorite recipes on back <u>flyleaf</u>. I can't over-emphasize how important it is to make this a habit. It saves hours of hunting for a certain recipe, and also serves as a reminder of good things you once made and have forgotten about. If you collect old cookbooks, give special attention to the spotted pages. They contain the best recipes.

About a blender:

This is a fairly new luxury that has fast become a kitchen necessity. I can't imagine cooking without one, though some people say they can't think of anything to use one for! Read this book. There are suggestions on nearly every page. The blender has brought mousses and purées (that formerly took infinite patience and hard work to produce) within easy reach of any cook who has the ingenuity to press a button. Gravies, salad dressings, soups, sauces, frappés, are achieved in minutes.

Just remember not to put something very hot in a blender and turn on full speed. It is liable to erupt like a small volcano. Wait for whatever you are blending to cool a bit. Don't fill a blender too full. The liquid enlarges with blending, and may overflow. Do several loads instead of just one.

A buffet supper I served to 40 young people not long ago was made infinitely easier by the faithful blender, which never had a chance to cool off. Preparation of a large ham loaf called for 5 onions, 10 eggs. Instead of grating and beating by hand, I blended onions and eggs together in blender, speedily and effortlessly, before mixing with the ground ham. Macaroni and cheese, served with the ham loaf, called for 3 pounds of grated cheese. I put the necessary amount of milk The recipe called for into the blender, and kept adding chunks of cheese. The tedious task was completed in a jiffy. Then I made a large blender fruit punch (page 8). This suggests a few of the many uses of this boon to the cook. Be sure you have a blender!

~~~~~~~~~~~

A <u>mortar and pestle</u> is as useful as it is ornamental. The macaroni and cheese dish, mentioned above, was generously topped with buttered cracker crumbs. There was a great gathering-up of half-empty boxes of Saltines, Ritz, and Wheat thins, which were pounded to fragments in the mortar. Much less messy than the rolling pin method. Great for a graham cracker pie. Who needs to <u>buy</u> crumbs?

~~~~~~~~~~~

About an old-fashioned meat grinder:

A grinder like this will probably be a museum piece by the time my granddaughter is using this cook book. Its name is deceptive, for it grinds many things in addition to meat, and, to me, is a kitchen necessity, as some of the recipes in this book testify. There are various electrical grinders on the market these days, but I prefer the dependability of certain hand-powered appliances, and don't mind a bit of exercise. If you are grinding anything juicy, be sure to place a bowl on a stool, under the grinder, to catch the drips. It is wise to have a special place on a solid counter for grinding. There is a metal plate sunk into my work counter, which gives a firm gripping place for the grinder.

About a French chef's knife:

Try to get one of carbon steel, rather than stainless, for it sharpens better. A good stout chef's knife looks dangerous, and like what the farmer's wife went after the three blind mice with, but it is harmless, and will do the most delicate work. It will do things that cannot be accomplished with either blender or grinder. It takes only minutes to master the technique of the knife held firmly with the right hand, with the heel of left hand placed on top of knife, pressing down near the point. Then one chops down with speed and force, moving the knife back and forth in an arc. Parsley, nuts, vegetables, various herbs, are reduced to the chopped degree you desire in very short order.

This is no temporary

gadget, but a tool as indispensable to Western cooking as the cleaver is to Chinese.

A square grater like this belongs in every kitchen. Though cheese may be grated in a blender if it is combined with liquid, there are many times when it must be grated dry, by hand. Always place a piece of waxed paper under the grater to catch whatever you are grating. In this way the counter is not soiled, and all you need do is pick up the paper and slide the gratings into receptacle to be used. When grating onions, carrots, etc. — leave some of the tops on, as a handle to grip. It prevents scraping fingers.

This is the old-fashioned way of cutting up hard winter squash. See page 137 for an easier way out of this difficult and dangerous method.

There is a vast difference between freshly ground pepper and the kind that one buys already ground. The latter will make you sneeze, the former won't. The shelf life of good peppercorns is forever, whereas the store-ground variety loses flavor rapidly. So have a first class pepper grinder, and try to get tellicherry peppercorns, the world's best kind. It will pay off in superior flavor.

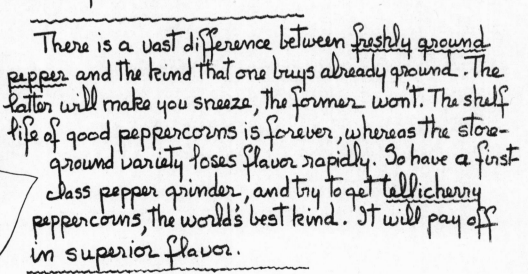

Keep a supply of <u>pinch clothespins</u> in a convenient spot in the kitchen. They are so much handier for securing plastic bags than those wire twists that are difficult and time-consuming to unwind. Anything kept in a plastic bag — bread or greens, for instance, or any half-used package that might spill, all respond to the clothespin treatment.

Put a <u>bay leaf</u> in with (on top) of any flours, meals, grains, or crackers that are prone to become infested. The bothersome pests avoid any container with a bay leaf in it.

Use <u>real lemons</u>! A plastic lemon is a modern abomination that, incredibly, costs more than nature's own.

<u>Sea salt</u> is available at health food stores. I use it in everything. <u>Raw sugar</u> is likewise available, and wherever practicable, I use it in place of the usual granulated. Sweeten with <u>honey</u>, <u>maple syrup</u>, <u>brown sugar</u>, <u>molasses</u>, as often as possible. Don't forget that <u>yogurt</u> may be substituted for sour cream in many instances. <u>Wheat germ</u> and <u>sesame seeds</u> make fine toppings for casseroles, and, incorporated into various foods, add much to their nutritive value and to their flavor.

A friend of mine once worked in the Stouffer kitchens. Their restaurants and frozen foods are tops. My friend said there were signs in the kitchens alerting the cooks to "put a bit of sugar in everything". Sugar is the great flavor enhancer. Skip the monosodium glutamate.

~~~~~~~~~~~~~~~

When flour or all-purpose flour is called for in various recipes, I mean one and the same thing, and always unbleached.

Never throw out the water in which potatoes have been boiled. Use it in gravy, soup or stew. Used in place of water in bread making, it adds nutrition and extra tenderness.

~~~~~~~~~~~~~~~

When browning anything in butter for any length of time, add a little corn oil. It keeps the butter from getting too brown.

~~~~~~~~~~~~~~~

Biscuits or cookies burned on the bottom? Let cool. Grate on fine side of grater. Cheer up, brides.

~~~~~~~~~~~~~~~

There are special little metal racks available to put on a burner, so that cooking utensil does not come in direct contact with heat. It is terribly important to use one if you are heating something that might scorch. I learned a bitter lesson when I had a goulash ready for a crowd, many years ago. I heated it (foolishly) directly on burner. It scorched. The meal was ruined. I have long since equipped myself with large double boilers (available at any hotel supply store). Another method with a mass of thick something-or-other, is to heat it in the oven. But there are still times when one uses a burner directly, when it is wise to place a rack between heat source and kettle.

Experience has taught me that aluminum is the least likely to scorch, and Corning ware (though I love it) the most prone. Stainless steel and enamel-ware fall somewhere in between. Knowing the propensities of various kinds of cookware helps one to be alerted. My niece, who did the drawings for this book, says, "The only thing that tastes good scorched, is rice".

Having acquired all the pots and pans I needed, before Teflon was invented, and because they are like old friends I couldn't cast aside for new ones, I have not gone in for this type of kitchen ware. But I have observed and discovered that Teflon does wear off in spots. Then what does one do? Butter the pan in spots? It's a little like having brass and silver lacquered so one need not polish it. (I tried it once). Pretty soon one is left with something that has acquired freckles. So I prefer to stick to basics, and know where I'm at; and things that endure are the best investments.

If you have a self-cleaning oven, put pans that can stand the heat (and have accumulated stubborn soil) in for a good high-heat treatment. They will come out sparkling clean.

Always, always have a _thoroughly preheated oven_ for everything you bake or broil, unless a recipe specifically calls for starting with a cool oven.

Don't let your herbs be "hippies"! Whether grown indoors or out, they need frequent haircuts to prevent them from getting leggy and going to seed. Save the clippings and add, chopped, to a green salad. If cuttings prove too bountiful, tie them in small plastic bags, and hand them around to friends who lack gardens. Herbs keep well in plastic in refrigerator.

~~~~~~~~~~~~~~~~~~~~~~~~~~

Do you have hanging plants that are difficult to water, or plants on good tables that you are in fear of water-spotting? Just place ice cubes in the flower pots. Harry Chandler, our local florist, gave me this hint. He says that the slow watering that results is good for the plants. I said, "How do I fertilize if I don't use water?" He said, "Freeze the fertilizer solution in an ice tray."

~~~~~~~~~~~~~~~~~~~~~~~~~~

My friend, Gladys Elvriken, says she has always meant to write the hot cereal manufacturers and tell them that to boil the cereal water first, then slowly stirring in the cereal, is the more difficult and lump-prone procedure. She has taught me to mix the required amount of cold water with the cereal. Then bring to a boil, stirring, not frantically, but occasionally, for a better result. I cook rice this way, too. Try it. It works.

~~~~~~~~~~~~~~~~~~~~~~~~~~

The secret of a tidy house: Don't put it down. Put it away!

~~~~~~~~~~~~~~~~~~~~~~~~~~

Plants that Repel Pests

Why not make plants useful, as well as ornamental?
Making separate gardens of herbs, flowers, vegetables, is a
common practice that can bring on problems which might better
be solved by some well-planned integration.

Here are some practices that I have found helpful:

Sage ~ Rosemary ~ Plant near vegetables in the cabbage family (broccoli,
cauliflower, Brussels sprouts). They repel cabbage moths. In
warmer climates, rosemary hedges are encouraged in orchards
to protect fruit trees.

Borage ~ Basil ~ Parsley ~ Plant next to tomato plants. Tomatoes
should not need spraying. (Borage seems best.) Borage makes
heavenly bouquets, and tender new leaves and flowers make good
eating.

Parsley ~ Plant next to roses to prevent aphids. There is no fluffier,
prettier border for a garden than parsley — and what dividends:
insect control, beauty, all the parsley you can eat. (Think of it as
food, not just as a garnish.) Emulate the old Romans, and have
bouquets of parsley decorating your dining room. Garlands of
parsley placed on one's head are said to prevent inebriation. Parsley,
chewed, masks even a garlic breath.

Nasturtiums ~ Plant beside cucumbers. These tender flowers seem to guard
cucumbers against their attackers. Remember that nasturtiums are
good to eat — flower, leaf, (and seed), and so decorative.

Onions ~ Garlic ~ Chives ~ Plant between potato rows to prevent
potato bugs. It really works!   Plant near roses to ward
off aphids.

Savory — This herb is the protector of <u>string beans</u>, and, interestingly, is <u>the</u> herb used to season beans in cooking. As with the chicken and the egg, I wonder which came first.

Tansy — Plant near <u>grapevines</u>, also <u>blackberry</u> and <u>raspberry</u> patches. Place a clump near screen doors to repel <u>flies</u>. Strew its pungent foliage where ants give trouble. There is no nicer flower for dried bouquets.

Mint — <u>Mice</u> hate it, <u>ants</u> likewise, along with members of the Women's Christian Temperance Union. Certain zealous females are alleged to have destroyed many southern mint beds, in the early days of the organization, due to mint's happy association with bourbon whiskey.

Basil — One of the greater <u>fly repellents</u>. Make lovely double-duty bouquets of this easily grown herb. Strew it fresh or dried on window sills that harbor <u>cluster flies</u>.

Yarrow — <u>Moth repellent</u>. So is <u>rosemary</u>. In New England we also gather <u>cedar</u> to protect woolens.

Wormwood — Reputed to keep <u>dogs</u> and other animals away from places where they are not wanted.

Marigolds — <u>Deer</u> and <u>rabbits</u> won't touch them. They seem to be a general repellent, yet marigold petals are good for human consumption. Sprinkle them on summer salads.

More Hints and Hang-ups

Keep a blackboard as near the kitchen exit door as possible, so it can flag you down with reminders of things needed. Here's mine, an old-time double slate that I prize for the following reason.

An old man named Charlie Raddatz, who was a friend of ours in our years in Phillipsburg, New Jersey, called often, with armloads of perfect flowers from his garden, his faithful dog beside him. He never left without telling us that the three things in life he loved above everything were his wife, his garden, his dog. The years took their inevitable toll. First the dog died, then he became too old to garden, and then his wife died. One day he appeared with this slate in his hands, and he gave it to me saying, "I want you to have this; it belonged to my wife. I remember when she brought it to the first grade. Only rich kids, we thought, had double slates. Mine was a single, like all the rest of the class. It was love at first sight —— not that the slate had anything to do with it."

We all save extra jars and tops for innumerable uses. But try and find the right top for the right jar. If one keeps the tops on the jars, they smell musty. Just tape the lid to the side of its jar, with magic tape, before putting it away. Oh so efficient!

When making a <u>molded salad or dessert</u>, it is wise to wipe the mold with a little tasteless vegetable oil. It makes unmolding so much easier. (Don't use butter, as it solidifies when chilled). Of course it is still necessary to dip mold in hot water. The results are nearer perfection with the use of oil, that's all. This has been mentioned before, but bears repeating.

<u>Cooking for one or Two</u>, and you don't want to use a whole package of frozen food? Take your stout French knife, and, cutting through box and all, slice off what you want. Return unused portion to freezer in a plastic bag (so exposed edge won't dry out).

Our <u>freezers</u>, and the foods they enable us to have on hand, are a blessed miracle. Short of a garden of one's own, frozen fruits and vegetables, which are picked at the peak of ripeness, are excellent fare. It has been said that the modern child no longer says, "What's cooking, Ma?" but, "What's thawing?"

When taking <u>dishes out of dishwasher</u>, remove those from lower rack first. Then any water spills from upper rack won't get on clean dishes underneath.

If dishwasher is <u>not full</u> when you are ready to turn it on, gather up some of those objets d'art around the house, that are dusty and washable — figurines, ashtrays, candlesticks, etc., and fill up the washer. They'll come out pristine.

Nothing like a supply of <u>bath towels in the kitchen</u>:
1) To line utensil drawers. It prevents clatter and clutter, keeps things in place, looks attractive. Buy thin, inexpensive

terry towels in your kitchen color.

    2) To dry salad greens.

    3) To place on drain board when washing extra-fine dishes that don't go in dishwasher. Absorbs water and noise and prevents chipping.

    4) They make very satisfactory dish towels.

On my radio program a prize of $25.00 was offered for the best household hint. Many poured in, but this picture illustrates the one chosen, because so many children are terrified or difficult _about having their hair cut_. A mother of many children said that all she needed to do was place a blackboard eraser on the child's head (as in eraser tag), make it seem a game to sit so still it won't fall off. No tears, no wiggles, just narcissistic enjoyment of one's mirrored image, and the hair-cutting job proved a cinch.

    No doubt this clever suggestion appealed to me because I have strong brain recordings of taking my little brother to the barber for his first haircut. The guillotine couldn't have seemed more ominous to him. His screams and tears were so heart-rending that I had to take him home with shaggy locks unshorn.

    Another great idea given me by a mother of seven: When a child has just graduated from crib to a regular bed, and is liable to get turned around and lost in the bottom of it — _make a pie bed_! This takes only one sheet instead of two, and keeps the little darling where he or she belongs.

Bill Henrich says to pipe smokers:

Save ½ an orange skin after it has produced the breakfast juice. Place it, cut side up, in tin of tobacco. Leave there for 2 or 3 days. Then discard skin and mix tobacco around a bit. The orange lends moisture, plus the slightest pleasing aroma.

Tom Sawyer's never-fail hiccup cure:

Onto 1 teaspoon of granulated sugar shake sufficient Angustora bitters to saturate lightly. Eat thereof and be convinced.

Orange or Apple Pomanders

Choose perfect oranges or apples. Prick the fruit all over with a tooth pick or heavy needle. (A needlepoint needle is fine for this.) Stick whole cloves into the holes, as close together as is possible, until the fruit is studded with one solid mass of cloves. Plunge a hairpin firmly into top of fruit, leaving enough of top of hairpin showing to run a ribbon through later. Dust all over with cinnamon. Wrap in tissue paper and set aside several weeks to dry. After drying, wrap in gay colors of tulle tied with matching bow.

Pomander-making is a pleasant project for children at Thanksgiving time. They will be ready for gifts at Christmas, or to hang on the tree, for ornament and fragrance. Their purpose is to perfume closets and bureau drawers, Their production an ancient household craft.

Plan to have a <u>desk in kitchen</u>. Between cooking bouts one can catch up on a lot of secretarial work, without burning the biscuits.

~~~~~~~~~~~~~~~~

Scrap Book Paste
(Totally non-staining, non-toxic, and adheres with a vengeance)

Mix 2 tablespoons of <u>corn starch</u> with 1 cup cold water. Bring to a boil, stirring the while, until it thickens and clarifies. Store in jar in refrigerator (or it will mold).

This is the paste Mrs. Mildred Bacon of Danville, Vermont, uses in her carefully-kept scrap books concerning local history. Some of the books are many years old, and there is no darkening of the places where paste was applied. My old albums are a mess, certain commercial "stickums" having worked their deteriorating mischief.

A fine paste for children pursuing some rainy-day project. The cost is zero.

~~~~~~~~~~~~~~~~

When washing doeskin or <u>leather gloves</u>, put a few drops of <u>baby oil</u> in the rinse water. Gloves dry soft as new.

~~~~~~~~~~~~~~~~

To <u>clean piano keys</u> (whether real ivory or simulated): Mix <u>rubbing alcohol</u> and <u>water</u>, half and half. Dampen soft cloth with this mixture and rub keys clean. They will sparkle. A professional taught me this.

~~~~~~~~~~~~~~~~

Moisture rings on some nice wood surface of furniture? Anoint with corn oil, sprinkle with salt, and rub and rub until spot disappears.

~~~~~~~~~~~~~~~~~~~~~~

Unless you have a silver chest that holds your flatware, have the top drawer of your sideboard fitted to hold the same, and line with tarnish-resisting flannel. This miracle cloth is available at certain stores, or a jeweler could get it for you. It will pay off in convenience, lifelong. Plan somewhere in dining room to have a long shallow drawer, upholstered in the same flannel, in which to line up all your flatware serving utensils. One can fumble endlessly for the right piece of serving silver if it is kept in a deep drawer. No need to clean any flatware, except once in a blue moon, if ensconced in tarnish-resisting flannel.

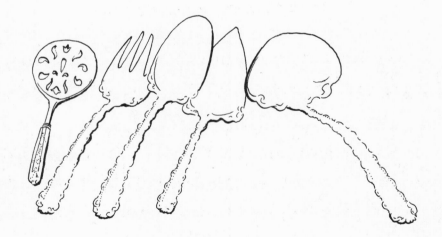

About House-building and Remodeling:

1) Don't have cupboards go to the floor around the entire kitchen. Leave some space under the main work area for a stool or two, and for several waste containers. It is a nuisance to be forever opening cupboard doors.

2) The majority of people today have a double sink and a one-oven stove. Try switching that. Have one large sink, and a stove with two ovens, if possible. A large sink lends itself to all sorts of flexibility. There can be one or several dish pans, according to the needs of the moment. And when it comes to the occasional large pans or kettles, a big sink will take care of them. Ever try to wash a turkey pan in a divided sink? Their popularity puzzles me. The pretty pictures one sees of a single oven, with a whole meal therein, is an advertising hoax. Very few foods are cooked at the same temperature. One oven, with company arriving, narrows the menu possibilities alarmingly.

3) Plan to have a utility room as near the kitchen as possible for a washing machine and drier, and — above all — an old-fashioned set tub! Don't let any architect, contractor, or interior decorator, talk you out of this great blessing. It's the place for a quick wash of delicate things that can't go into the washing machine, a place to fix flowers, to soak the baby's diapers, to wash off muddy boots, for the home mechanic or gardener to remove the first layers of grime. (Needless to say, one uses a disinfectant on the set tub between some of these activities.) The set tub has

343

myriad functions, but I love it most when entertaining. I fill it
with soapy water, and into it go any last minute pots or pans
before the arrival of guests. The kitchen looks spotless, and when
the late-hour cleanup comes, in go all the difficult baking
dishes that need scouring. They soak clean overnight, and require
no elbow grease the next day.   Have shelves over the
set tub to hold soaps and such for the aforementioned projects.

Another thing to be sure to have in a
utility room is a place for wrapping
packages, be it Christmas or any day
of the year. Here's a picture of my
wrapping corner. It really takes the
sting out of a dull chore. There is no
frantic running around the house for
twine, scissors, wrapping paper, sealing
tape, etc. It's all there, ready for action.
The cupboards hold fancy paper,
ribbons, stickers, and what-nots for gift wrapping. There is
scarcely a day that I don't use and bless this convenient set-up.
        Also in the utility room is my sewing
machine, a small work bench with the tools one runs for, several
times a week, an ironing board that is always up and
ready for use, a place to shine shoes, a place for brooms,
vacuum cleaner and general cleaning equipment, wooden
racks* that fold against the wall when not in use, but pull

* Available at Vermont Country Store, WESTON, Vermont 05161

out into many arms for drying hand-washables, and a supply of plastic hangers for drip-dry garments. The utility room won't take any prizes for neatness, for it gets so much use. But all I need do is shut the door, and the kitchen looks great.

4) <u>Houses without attics or cellars or sheds</u> bring all sorts of questions to mind. For example: Where will you store that carefully cleaned wedding dress? Where does one put the Christmas decorations that proliferate from year to year, the children demanding that the most desiccated ornaments be preserved for reappearance? Where put junior's play pen, high chair, bed, treasured toys, when he is through with them? It's amazing how fast one becomes a grandma and needs such things again, or how great it is to have them to loan out. Where keep games, records, old letters, etc., etc.? Where put hoses, wheelbarrows, lawn mowers, rakes, shovels, lawn furniture, peat moss, flower pots, bicycles and their ilk? Do you plan to fill your garage with them so you have to keep the car outdoors, or have you planned space?

5) Lean toward small rooms with large <u>closets</u>, rather than large rooms with small closets, unless you are in a position to have everything large. Nothing makes a home as functional, livable, easy to take care of, and saleable, as great, generous closets, and plenty of shelf space. Architects still haven't gotten the message.

6) If you have a garden and <u>want to keep root vegetables</u> through the winter, have you planned a section of cellar that remains cool and has an earth floor?

7) People used to have <u>cold pantries</u> off the

kitchen. They are still a boon for keeping certain food supplies canned goods, preserves. An outside wall of utility room could be partitioned off for this. A good place for wine racks also. A warm kitchen is not the best place to store wine, decorative as the whole set-up may be.

8) Think twice before you spend a fortune on metal storm windows, screens, doors. Wood is still the miracle material, and if something doesn't fit just right, it is easily remedied. When metal gets out of whack, drastic surgery is called for.

9) No one has ever come up with anything better than a double-hung window. Consider carefully before you fall for louvres, casement gadgets and such, unless there is a very special reason for their use.

10) If you live in the North country where there is lots of snow, save heaps of money and problems by not having a concrete floor in your garage. A concrete floor is awash with salty snow water dropping in great chunks from the automobile all winter long. Even a drain in the floor is not effective. Just cover the good earth with buckwheat gravel (small, roundish pebbles, easy to walk on) and let nature do the rest. All you need do is rake the gravel now and then for neat effect, and in the summer put a plant or two in your garage and you have a Japanese garden. Great place for a little Buddhist meditation. Be sure this shrine has a regular exit door in addition to garage doors; and also make the garage large enough so you don't have to inch along a wall sideways to extricate yourself. Parsimonious planning

of size has turned many a garage into a catchall rather than a convenience. The car or cars sit outside. A mess of this and that is housed.

11) If you serve <u>drinks</u>, plan <u>a special place for their preparation</u>. All the paraphernalia of drink mixing is a nuisance around the main sink of the kitchen. I have a table in my utility room, with shelves over it holding glasses, cocktail shakers, liquor, everything ready for the cocktail hour (see pages 4,5). Being a widow, when guests arrive I invite them to help themselves, or ask a couple of the men to take charge. This takes a load off my shoulders, and no one seems to mind. When the cocktail hour is over, I can close the door on the confusion that is the inevitable part of the before-dinner libation.

12) Because the old spring on my farm runs by gravity into the house, and then down into a pond, it seemed natural to steal a little of that steadily-running water, and have it go through a fountain on the south side of the dining room. This humidifies the whole house, as well as looking lovely and encouraging house plants to prosper unbelievably well. Few are lucky enough to have an endless supply of spring water, but why can't some manufacturer who turns out all those ugly humidifiers for the home, make <u>an aesthetically pleasing recycling fountain</u> that would achieve the same result? Much more fun to carry a bucket of water to a fountain than to a homely humidifier. Every home should have those two soul-sustaining elements — water (a fountain), fire (a fireplace).

About Entertaining:

So you're going to have a party? Great. I've sung the praises of home entertaining throughout this book, not dodging the fact that it is hard work: part of a day to plan and shop, another to prepare everything, another to pick up all the pieces (unless one has a staff). But rewards are great.

First, write out the menu on a large sheet of paper, writing down your shopping list at the side of the page, with date and list of guests at the top, and the battle strategy is well begun. File away this tattered work-sheet when shopping and party are over. It makes fascinating reading in future years, lets you know what you fed so-and-so way back when, suggests menus you'd forgotten you had, keeps one from serving the same people the same thing. Scribble in a few notes concerning disasters, successes, quantities, maybe a few prices. You soon build up a valuable reference file.

Do as many things the day before the party as are possible: set the table, fix flowers, make the main dish (unless it's a roast), and the dessert. If planning a tossed salad, for which the preparation of the greens is long and tedious, remember that readied greens keep perfectly for 24 hours, wrapped tenderly in a bath towel in the refrigerator, and emerge at party-time both dry and crisp. A good head start gives one satisfaction and motivation beyond compare, and comparative ease on the day of the party.

On the day of the event, get into action early in the kitchen, and prepare every other last thing that you are going to serve, potatoes, vegetables, everything. This book is filled with recipes for early cooking, later heating.

Oven-to-table equipment becomes more accessible and attractive every day. Collect it as you would rare antiques, for it greases the wheels of entertaining. It has been years since I've shifted food from cooking utensils to silver serving dishes. This takes help in the kitchen, or youthful vitality of a high order. I have neither, at this point, but still give parties with enthusiasm.

If there is something that needs unmolding, do it hours ahead, and put back in refrigerator — _ready._ It will wait in the cold, endlessly.

If gravy is to be part of meal, make it as far ahead as pan drippings allow, shifting roast to another pan. Keep finished gravy hot in a double boiler. (This is one thing that lends itself to long heating.)

The _buffet meal_ is my way of managing a party, and I make it a _kitchen buffet._ With kitchen in order, why haul everything into the dining room? People help themselves to hot plates, and go down the line of stove and counters, taking what they want. Perhaps someone stands at the roast, carving and serving, and perhaps I stand at the salad bowl, tossing it with its dressing at the last minute, and serving onto individual salad dishes, ready for the guests as they come my way. Then we graduate to the dining room to a nicely set table, candlelight, flowers, wine.

Here's a small check list, along with the assumption that table is set, all food ready:

1) Is kitchen waste basket empty and ready for business?

2) Is coffee situation entirely cared for, percolator, or whatever, ready to go; sugar on tray waiting for its cream pitcher partner chilling in refrigerator; cups and saucers conveniently located? Or is after-dinner coffee tray ready, if you serve coffee that way?

3) Is fireplace (if you have one) ready to light? "A fire laid is half lit," said Arnold Bennet, or words to that effect.

4) Candy and/or nuts on table? Salts and peppers? Ash trays?

5) Seating figured out in your mind, or on place cards?

6) Is ice ready?! And is bar set up for everything you plan to serve?

7) Are serving implements all set out? Plates warming?

8) Is dessert ready for serving from sideboard, or a small table beside the hostess?

9) Are liqueur glasses and bottles ready in the living room (if you plan to serve them)?

If the answers are all "yes", then go take a nap, luxuriate in a hot bath, and while you are dressing to look your best, sip your first drink. You have earned it. This is my formula for feeling like a guest at one's own party, and for savoring those golden moments of anticipation, before friends arrive.

Want to give a party with lots of people and little work? Set everything up for self service. Don't set any tables. Have food that may be eaten entirely off one plate, with a fork only. (Knives fall off plates too easily.) Use paper plates (if they're firm), paper napkins too, if you want to. Let people sit anywhere they choose, including the floor. And don't wait on them. Have a dessert that may be eaten without any utensil, such as Spice Cake (237), Orange Cake (234), Marguerites (242), Brownies (241). Have a coffee area with everything ready for self service, some ice water for the thirsty. If you start serving people, they will let you, so don't begin! Don't flit about, except to enjoy talking with guests. Encourage them to partake, provided they do it themselves. You have provided amply. Having done that, it is every man for himself.

With all this talk about how to be good hosts, I have two suggestions for guests:

1) <u>Don't ever arrive early!</u> If you do, you will deserve the forced, wolf grins that distort the faces of your hosts.

2) <u>Be a little bit helpful</u>, unless there is help in the kitchen. Such things as pouring water, lighting candles, clearing the table between courses, passing coffee, are hardly arduous, and of genuine assistance. Don't stack plates in the kitchen unless you rinse them, or your hostess is left with dishes not only stuck together, but soiled on <u>both</u> sides. Better to leave them spread all over the kitchen.

A pan of <u>soapy water</u> in the sink, to receive the used silver, and an obvious <u>place for plate</u> scrapings, will encourage the helpful guest. This makes for painless clean-up later on, when guests have departed.

On the following page is the menu for my greatest effort party-wise, followed by the story of how it came about. As recipes for most things on the menu are to be found in this book, it might be of interest to include it. Aware that the appetizers were mostly brown in color (though varied in texture and type of food), I overcame this apparent disregard for what I've been preaching, by using colorful dishes, and embellishing with lavish touches of parsley, radish roses, even marigold and chive blossoms.

Buffet Dinner for United Nations Diplomats, October 2, 1971 (35 people)

Appetizers

Meat Balls (page 20)) served hot   Beer Bread (page 204), sliced thin
Fish Cakes (page 114)) from candle warmers   and spread with sweet butter, with
                                           Liver Pâté (page 18)

Peanuts   Tray of Finger Greens : carrot curls, celery and cucumber sticks

Chicken à la King (page 74)   Baked Ham (page 99)
Merrymount Lobster (page 110)   Hot Mustard*

Bowl of Potato Chips

Baked Macaroni and Cheese (page 131)   Baked Squash with Pecans (page 190)

Stuffed Eggs (page 123) Tomato and Onion (page 156) Cold Gingered Fruit (page 307)

Pickled Garden Relish** Bowl of Mc Intosh Apples (shiny and red from my orchard)

Large Tossed Green Salad (page 134) containing marinated zucchini, and croutons
                    French Dressing (page 139)

Hot Rolls (page 207) and a plate of swirls of butter pats for self-service

Tipsy Pudding (234)

Coffee   Sanka

Crême de Menthe (white, on cracked ice)

* page 51 in Let Herbs Do It by V. W. Bentley, Houghton Mifflin Co. Boston
** page 60 " " " " "   1973

Adlai Stevenson believed that United Nations people do not see enough of the U.S.A. outside New York City. So, some years ago, an organization was formed to get the delegates to various parts of the country on pleasant outings. Fall foliage season of '71 found a bus-load of distinguished people arriving in Peacham, Vermont, to be billeted in friendly homes there. They saw one of our loveliest Northern villages in all its fall splendor, and many were the activities planned for their enjoyment, winding up with a dinner at Bentley Farm on Saturday eve (in Danville, about 10 miles north of Peacham). The menu I planned is here for you to see, and I include it because every recipe is in this book, or my previous herb-book. It also corroborates my preaching about variations in taste, texture, color, and never repeating a theme at the same meal.

Needless to say, it took me a full week to get ready, and almost another week to clean up, and decide what to do with all the leftovers. I had much too much food, but guess I'd rather be accused of profligacy than parsimony. Also, there were people from all over the world, and I hoped that with so great a variety of food, everyone would find something to his taste.

The bus, with its interesting passengers, drew up beside the garage, right on schedule. The garage had been transformed with fall leaves, rugs, and a wide U of three tables covered with red checked cloths. At the center table my brother held forth as bartender. It bore everything potable that the heart could desire or the baby cry for, and was so arranged that people could help themselves, or be waited upon — whichever they desired. The sides of the U held the appetizers, as listed, and behind each of the tables stood one of my very pretty nieces. They oversaw, passed things, attracted more attention than the food and drink.

When the cocktail hour was up, we moved on through the adjoining woodshed and breezeway, to my large country kitchen. While the cocktail party progressed, I had the chicken heating in large double boilers on the old wood stove, the lobster removed from electric ovens and placed in wood stove warming oven; the macaroni, squash, and rolls then took over the ovens. The cold dishes were arranged all around the center island. My brother progressed from bartender to carver of ham at the head of the island. Because the garden was bursting with buttercup squash and zucchini, they appeared as hot vegetable and cold embellishment to the salad. The chicken, lobster, macaroni, squash, rolls, were prepared days ahead and frozen, like-wise all the appetizers. The day before the party was devoted to the preparation of all the cold dishes listed. Salad greens were washed and ready in bath towels in the refrigerator. The zucchini was ever so slightly cooked and marinated in sufficient French dressing to pour, dressing and all, on the salad at the last second, and toss with croutons. Tipsy Pudding was also made 24 hours ahead, and the ham baked and decorated and kept at room temperature, because there wasn't an inch of space left for refrigeration. On this crucial day ahead, I had extra hands to help me. I'm no superwoman, and I did not want to be a basket case for the day of the party. Everything, and I mean every-thing, was completed 24 hours ahead. So when "hushed October morning mild" dawned on the 2nd, I could smugly go around, after a good night's sleep, attending to the last-minute, non-tiring, fun things.

All through the week I'd been setting tables with best linen and silver, 10 at dining room table, 12 at two tables in sun room, 8 in the living room, 6 in my downstairs bedroom. The bus driver ate with us. That made 36. Nature was kind and had not frostbitten my geraniums, so there were bright red bouquets on each table.

The guests picked up plates in the kitchen, went the rounds from hot to cold food, taking what they pleased, and then went and sat wherever they wanted to, in the four front rooms, where candles were lit, fireplaces burning. Not having place cards solved the problem of protocol. Not having wine simplified matters also, and no one had been stinted during the cocktail hour. Cold spring water is one of Vermonts' blessings, and thats what we had. I think everyone went back to the kitchen for second helpings, which was gratifying. The Tipsy Pudding I served from the sideboard, my nieces removing dinner plates as they passed the dessert, and then the coffee and Sanka from electric urns.

I was amused that the Russian representative kept asking me where the servants were, and who had prepared the meal. (Capitalists are supposed to have flunkies all over the place.) When I told him I had taken a week doing it, with little assistance, he expressed doubt. Fearful, in advance, that I'd stumble over a Russian name, it was enchanting to discover that his name was Smirnov, and a relief that I'd provided Smirnoff vodka at the bar, which he appreciated.

Somewhat overfed we advanced to still another location, the barn for liqueur (always walking out on the mess behind us was carefully planned strategy), and this time there was no choice of drink, just a choice digestive. The yawning open doors of the barn revealed the harvest moon coming up over the White Mountains, in unbelievable obedience to my wish.

I understand the group sang all the way home on the bus, international animosities forgotten.

Finally . . . .

to tell of the worst meal ever served to me, as a guest, seems a good way to dramatize my philosophy concerning food. This was the menu:

<u>Vichyssoise</u>
<u>Welsh Rabbit</u>
<u>Vanilla Ice Cream</u> — <u>Chocolate Sauce</u>

I think there was a dab of whipped cream on the ice cream, but as this would stretch anyone's imagination too far, I'll skip the claim. Furthermore, I'm beginning to feel frail just writing about it. Now, every one of these things I love —— but <u>all together</u>, oh dear! (Incidentally, mine host is dead, so I'm free to speak out.)

With vichyssoise, which is cold, and thick, and rich, and delicious, I'd serve a hot course next, of broiled or baked lean meat —— perhaps lamb chops, or chicken, with broiled tomatoes, and a crisp green salad, and the lightest of fruit desserts, but nothing even suggestive of creaminess.

See page 132 for the way to serve Welsh Rabbit, which is a supper dish calling for nothing before, and very little afterwards.

If one has ice cream with chocolate sauce to finish a meal, start off with a clear soup, have meat lean, vegetables non-creamy, so that the dessert provides an appetizing ending, not an emetic.

So here are some of the principles I try to adhere to:

1) Never repeat a theme at a meal — ever. A creamy course means that the other courses should be, in

contrast, light and non-creamy. If you have baked or broiled tomatoes for a vegetable, don't have tomatoes turn up in the salad. If cheese is served as an appetizer before the meal, don't have macaroni and cheese for dinner, or cheese with the dessert.

2) Make things taste <u>more like what they taste like</u> than what they taste like. If this sounds like gibberish, a true story may translate what I mean. One night a small boy was brought to our home for dinner. We had macadamia nuts with cocktails. The young man had never tasted them before, and stuffed his face enthusiastically, but not impolitely, saying, "These nuts taste more like nuts than any nuts I ever ate." That statement sums up a very important aspect of the culinary art. For example, make chicken taste more chicken-y. In making chicken soup, stew the bird in chicken broth, salt it with chicken bouillon cubes, bake it in cream of chicken soup, etc., etc. Make beef more beef-y by similar methods. Put celery seed in creamed celery, a touch of lemon extract in snow pudding to make it more lemon-y. Bring out the essence of every flavor. This does not mean to do away with all other seasonings, but to develop the greatest flavor in the thing you are preparing. Don't mask it, develop it!

3) Except in the case of hungry teen-agers with hollow legs and flat tummies, it is best <u>not to serve bread and potatoes at the same meal</u>. (There are exceptions, but it's a good general principle.)

4) Always have <u>one plain taste</u> as part of a meal. Doctored-up, spiced-up, herbed-up everything, is an assault

on the taste buds, and not good meal planning. The Japanese often end a big meal with a plain apple, nothing else. Plain finger greens in place of a salad with a strong dressing, are often the solution if other parts of the meal are heavily seasoned.

5) Plan that a meal have color, taste, and texture contrast, and chances are it not only has eye and flavor appeal, but is tops nutritionally. The best example of what I mean is, again, in reverse — a bad example:

<u>Chicken Breasts</u> in <u>White Sauce</u>
<u>Mashed Potatoes</u>   <u>Cauliflower</u>
<u>Vanilla Pudding</u>
(on white dishes!)

6) which brings me to the only sort of "vision" I ever had. For no reason at all I woke up one morning from a terribly insistent dream where someone kept asking me, "<u>why is there no blue food?</u>" — over and over. So I sat on the edge of my bed and thought and thought, and could only call to mind that dot in nature known as a blueberry, which turns purple when cooked, and the blue lobster that occurs only once in every fifty million. After further cogitation I thought of something that had never entered my head before — suddenly I knew why I loved blue china the most, always had a blue dining room, and lots of blue in the kitchen: to complete the one color of the spectrum that food lacks. As with a bouquet of flowers that, to me, is most beautiful when it contains every color of the rainbow, so do

foods, I think, look the most attractive on blue dishes, that color supplying the missing link. End of vision.

~~~~~~~~~~~~~~~~~~

When asked where I got my cooking hang-up, I tell people it is because my husband <u>praised</u> my culinary efforts, and, like most people, I lap up plaudits like a sick cat, and redouble my endeavors. So my advice to all husbands is — compliment the cook.

Also, my husband's work was such that he was often late for dinner, very late. So I <u>learned early to hold a meal</u> indefinitely without spoiling it. The same principle applies to a husband-ready meal as to a company-ready meal. You get everything prepared and then <u>let it cool off</u> — completely, if necessary. And you don't reheat anything until you see the whites of his eyes. <u>Never keep anything hot for any length of time</u>. The remark so often made, "My husband's dinner was burned to a crisp when he finally got home" conveys one of two things. Either the wife is stupid, or she's working out hidden resentments against the late and hungry alleged chauvinist pig.

Of course there are times when the family can't wait for the late return of the man in question. That's where <u>homemade TV dinners</u> come in. Dish up the late-comer's meal on a slightly buttered oven-proof plate. After it has cooled, if he's still not there, cover with foil so it won't dry out, and put in refrigerator. Heat rapidly, covered, in a very hot oven, at the last minute, when he is ready. You and the children have been fed, and everyone is cheerful. (The home made TV dinner is a great trick after any meal where there are left-overs. I keep aluminum foil plates for this. Sometimes I freeze the prepared dinners, or just refrigerate them for the next night. In any event, some meals are all ready, with no work whatever.)

Sometimes the shoe is on the other foot, and you are the late one, with nothing ready for dinner, and that is always the night your husband comes home early. My sister taught me this subterfuge: <u>Set the table</u>! This symbol of preparedness gives the impression to husband and children that food is imminent, so they wait patiently.

It is my theory that "Women's Lib" began with the back yard barbecue. Time was when children languished in hammocks on front porches, hoping for something to go by on the quiet street. Women were attending to kitchen matters. Men were reading the evening paper in the living room. The wash hung in what was called the back yard. No one ever thought of eating there. <u>Plenty</u> drove by those shady verandas, in time —— too much. Off came the porches, and in the flight from noise, and the need for privacy, the back yard became what is known as a patio, where the men donned chefs' hats, and started reading the food page of the newspaper. With the rise of the patio barbecue, men have become excellent cooks, so this book is for them, too. The trend is dangerous, and we women had better watch it, for through our sloth and indifference to the power traditionally ours in practicing the fine art of feeding people, we are allowing men to appropriate the role.

After all, it was men whose culinary competence and raptures were so great that it killed them. What woman could claim such dedication? Apicius poisoned himself when he ran out of money to spread the festive board. Vatel is said to have thrown himself upon a sword when the fish planned for a luncheon for Louis XIV failed to arrive on time. Carême died young, "burnt out by the flame of his genius and the fuel of his ovens." Alexander Dumas experienced a sudden loss of energy and died trying to write a cook book!

Somehow it's difficult to imagine Fannie Farmer committing hari-kari. So we women had better plug along, as always, stick to our guns, and not allow the men to usurp the glory.

Dumas fills me with empathy, and to avoid his fate, I now lay down my pen.

Index

Index

Index

Index

Index